D1035553

Explorations
in the
Development of Writing

Theory, Research and Practice

Explorations
in the
Development
of Writing

Theory, Research and Practice

Edited by

Barry M. Kroll

Indiana University

and

Gordon Wells

University of Bristol

JOHN WILEY & SONS

Chichester · New York · Brisbane · Toronto · Singapore

Library of Congress Cataloging in Publication Data:
Main entry under title:

Explorations in the development of writing.

   Includes indexes.
   1. English language — Composition and exercises — Addresses, essays, lectures.   2. English language — Rhetoric — Addresses, essays, lectures.   I. Kroll, Barry M., 1946-   II. Wells, C. Gordon.
LB1576.E97   1983   808'.042   82-23774
ISBN 0 471 90136 9

British Library Cataloguing in Publication Data:

Explorations in the development of writing.
   1. Children — Writing
   I. Kroll, Barry M.   II. Wells, Gordon
   372.6'23   LB1139.W7

   ISBN 0 471 90136 9

Phototypeset by Dobbie Typesetting Service, Plymouth, Devon
Printed by Pitman Press, Bath, Avon

Contents

PRACTICE

Introduction

A decade ago the contributors to a volume on the development of writing abilities would probably have been a rather homogeneous group. The development of writing was almost entirely the preserve of educators and their concern was chiefly with the writing carried out in school or college. Today, however, the situation is quite different. Increasingly, in addition to educators, researchers from such fields as linguistics, psychology and sociology are turning their attention to the study of children's writing, leading to a diversification of perspectives and purposes.

Surveying the field today, one is aware of a blossoming of interest in the development of writing that parallels to a considerable extent the explosion of work on the development of spoken language in the late sixties and early seventies. The sorts of questions that are now being asked include the following:

> What form does the development of writing take in a literate society if it is not deliberately tutored?
> Is there a universal sequence of stages in development, and if so what is it?
> What are the cognitive processes most centrally involved in writing? How different are these from the skills involved in speaking?
> What role does writing play in the lives of individual members of societies which have achieved different levels of literacy?
> What should be the goals of writing instruction?
> Should different component skills be practised separately and where should the balance in emphasis come between writing as 'craft' and writing as 'art'?
> How can adults—parents and teachers—best facilitate their children's development as writers?

In inviting contributions for this volume, these were the sorts of issues that we hoped would be addressed. Our aim was to demonstrate the scope of current work on the growth of writing abilities and at the same time to show

how advances in understanding are emerging from a two–way traffic between theoretical research and educational/classroom practice. We also wished to indicate the geographical scope of the current interest in writing, and so we have included authors from many of the major English-speaking countries: Australia, Britain, Canada, New Zealand and the USA. The collection thus brings together papers which represent some of the best of recent explorations into the development of writing abilities in the English-speaking world which, we hope, will prove stimulating to both researchers and practitioners.

Given the scope of the papers which follow, a lengthy editorial essay would be inappropriate. Our purpose in this introduction is simply to guide the reader into the collection by laying out the organization of the book and providing brief commentary on the chapters. As our subtitle indicates, we have organized the book in three sections, around the categories of theory, research, and practice. Those chapters which we categorize as 'theory' have the aim of providing new frameworks for thinking about writing development, or of identifying issues which seem to be central to an understanding of the growth of children's writing. Those chapters which we label 'research' entail some type of empirical investigation of what writers of various ages are able to accomplish in written language. And those essays which we call 'practice' explore school procedures and programmes which are likely to aid in the development of children's writing abilities. Of course, explorations of theory, research, and practice will often overlap, and it is not surprising, therefore, to find that many of our chapters could have been categorized under more than one of the labels. Nevertheless, it seems useful to identify a central aim for each chapter and to group it with papers that have similar purposes.

Theory

Our first category of explorations involves theoretical explication and conceptual analysis—such activities as elaborating a general framework or model for thinking about growth in writing, or identifying the key issues, problems, or questions concerning children's use of written language. There have been relatively few attempts to formulate general theories of writing development. Easily the most influential effort to date has been the scheme proposed by James Britton, Emeritus Professor of Education at the University of London. Britton's model is, in part, an attempt to account for the development of two differentiated forms of writing: transactional (persuasive and informative) writing and poetic (or 'creative') writing. According to the model, in the early stages of writing development children tend to compose in a kind of 'written–down expressive speech', a form of writing that is relaxed, intimate, and free from the constraints of a specific task or audience. Through exposure to more varied forms of written language in their reading and through attempts to cope with transactional and poetic tasks, children learn to modify expressive writing to meet the demands of two diverse purposes: to *do* something by means of writing (a transactional purpose) or to *make* something in written language (a poetic purpose). This movement from expressive writing towards the other forms involves more than learning new modes of expression; development is associated with two different cognitive activities, or what Britton calls two 'roles': the role of participant and the role of spectator. Transactional writing involves the participant role because the writer seeks some outcome in the actual world. Language is used to accomplish some end. Cognitively, the writer must make his representation of reality accessible to a reader — he must 'enmesh' his reality with the reader's knowledge, experience, interests, and so forth. Poetic writing, on the other hand, involves the spectator role, in which the writer uses language for its own sake. Freed from the demands of participation in some transaction, the writer can focus on forms and patterns of language itself, creating a verbal object as a work of art. Cognitively, the writer can reflect on the potentiality of experience — imagining, contemplating, reconstructing — operating directly on his representation of reality.

In the first chapter in this volume, Britton elaborates his view of spectator-role writing, focusing on the emergence and evolution of the 'story world', an organized representation of fictionalized experience. Britton explores the ways that exposure to fictional narratives influence the development of those internal fictions — or world pictures — by which we construe experience and anticipate events. In brief, the story world provides an early framework for thinking, an understanding of the real/make-believe distinction, and, ultimately, an ability to think about the world as it might be.

In the second chapter, David Olson and Nancy Torrance, from the Ontario Institute for Studies in Education (Canada), are concerned with the cognitive and social consequences of literacy. In previous work, Olson has pointed to a distinction between 'utterance' and 'text', a distinction which has implications for the development of writing. Utterance is closely allied to conversation, includes primarily informal structures, and performs largely interpersonal functions. The meaning of an utterance depends on the interaction of speaker, listener, utterance, and context. On the other hand, text is closely connected with writing, includes predominantly formal structures, and performs ideational functions. Text is 'autonomous'; the meaning is, to a much greater extent, to be found in the text alone. Thus, writing and speaking differ in terms of the nature and status of meaning in each of them. When children begin to communicate in writing, they must learn that, contrary to the case in speaking, linguistic forms are the only clues to the author's intentions and that it is therefore crucial to find the right words to fit one's intentions. But writing and speaking also differ in terms of *authority*. In oral discourse, the authority resides in the speaker; however, written texts have an authority independent of their authors. Olson and Torrance point out that this inherent authority of texts poses a problem for young writers: the problem of how to cope with the authority relations between writer and reader, including both how to write with a sense of authority and how to read with a critical attitude. The solution involves a realization that authority resides not in personal status but in the text, in the adequacy of reasons and evidence, and hence that writers and readers are fundamentally equals.

The third paper in the theory section spans our theory-research categories, but we have placed this chapter by Andrew Wilkinson and associates in this section because of its exploration of new possibilities for analyzing children's writing. Wilkinson, now at the University of East Anglia (England), reports the results of some of his work at Exeter with three former associates: Gillian Barnsley (Rusden State College of Victoria, Australia), Peter Hanna (Roehampton Institute of Higher Education, London), and Margaret Swan (Nova Scotia Teacher's College, Canada). The paper discusses in detail two 'models' for assessing writing development: an affective model and a moral model. These two dimensions of written texts—unlike the cognitive and stylistic dimensions—have previously received very little attention. Thus the principal contribution of the Wilkinson *et al.* chapter is to develop a new set of categories for analyzing changes in the content of children's writing.

Research

A good deal of the research on writing development has had a predominantly descriptive aim: to document what individuals can do at various points in their development as writers. Because of this developmental-descriptive aim, a popular design for studies has entailed asking groups of children of several ages to perform the same (or similar) writing tasks, and then to examine the resulting scripts for the features one is interested in. The paper by Wilkinson *et al.*, chapter three, illustrates such a design. Groups of children aged 7, 10, and 13 were given a set of writing tasks and their scripts were examined according to the researchers' models of affective and moral growth, yielding some generalizations about changes in the content of children's writing across these ages.

Such cross-sectional descriptive studies are useful for providing an overview or general 'map' of growth sequences. But the resolution and detail of such a map can be amplified through intensive studies of a few children over longer periods of time. In chapter four, John Collerson, Milperra College of Advanced Education (Australia), uses the case study approach to examine intensively the body of letters written by his daughter, Juliet, between the ages of 5 and 9½. Although the study involves only one child and one genre of writing, and thus has limited generalizability, its findings are rich and suggestive. Because Collerson studies his own daughter, he is able to place letter writing within the broader context of a child's life experiences, particularly within a network of significant others and various social obligations. Collerson looks carefully at the endings, beginnings, and bodies of Juliet's letters, noting a trend from the simple and formulaic towards variety, more personal feeling, and increased elaboration.

Chapter five, by Barry Kroll, Indiana University (USA), takes a related approach to the study of writing development, in that the nine-year-old children in Kroll's study were part of an on-going longitudinal study of language development. Thus, while Kroll focused on the writing abilities of a group of only 18 children, all of the same age, he had at his disposal a large number of indices collected over the previous six years, including measures of preschool language and knowledge of literacy, reading attainment at age seven, and various indices of parental background and interest in literacy. Kroll's aim was first of all to describe what these nine-year-old children were able to do as writers. His principal measure of writing attainment was a composite of scores on four writing tasks. But Kroll's major intent was to examine which of the various background measures would be most predictive of writing attainment. His findings were that parental interest in literacy and the child's preschool knowledge of literacy were most strongly related to writing attainment, pointing to the importance of the home in children's development in writing.

In chapter six we jump to the end of the developmental spectrum to look at the uses which adults make of the writing skills they have acquired. As in several of the preceding papers, the study by Morwenna Griffiths and Gordon Wells, from the University of Bristol (England), is primarily descriptive in aim, though its methodology differs from other research in this volume. Griffiths and Wells interviewed 160 adults, asking them a series of questions about the frequency and type of writing they did, as well as questions about their enjoyment of and reasons for writing. While it may seem that a study of adults' behaviour extends the bounds of developmental work beyond what is normally included under that heading, the authors argue strongly that the study of development necessarily requires a clear view of its endpoint, that is to say of the nature of the fully developed abilities and of the uses to which they are put. Answers to such questions are also relevant to the study of development in another sense. Writing is a social, as well as a purely individual, activity and the practices of adults and their attitudes toward writing may play an important role, as Kroll shows, in their children's development as writers. Many of the participants in the study by Griffiths and Wells were parents, so the information obtained from the interviews can be seen as having a double significance, firstly in giving a fairly comprehensive picture of the way in which various groups of adults make use of their writing abilities and secondly in suggesting the differing models of writing that are made available to children in different types of home. The picture of adult writers that emerges from this study also reminds us that development in writing is a process which continues beyond secondary school, extending into the world of work as well as into adults' personal lives. Too often, developmental studies seem to imply that development ends when formal instruction in writing ceases. But, most importantly, this study raises a series of questions which are too often glossed over in research on writing: Just how important are writing abilities in our modern, technological society? Is there justification for the time and money spent on teaching people to write? How often do adults put their writing skills to any practical or personal uses and how confident do they feel on those occasions? The responses to the interview questions were tabulated and analyzed in some detail, with particular attention to the ways that such factors as sex, social class, and level of educational attainment were related to people's tendencies to write for certain audiences or to use writing of a particular form. The results indicate that, although many adults dislike writing, they never-theless view it as having an important bearing on their jobs and prospects for employment. Taken as a whole, the results show that writing plays a significant role in the lives of a majority of people.

The research papers which we have discussed thus far have all involved describing what individuals do as writers, either by asking them about their writing (as in Griffiths and Wells) or by examining their written products (as in Wilkinson *et al.*, Collerson, and Kroll). The analysis of written products — whether from many children of several ages or from only a few children across a span of time — constitutes one of the major thrusts in research on writing development. Another important emphasis in developmental research is to study the writing process itself — the ways writers behave in the act of composing — rather than simply to look at the end-products of a writing episode. The seventh chapter, by a group of researchers in Ontario, Canada — P. J. Burtis (York University), Carl Bereiter (Ontario Institute for Studies in Education), Marlene Scardamalia (York University), and Jacqueline Tetroe (Ontario Institute for Studies in Education) — focuses on the development of planning in children's writing, and in so doing examines one of the most important processes involved in the production of mature writing. From an exploration of thinking-aloud protocols from writers between the ages of 10 and 18, the researchers discovered a tendency for younger children to compose by thinking of content and then immediately writing it down, without engaging in much planning. The Ontario group then pursued their investi-gation of planning with groups of children aged 10, 12 and 14. Instead of simply describing what kinds of planning children do spontaneously, however, the researchers used the technique of trying to induce planning before writing. The rationale for such a method is that it drives children's performance closer to their competence. By merely observing children we may see what they do on one or more occasions, or perhaps even habitually in a particular context, but we may miss what these children are capable of doing. So the researchers introduced their subjects to a variety of guides designed to induce them to plan before writing—for example, a set of five cards which served as reminders of different kinds of planning. The results, in brief, showed that, for the youngest children, writing is so closely tied to content generation that it is difficult to get them to make plans that are significantly different from a first draft. As writing ability develops, there is a separation of the problem of finding content from the problem of producing text—but plans are still closely tied to content. Still later, children begin to produce plans that have properties and contain elements which are not so directly related to content.

Practice

Of the two major types of research on writing development—product and process research—those studies which focus on writing processes often hold special relevance for educational practice. While teachers are interested in exploring various ways to assess development on the basis of written products, they are primarily concerned with influencing the processes their pupils engage in when they write. The first two chapters in the 'practice' section, although centrally concerned with pedagogy, are also based on systematic observation of pupils in the process of writing in school. These chapters illustrate the close connection between process studies and the exploration of educational practices. The paper by Barbara Kamler and Gary Kilarr, from Riverina College of Advanced Education (Australia), presents two accounts of children in the act of learning to write. In the first account, the authors examine five 'writing episodes' in the experience of a kindergarten child, 4½-year-old Coline, tracing the emergence of conventional orthography in her writing over a five-month period. In Coline's classroom, children are given the freedom to determine what they want to write and to figure out how to do it on their own. Thus Coline provides an illustration of the way a child can invent and discover the conventions of written language—when children are given control over the writing process and shown that writing is, fundamentally, an effort to make meaning. In the second part of chapter eight, Kamler and Kilarr analyze a writing conference between a fourth-grade teacher and two nine-year-old children. These children are also in a classroom with considerable freedom— freedom to choose their own topics and then to rehearse, draft, and revise their stories before selecting the ones for 'publication'. The two children in this account have chosen a jointly written piece to talk over with their teacher. The transcript of their discussion shows, in fascinating detail, the thought processes of the children as they revise their work together and the means by which a teacher can be a facilitator for writing development. The teacher lets the children do most of the talking in this conference, encouraging them to experiment, and when she intervenes it is to help the children clarify their meaning.

Chapter nine reiterates many of the same themes of individual choice and control over writing, pupil collaboration, and teacher facilitation, but in this case in the context of work with secondary-school pupils. While the paper focuses on educational practice, it is, like Kamler and Kilarr's, based on close observation of both written products and pupils in the process of writing. The chapter comes from a group of teachers and researchers in London: John Hardcastle (Hackney Downs School), Alex McLeod (University of London), and Bronwyn Mellor, John Richmond, and Helen Savva (all with the Inner London Education Authority). This essay ranges across a number of central issues in the teaching of writing, but perhaps its main point is that secondary-school pupils know a good bit more about writing than is often realized, and that the teacher's most important task is therefore to help them organize, extend, and make explicit this tacit understanding. In the first part of the chapter the authors examine the 'errors' in a pupil's piece of writing, demonstrating that, when we look for the system behind the errors, we can see evidence of what the writer knows, as well as what she needs to learn. Thus the authors recommend a perspective on writing which emphasizes progress and development rather than deficit and defect. In the second major part of the chapter the authors focus on the concept of 'collaborative redrafting' — encouraging pupils to work in pairs on their written drafts, thus putting to use the things they know about written language. The authors present guidelines for promoting collaborative work, and they discuss several videotaped episodes of such work in progress. In the final part of the paper the authors introduce a process-based writing curriculum which recognizes individual differences among pupils and offers opportunities for pupils to search out their own ways of developing as writers.

The emphasis on the child as an active participant in the process of learning to write is not, as Robert Shafer's chapter shows, a novel concern of contemporary educators. Shafer, from Arizona State University (USA), points out that the emphasis on informal learning and personal inquiry through writing had its origins in the progressive movement, roughly in the period between the two world wars. Shafer begins with a brief account of his experiences as a participant-observer in an English primary school, during which he saw children's writing unfold partly through a sharing of personal experience and partly through group interaction. Shafer then goes on to explore the origins and development of this 'personal experience' model of the writing curriculum. He maintains that this model, as it has evolved in Britain from the 1920s to the present, represents a coherent and well-validated approach for language-arts instruction.

The final paper, by Marie Clay of the University of Auckland (New Zealand), provides an appropriate conclusion for this section in that it summarizes many of the key themes from prior chapters. Clay contrasts two views of learning to write: one based on strict teacher control of concepts and topics, on practice of a skill until it is performed perfectly, and on the attempt to prevent pupils from making mistakes; the other based on the child's control of many aspects of writing, on the encouragement of novel responses, and on permitting children to make discoveries by making mistakes. Clay advocates — along with all of the writers in this section — the second view, since it places primacy on the creation of meaning. Children who are encouraged to create meanings through the use of graphic form and to explore the world of print are building a personal 'theory' of writing, a theory which will enable them to pay attention to information which confirms or contradicts the theory, and thus to advance their writing skills. Clay also argues for the interrelatedness of all language activities — oral language, reading, literature, and writing — and hence for a style of working which integrates these activities in a whole language curriculum. The teacher's role in such a curriculum is to serve as an observer-facilitator, watching for what children can do, encouraging them to venture into new territory, and guiding them toward making their own discoveries about the process of writing.

As our comments indicate, the chapters which follow offer a rich diversity of perspectives on the experiences of becoming and being a writer and raise many issues for further exploration. We believe that they will prove interesting to theorists and practitioners alike, challenging them to develop richer and more powerful models of writing, and helping them to become more effective in enabling their pupils to master the art and craft of writing with confidence and enthusiasm.

BARRY M. KROLL
GORDON WELLS

THEORY

Explorations in the Development of Writing
Edited by Barry M. Kroll and Gordon Wells
© 1983 John Wiley & Sons Ltd.

1

Writing and the Story World

James Britton

ASK ME ABOUT MY GRANDCHILD

Since my retirement I have acquired a grandchild. Now my granddaughter, Laurie, is in no respect experimentally controlled, and I am not in any strict sense in the data-collecting business. Yet I can't help observing, and some of the observations, taken over a period of time, present very intriguing configurations.

There is, for example, the matter of the 'play face'. I had picked up enough about anthropologists' use of the term to be interested in the phenomenon when it appeared, though it was my daughter (who knew nothing at all of the matter) who first noticed it. 'Have you seen Laurie "duck"?' she asked, 'to be comic, to be un-serious?' Laurie was 1 year 15 weeks' old at the time, and we duly witnessed her performance. The 'duck' was a kind of crouch, as though an attempt to get nearer the ground: her shoulders raised, her head at an angle. Her face wore a particular expression, slightly apprehensive, as though to say, 'You *do* know I'm only playing'; and her gait was what my daughter described as a Groucho walk. In this stance on this occasion she proceeded to do what she dearly loved to do, but knew was forbidden—she went to the nearest bookcase and began pulling books out on to the floor! A little later—another forbidden delight, similarly 'protected'—she went over to fiddle with the knobs on the television set.

Bruner's (Bruner, Jolly and Sylva, 1976) attention seems to have been attracted to the notion of 'the play face' because it serves 'to reduce the apparently dizzying variety of forms that play could take'. 'On closer observation,' he goes on, 'it turns out that play is universally accompanied in subhuman primates by a recognizable form of meta-signalling, a "play face", first carefully studied by the Dutch primatologist van Hooff. It is a powerful signal—redundant in its features, which include a particular kind of open-mouthed gesture, a slack but exaggerated gait, and a marked "galumphing" in

3

movement' (p.14). The kind of behaviour most frequently associated with the play face in monkeys is the play fight, and instances of this have been observed in creatures from a few weeks' old through to the adult stage (van Hooff, Chevalier-Skolnikoff and Lawick-Goodall in Bruner *et al.*, 1976). A somewhat attenuated form of the play-face signal has also been claimed to occur in the rough-and-tumble play of three- to five-year-old children (Burton Jones in Bruner *et al.*, 1976).

In Laurie, use of the play face was short-lived—after about three months we did not observe it; and I shall speculate on why this was so. Not very long after that first observation I have referred to, Laurie began to take an interest in picture story books and photographs of members of the family. This seemed at first to be principally an interest in recognizing familiar people or objects. She liked to sit on somebody's knee, follow the pictures and listen to what was being read. The reading in the early stages was punctuated by pointing and vocalizing. (At 1 year 6 months, *Ba-ba*, *Da-da*, *Mummy*, *cheese* (for any kind of food), *outside*, etc. At 1 year 9 months, *Teddy*, *there he is*, *blanket*, *towel*, *birdie, quack-quack, nose*, etc.) No doubt this behaviour can be explained simply as part of the familiar 'naming game'—applied here to pictures of objects as it had already been applied to objects themselves. But there may be another aspect: if indeed stories are to open up a new world of the 'possible' as distinct from the actual, then the sustained interest in finding what is familiar from first-hand experience now recurring in pictures and stories may be seen as a process of making herself at home in the newly approached alternative world, the world of story. Very soon her performance began to reflect a more substantive interest in what goes on in that world. At 2 years 2 weeks, she had a picture story book called *The Naughty Pussies*. Sitting on her mother's knee, turning the pages over and listening, she kept up her own commentary, 'pussy table', 'naughty pussies', 'cup of tea', 'tea cloth' and so on, until the 'catastrophe' happens—the table cloth is pulled off and everything falls over: at this point she cried out 'Naughty!', then, hitting the page at every repetition, she shouted, 'NO! NO! NO! NO!'.

Her enjoyment of stories and ability to participate in them grows rapidly. Her comments begin to include anticipations of what is going to happen and her own opinions regarding what does happen.

At the same time, there is, as one would expect, a reciprocal movement by which story material begins to affect her own play. What in the early stages was manipulative play imitative of daily experiences (dressing and undressing the teddy bears and dolls, bathing, feeding, changing them) is increasingly accompanied by explanatory comments that draw upon her own feelings and purposes and so elaborate make-believe behaviour in a way that both parallels narrative structure and incorporates incidents from particular narratives. Her toys, it seems to me, become coinhabitants with her of a story world.

If the play face was a device for opting out of the actual social world in order to suspend its sanctions, then I believe she no longer needs it: the story world, once established, provides that refuge, enabling her, within limits, to make happen what she wants to happen.

We should do well not to underestimate the importance of this first encounter with the story world. I think it has a double impact. In the first place, verbal narrative form presents an organized representation of the kinds of experiences a child has hitherto participated in or observed or heard talked about—modes of involvement which frequently intermingle, and each of which must in itself appear as partial, diffuse, fragmentary when compared with a verbal narrative. Secondly, a vast range of new and unfamiliar participants in events is brought on to the scene. Their novelty and strangeness no doubt tend to put events into a more distant perspective, so helping a child to perceive the forms or patterns that events can take. Laurie's experience of being reproached for something she has done, for example, may now be set alongside the tale of the naughty kittens.

Precisely how a child sees the relationship between experienced events and narrated events we clearly do not know; yet it must surely be the case that narrative form perceived in stories begins to influence the interpretations he makes of what happens to him.

How in fact does an infant make sense of his early experiences? Speaking from a phenomenological perspective of the process of construing in general, George Kelly (1963) offers us this: 'The substance that a person construes is itself a process . . . It presents itself from the beginning as an unending and undifferentiated process. Only when man attunes his ear to recurrent themes in the monotonous flow does his universe begin to make sense to him. Like a musician, he must phrase his experience in order to make sense of it. The phrases are distinguished events' (p.52). Under the influence of Vygotsky's work, interpreted and extended by Bruner and Roger Brown, we have become accustomed to recognizing the role that language plays in this process of 'phasing our experience'. In the course of social interchange—speaking and doing in close association—a child acquires words which then become, as it were, 'filing pins' upon which categories of experiences are constructed. The categories are crude at first but continuing use of the terms in increasingly sophisticated ways over a period of years leads eventually to the development of 'true concepts', modes of thinking typical of the adult user of the language in question.

This explanatory theory has been considerably modified in recent years as a result of studies of prelinguistic behaviour. Bruner (1975), for example, has found that cooperative activity between parent and infant, principally in the form of play, establishes 'formats', routines of behaviour into which the infant is increasingly drawn, and which become increasingly meaningful to him. In this way meanings are exchanged by the joint recognition of behavioural patterns—the infant begins 'to phrase his experience in order to make sense of it'. A child's own vocalizations accompany these activities and are in course of time assimilated to the mother's speech. Thus speech first functions in such a way as to *highlight meanings already established in terms of cooperative activity*. Such observations allow Bruner to speculate 'that language is a specialized and conventionalized extension of cooperative action: its acquisition is a transformation of modes of assuring cooperation that are prior to language' (p. 3).

Katherine Nelson (1974) is directly critical of what she calls 'the abstraction theory' of concept formation—the gradual extraction of common features from successive encounters pivoted upon words. Instead of asking 'How does a child form a concept to fit the word?' she suggests we should ask 'How does a child fit words to his concepts?' For she believes that young children form a few powerful 'core concepts' from their experiences of, and action upon, objects, people and events. These core concepts are dynamic in the sense that they are constructed in response to things that move, change, can be manipulated, that they are based upon functions rather than features, and that they are holistic rather than analytic. Drawing a similar picture, John and Elizabeth Newson (1974, 1975) stress the importance of the adult's role in the interaction: 'The object with which the human infant interacts most often and most effectively, particularly in the earliest stages of development, is almost invariably another human being.' This 'intersubjectivity', a process of negotiation between individuals, is, in the Newsons' view, the source of human understanding; of its acquisition they say: 'Only through the delicate ballet of action and reaction between a more experienced and a less experienced communicator can shared meanings be arrived at.'

All this begins to suggest that the earliest framework by which children construe experience may be one of human motives and intentions and the ways in which they interact. When Margaret Donaldson (1978) distinguishes between 'embedded' and 'disembedded' reasoning, it is clear from her account and from the experiments she describes that human intentions are the matrix in which the child's early thinking is embedded; and when she wants to illustrate young children's ability to reason deductively, she quotes their comments while *listening to stories* (p.55).

We may surmise, then, that a general sense of how human beings interact provides a powerful framework for a child's early thinking, a framework which later accommodates and influences the kind of concept formation Vygotsky has described, pivoting on words as they are acquired; further, that this framework both assists a child in making sense of the stories he hears and is itself elaborated and extended from that source. It is interesting to note, in this connection, that an American psychologist has claimed that story comprehension provides 'A Royal Road to an understanding of the human mind' (Bower, 1978); and a British psychologist goes so far as to suggest that the paradigm needed for psychology to become a respectable science is one that recognizes 'the notion of the perception and behaviour of higher organisms as being given by a kind of running internal fiction, rather than from stimuli directly related to events' (Gregory, 1977). What we need, in other words, is a psychology committed to studying the internal fictions by which we store versions of our experience, anticipate events, etc.

REALITY AND THE STORY WORLD

Let me consider in more detail one aspect of the relationship, as a child sees it, between events experienced at first hand and the events represented in the story world. I have suggested that the distinction marked by 'the play face' when Laurie was about one year old—a distinction between 'in play' and 'in earnest'—rapidly gave way, once she had established a sense of the story world, to a distinction between that world and the real world we live in; further, that in her make-believe play she was operating, along with her dolls and other toys, in the story world. The relationship I am concerned with, then, is that between reality on the one hand and make-believe play and fictional stories on the other.

From the age of two Laurie was accustomed to hearing her voice on the tape-recorder, and often demanded it by saying, 'Want Laurie'. At 2 years 7 months, this exchange with me took place:

L.   What's that on your lap?
Me   That's a tape-recorder.
L.   Where's tend Laurie?
Me   Mm?
L.   Where's tend Laurie?
Me   Where's what?
L.   Tend Laurie.
Me   Tend Laurie? What's that mean?
L.   Tend Laurie in that.
Me   On yes, Laurie in there.

I finally made it: 'tend Laurie' means pretend—a word she had previously used only as a verb ('Tend Laurie telephone—"Hello" '). Thereafter she used 'tend' to acknowledge the play function of objects: when she 'pretended' to cook a meal for her teddies it was 'tend scrambled egg' on 'tend plates' (2 years 7 months), and when she put a doll to bed she wanted 'a hot bottle' and commented, 'cold—tend hot' (3 years 1 month). A verbal means had been found, it seems, of marking the distinction between the meanings associated with everyday reality and the meanings assigned for the purposes of make-believe. But it is not a simple distinction to make and Laurie's use of the term shows interesting developments. At 3 years 3 months, there was this exchange:

L.   Want hear Laurie.
Me.   Mm?
L.   Hear Laurie.
Me.   Pretend Laurie?
L.   No, *real* Laurie.
Me.   (*pointing towards her*) But *that's* real Laurie!
L.   No, want Laurie in there.

I suppose there must be some growing sense of the difference between somebody mimicking Laurie, which would count as 'pretend', and the function of the recording machine. Again, if dolls that are constantly 'fed', 'bathed', 'put to bed' are clearly associated by function with the pretend world, what is the status of art objects, things we display but don't *use*? At 3 years 4 months, Laurie walked around the Victoria and Albert Museum and persisted in asking 'pretend' or 'real' of a variety of objects, mostly in glass cases, but including a very real orange that somebody had put aside for lunch!

In a recently published posthumous book, *Mind in Society*, Vygotsky (1978) assigns an important role to the use of play symbols as a stage in what he calls the 'prehistory of written language'. The use of gestures and visual signs constitutes the first stage in this prehistory ('Gestures, it has been correctly said, are writing in air'), and the incorporation of objects to facilitate gesture introduces the second stage, that of the use of play symbols: 'A stick becomes a riding-horse for a child because it can be placed between the legs and a gesture can be employed that communicates that the stick designates a horse in this instance' (p.108). From repeated use in this way in the play situation, the object itself gradually acquires an appropriate meaning. In this early stage, Vygotsky suggests, 'perceptual similarity of the objects plays no noticeable part in the understanding of the symbolic notation'—a characteristic, clearly, that applies also to a written word. At a later stage, however, 'children begin to make one exceptionally important discovery—that objects can indicate the things they denote as well as substitute for them' (p.109). At this stage aspects of the play objects themselves begin to influence the interpretations given to them in the play activity. Laurie's 'pretend scrambled egg', for example, when she first played the game was anything that could be put into a 'pan' and dished out on to 'plates'; but, after several months of the game, once having used *yellow* torn-up paper she was unhappy with anything else. This interpenetration of perceived aspects of the play object with its symbolic significance will have the effect of stabilizing the use of the object and so making it meaningful without the support of the gestures that first gave it meaning. Vygotsky quotes an experiment in which he consistently used a variety of everyday objects to represent the people and places in a game; thus, a watch represented a drug-store, a pencil represented a nursemaid, and a knife, a doctor. When, quite outside the play situation, a knife fell to the floor, a child said, 'The doctor has fallen' (p.110). Vygotsky believes that developing such a secondary meaning for a play object independent of the play situation is an important step towards handling the second-order symbolism of the written language (where a written word is a symbol for the spoken word which in turn is symbol for its referent).

Vygotsky's example of the knife/doctor may seem a little over-induced, but the interaction of the play purpose and the nature of the play object may be observed in spontaneous play. Two boys, a five-year-old and a seven-year-old, were recently recorded playing with an assortment of toys, mostly model cars. But in the course of the play, the story framework changed from an accident involving a car to one involving a space-ship. New roles were happily allotted to the toy vehicles until they came to this point:

Five-year-old   Pretend this was the space-ship. All right, Batman car the space-ship.

Seven-year-old   I've mended it. We needs a mechanic. See if I can make a mechanic. Oh yes, this is the mechanic. (*holding up a squeaking toy mouse*).

Five-year-old   No it isn't! He squeaks, so he must be a mouse!

Together   (*with delighted giggles*). A *gigantic* mouse!

And the game proceeds, with the space-monster mouse-mechanic playing his appointed role. (With acknowledgements to Pat Jones, Advisory Teacher, Wiltshire County Council.)

I am inclined to believe that in the early stages the distinction between socially determined reality and the story world is essentially a distinction between two orders of meaning, those derived from first-hand experience, and those *assigned* for the purposes of make-believe play and fictional stories. There is in make-believe play a freedom to invent, and in fictional stories a freedom to interpret, that is in sharp contrast to the demands of given meanings in social interaction. Further, I believe that the two orders of meaning are in the earliest stages held in paradox rather than set over against each other. I take the word 'paradox' from Donald Winnicott's comments on play in his book, *Playing and Reality* (1971). His primary example of paradox relates to the 'transitional object'—the scrap of blanket or other handy item that forms the first bridge from the wholly inner life of the infant to the world of objects that constitutes his environment. That paradox is a sharp one—the child has 'created' the transitional object that is at the same time something that was 'lying around'. Winnicott goes on to claim 'that when we witness an infant's employment of a transitional object, the first not-me possession, we are witnessing both the child's first use of a symbol and the first experience of play' (p.96). He sees a direct development from playing to cultural experiences in general and throughout this development an element of paradox remains.

My paradox seems to be a double one. The child's active involvement in the stories he hears is, I believe, tantamount to an act of invention on his part, not distinguished from the inventiveness of his make-believe play. And, in the second place, his activities in the story world exist alongside his first-hand experiences without at first challenging direct comparison. Clare, aged 2 years 9 months, *differentiates* when she says, leaving her toy farm to go to bed, 'Oh *why* am I *real* and I can't live in my little farm!' — but she will be many months older before she first asks of a story she likes, 'Is it true?' I would agree with Winnicott when he advises adult observers of children's play that 'the paradox needs to be accepted, tolerated, and not resolved' (p.53).

In course of time, however, the child will come to raise the question himself. A conversation between Andrew, aged 3 years 11 months, and his nursery class teacher, reported by Nancy Martin (1976), illustrates what is probably an early stage of that enquiry. Andrew discovered his teacher writing up events in her log book, and asked, 'What are you writing?'

T. Some of the interesting things that have happened here in the Nursery.
A. Tell me them.
T. This one says, 'Mrs T and Mrs S visited the Nursery during the afternoon session to see the climbing frame and make arrangements for its removal'.
A. What did they want to look at it for? Drew says they are going to take it away in a lorry.
T. I'm hoping so. It's very rusty and dangerous for you all to use. That's why I asked Mrs S to come and see it. Then, after she'd been here I wrote all about it in this book.
A. Read some more. (*The teacher does so and Andrew asks:*) Is it all real? Is it a true story?
T. Everything in here is true. I only write down the things that actually happen . . . .
A. It's a nice story book. Why have you never read it to us?
T. I'm sorry that I didn't think of it. It's a lovely idea . . . .
A. Are all books real? They're not, are they? Some of them are. The one about the farm, and the car book, and the seaside, they're real. But it's hard to know. Is *Monkey Island* real? That's my favourite.
(*The teacher suggests that he should fetch it from the library so that they can find out.*)
A. (*returning with the book*) It's not a true story. I asked in there. I don't know whether it's my favourite any more.

This reluctance to accept that a familiar story may not be true — may be an account of events that never happened—seems to be part of a typical developmental pattern. Applebee (1973), in a study of the stories that five- to seven-year-olds hear, read and tell, recorded this exchange with a five-and-a-half-year-old:

(Where does Cinderella live?)	In a little house.
(Do you know where that is?)	In the woods.
(Where are the woods?)	—
(Do you think you could go to the woods to visit her?)	No.
(Why not?)	There might be a wolf there.
	(p.136)

Applebee found that the younger children were usually confident that the fictional characters could be visited, though for a variety of reasons it would not be easy. In developmental terms, 'the progression seems to be from total acceptance of story characters to a stage at which they are real but very far away, to an awareness of insurmountable contradictions between what story characters do and the child's knowledge of the possible. At this last stage, story characters become "just a story", often being assimilated to puppets and other active but clearly "made-up" characters' (p.141).

In his longer study, *The Child's Concept of Story*, Applebee (1978) documents the kind of reluctance we caught a glimpse of in Andrew's comments on *Monkey Island*. By the age of nine or ten, he found, most children have come to accept the fictional nature of stories as 'just stories', but the progress has been gradual, one of elimination, so to speak, since an individual's best loved stories are the last to be admitted to be 'untrue' (p.46). The progression is also complicated by the fact that obvious unreality is accepted and enjoyed from an early age. Nonsense rhymes, for example, 'are accepted and enjoyed precisely because they are *not* real; instead they invert the normal order of events in a way that the child recognizes and greets with laughter' (p.40). (Clare, at four and a half, produced inversions for her own amusement, as for example:

I danced over water, I skipped over sea
All the birds in the air couldn't catch me
I skipped as slow as I could over water
I danced as slow as I could over sea
All the silly birds in the air couldn't catch me.)

Applebee suggests that it is the young child's inability to recognize the respective roles of real and make-believe experience (the 'paradox' I have referred to) that allows the story world to be 'a powerful mode for extending the relatively limited experience of young children'. From stories they learn, in short, what to expect from people and places 'without the distracting pressure of separating the real from the make-believe' (p.52). When, with reluctance, the true/not-true dichotomous distinction is progressively applied, I think it likely (though I know of no evidence) that some children lose interest in stories and do not recover it. For those who come out at the other side, however, recognizing and differentially valuing both modes of experience, stories will acquire an important new role. In Applebee's words: 'As long as stories are seen as true, or at least (as in nonsense) simply an inversion of the true, they can only present the child with the world as it is, a world to be assimilated and reconciled as best the child is able. It is only after the story has emerged as a fiction that it can begin a new journey toward a role in the exploration of the world not as it is but as it might be, a world which poses alternatives rather than declares certainties' (p.41).

What, then, do we mean by 'emerged as a fiction'? There is a simple sense in which a true story reports real events and describes a real world, while a fictional story is free to do otherwise—to describe as though they happened events that did not take place and to locate them in a world in which what we know to be *im*possible is possible. But of course the freedom to do so is very different from an injunction to do so, and many a paragraph in a work of fiction is fictional only by reason of the context in which it is placed. [As Gregory, (1977, p.394) has observed, 'Novels describe recognizable people, with the usual number of heads and arms, living in ways which are broadly familiar'.] The writer of the true story is under an injunction; the writer of the fictional story is not. Where in fiction the 'real' ends and the 'fictional' begins may well puzzle us as it confused Laurie when she listened to herself on the tape-recorder. What we meet in fiction, then, is a conglomerate of the real and the fictional. The child's ability to respond appropriately to that conglomerate marks the sophisticated end of the developmental sequence that began with a paradoxical indeterminacy, moved through a true/untrue dichotomy, and successfully emerged. There remains the further question as to how direct and unassailable is our conception of 'the real', but that question I shall defer to a later context.

THE WRITTEN LANGUAGE

My concern so far has been to explore the effects upon young children of coming to know the story world. It is high time I moved on to relate this to the processes of writing, and for that purpose I need to go back to Vygotsky's (1978) essay on 'The Prehistory of Written Language'. Though his references in that essay focus upon writing, it is important to understand that he sees writing as an inextricable part of the broader process of mastering uses of the written language, both in reading and writing, and in facilitating speech and thought. If teachers in their practices and psychologists in their theories see reading and writing as distinct processes, it is because they focus upon the motor skills required and ignore the effects of written language acquisition upon cognitive development, and the role it plays in relation to a child's own needs and purposes.

In tracing the development of the written language in the individual child, Vygotsky sees four modes of behaviour, each intricately—if sometimes deviously—related to the others. These, in order, are: (1) the use of gesture and visual signs, (2) the use of symbolism in play, (3) the use of symbolism in drawing, and (4) the use of symbolism in writing. Taken together they constitute what he calls 'the history of sign development in the child' (p.106). I was struck first, in reading this, by the fact that speech is not an item in that list; and I was reminded of a comment in Vygotsky's (1962) earlier book, *Thought and Language*, 'Our investigation has shown that the development of writing does not repeat the developmental history of speaking. Written speech is a separate linguistic function, differing from oral speech in both structure and mode of functioning' (p.98). One of the most notable lessons we learned from that earlier book was the view that infant speech lays the foundations for mature thinking. A child takes on the conversational speech of those around him, discovers that talking to himself about what he is doing is an aid to successful performance, and thereafter employs speech in two modes, conversational interaction and 'speech for oneself'. This latter mode, moving towards what we might call 'private speech' (increasingly freed from the constraints of both speech syntax and conventional word-meanings) becomes internalized as 'inner speech'—the 'post-language symbols', as they have been called, that we employ in mature thinking. This model by which overt social behaviour (that of speech) becomes internalized (and at the same time 'emancipated') is, I think, typical of Vygotsky's view of the development of human consciousness. Speech becomes the arena in which meanings are actively negotiated, in which understanding is generated. Its ability to perform this function arises from the fact, in Sapir's (1961) words, that 'it is learned early and piecemeal, in constant association with the colour and the requirements of actual contexts' (p.10). Add to this the dynamics of conversation, here described by Berger and Luckmann (1967): 'In the face-to-face situation language possesses an inherent quality of reciprocity that distinguishes it from any other sign system. I speak as I think; so does my partner in the conversation. Both of us hear what each other says at virtually the same instant, which makes possible a continuous, synchronized, reciprocal access to our two subjectivities, an intersubjective closeness in the face-to-face situation that no other sign system can duplicate. What is more, I hear *myself* as I speak; my own subjective meanings are made objectively and continuously available to me and *ipso facto* become "more real" to me' (p.52).

This interdependence of speech and context is crucial. In the earliest stages of speaking, 'context' refers primarily to the physical situation: a young child's conversational speech is more or less restricted to revealing the here-and-now—in fact to whatever of the here-and-now is taken up into cooperative behaviour. As 'represented experiences' in pictures, models, picture books, are taken up, the context expands and, as we have seen, the story framework itself provides schemas that facilitate that expansion. By such means the child reaches a stage where remembered experience can be brought into the context where it relates to present activity or where it is brought into a communicative exchange, whatever is 'between us' as topic of conversation. The stimulus of the interaction with the physical environment or with a partner in conversation seems to me to be crucial.

What then remains as a function distinctive to written language? Clearly the clue to the difference lies in the reduced dependence upon such a stimulus from the physical and social environment. What is read may be re-read across changing contexts, in varying physical situations and varying social relationships (with their concomitant attitudes and feelings). What is written may be returned to and considered afresh, each approach being influenced by a different set of circumstances and expectations. There is thus a superimposing of one situational, ideational and emotional context upon another and what is successively 'recaptured' grows less context-dependent than an item in a conversational exchange. The move is toward a *constancy* of meaning, towards an ability to handle relationships that are less and less 'embedded' in particular situations. This, as Vygotsky (1978) has suggested, parallels a move from arithmetic to algebra; and in terms of development, it constitutes the taking on of "a particular system of symbols and signs whose mastery heralds a critical turning point in the entire cultural development of the child' (p.106).

Speech certainly has an important role to play in the acquisition of mastery of the written language: it can be shown that at each of Vygotsky's four stages in that development it acts as a facilitator. Yet the four stages thus assisted by speech move in a direction that is *away* from speech; a direction I can only describe as a move from *intimacy* and *immediacy* of meaning towards *constancy* of meaning. Thus, while, generalization and abstraction, for example, have a role to play in the spoken language, it might be claimed that their home ground is the written language.

Vygotsky's first stage, that of gestures and visual signs, seems to cover a variety of early activities including 'the play face', pointing, waving goodbye, a good deal of scribbling and early drawing, where the marks made by the pencil may catch merely a residue of the gestural depiction produced by the child. The importance he attaches to gesture ('the initial visual sign that contains the child's future writing as an acorn contains a future oak'—p.147) must be related to the importance anthropologists ascribe to gesture in the primates, i.e. that it constitutes a stage in evolution at which an organism 'gradually ceases to respond quite "automatically" to the mood-signs of another and becomes able to recognize the sign as a signal: that is, to recognize that the other individual's and its own signals are only signals which can be trusted, distrusted, falsified, denied, amplified, corrected and so forth' (Bateson, in Bruner *et al.*, 1976, p.119). As precursor to communicative behaviour in general this is clearly a vital step: its relation to writing in particular emerges only at the later stages of the development to which it has contributed.

The use of symbols in play represents a more sustained and deliberate form of symbolic behaviour, a narrative enactment that is enriched and extended as it incorporates material from the stories children have read to them. Here, as we have seen, Vygotsky makes the particular point that the increasingly stable meanings assigned to play objects pave the way for 'the deliberate structuring of the web of meaning' (Vygotsky, 1962, p.100) demanded in the production of written language.

In considering the use of symbols in drawing, Vygotsky again stresses the important role played by speech. Drawing really only begins when a child is fluent in speech. What he draws is what he *knows* rather than what he can *see*, and he musters that knowledge in speaking as he draws. Progress is marked by the stage at which his speech *designates* what he is drawing: in the earliest stage a word used about a completed drawing (or scribble) may designate what he now recognizes after the event, but as time goes on the designating word comes earlier and earlier. Vygotsky sees this as an indication that the drawing becomes increasingly a carrying out of what has been designated in advance, and thus involves a process of *deliberate representation*, foreshadowing what must take place when we write.

The most tantalizing comment in this account is Vygotsky's suggestion that in order to master second-order symbolism—in order to learn to write—a child must 'make a basic discovery—namely that one can draw not only things but also speech' (p.115). He admits that we do not know how this shift takes place because no conclusive research has been carried out. He refers to experiments which suggest that the particular placing of 'meaningless and undifferentiated squiggles' upon a page does appear in some children to provide a kind of recording that is meaningful to them—a kind of topographical recording which they can use as an aid to recall. And he goes on, 'Children gradually transform these undifferentiated marks. Indicatory signs and symbolizing marks and scribbles are replaced by little figures and pictures, and these in turn give way to signs' (p.115). How the shift is made from squiggle to conventional orthography remains a fascinating speculation. Manipulative play is likely, I believe, to form an important element in that shift; make-believe play and the story world are likely to prove a facilitating context for it.

KNOWLEDGE OF LITERACY

Laurie at 3 years and 4 months cannot read or write, yet the written language has occupied a good deal of her attention for some while. Her interest in books began early: enjoyment of the first stories read to her was accompanied by curiosity about the books themselves — the pictures, the turning of pages, the printed marks — all this by 1 year 10 months. And though she has become an addict of the Muppets and one or two other television programmes this does not seem to have affected her concern for story books.

The first references to writing in my records came about a year later, at 2 years and 10 months, in a conversation between Laurie and her father:

F. What've you got there?
L. It's a book. I want to write in it.
F. You want to write in it? What sort of a book is it?
L. (*with emphasis*) Daddy's book!
F. That's Daddy's book, isn't it?
L. Want to write.
F. You know, it's Daddy's Italian notebook.
L. Want to write.
F. What do you want to write?
L. 'Ve you got a pen?
F. Yes, I've got a pen. What do you want to say?
L. I *can't* write!

One of her favourite games in recent weeks has been playing at restaurants, and there is a corner of 'the green room' where it takes place. I have played the customer several times. Amongst the talk of what she can offer her customers, reference to quantities and prices is fairly prominent. Here are the opening moves on a recent occasion (at 3 years 3 months):

L. Do you like three cucumbers?
Me I think I'd like some scrambled egg. Could I have some scrambled egg?
L. Yeah. Two Fifty P. And three yoghurts?
Me Yes, and some coffee.
L. O.K. Sixteen.

What particularly struck me was that the set-up included a tear-off pad and a pencil and whenever she took an order she made a scribble on her pad. I noted the order in which she wrote these down, pointed to the second of the four listed items and asked her what it was. She answered at once, correctly, 'coffee'. When after a while I said I wanted to pay the bill, she said "Three, please, six, seven.'

On that same day I was shown a letter she had written to her friend Anna.

Lines of cursive scribble were on the inside of a folded sheet, and on the outside rather more angular shapes looking like an address. Asking her what it said, we were told, 'Anna', 'Dear Possum' (a nickname), and 'Home for Christmas'.

Two weeks later, when she was on holiday with her parents, they noticed her walking up and down gazing intently at the cover of a book she had in her hands. When they realized that the author's name, boldly printed on the front, began with ALISON, they asked her if she knew what it said. (Alison is her mother's name and Laurie likes to call her that on occasion.) 'I don't know what it says,' she said firmly without taking her eyes off it. 'Go on,' they coaxed her, 'what do you think it says?' She looked up and asked, 'Does it say "mummy"?'

That was about two weeks ago. Laurie's visit to us yesterday, at 3 years 4 months, proved a splendid occasion for winding up my account. She had a particularly long session listening to my wife reading nursery rhymes out of a large picture book which has a kind of pictorial inventory of the contents inside the front cover and an index at the back. After a break she came bursting into the room shouting 'Danny!' (an earlier attempt of course at saying 'granny' which has now become fixed):

L. Come on Danny! I'll read you a story!
D. Oh, that's nice!
L. I'll read this story to you, O.K.?
D. You read me a lovely story—that will be nice.
L. (*Pointing at an item in the picture inventory*) Do you like this story. Do you like this one?
D. I like them all. You choose.
L. What, this one? This one?
D. Mm.
L. O.K. (*she turns to the index at the back*)
D. Can you manage?
L. Yes, I'll find it. Eighty Six. (*a 'pretend' operation, of course*)
D. Any one will do, Darling.
L. Four.
D. That will be around the beginning of the book.
L. Where is it?
D. About here, I should think.
L. (*having found the one she wants*) A man and an old lady had so much children (*pause*)
D. She didn't
L. Know what to *do* (*pause*)
D. She gave them
L. Some bread (*pause*)

D. Some soup
L. And sent them to bed!
D. Yes!

Laurie had brought with her a sealed envelope with a dollar note inside it. On the flap was a drawn line on which a line of cursive scribble rested. On the front was a line which began with the same sort of cursive scribble but changed into a string of double circles, eight of them, continuing in a straight line. When I asked her what this writing meant, she said 'Eggs'. It appears that it was, in imitation of something her mother had done the day before, a letter to someone asking them to buy her some eggs!

So what will come next? Shall I be able to document further Vygotsky's suggested shift from 'drawing objects' to 'drawing speech'? Perhaps the next stage will involve some manipulative play with the substance of the written language: alphabet books and letters — blocks or cut-out shapes. There would be little one could call 'analytic' in that manipulation: selecting and arranging — acts of synthesizing, on changing criteria, colour and shape, and perhaps culminating in word production. I believe such manipulative play with 'alphabetic substance' might be helpful, but I may be wrong; experience with print and with pen — in the stimulating context of make-believe play and stories — may itself be enough.

What seems perfectly clear is that 'pretend writing' and 'pretend reading' are crucial elements in the prehistory of writing. After all, we pretend to be the sort of people we *want* to be and we pretend to do the sort of things we *want* to do. Pretending presupposes some imaginative grasp of what writing and reading can do for us. Recent psychological, linguistic and other enquiries are revealing how our intentions release tacit powers favourable to successful performance (Bruner, 1975; Polanyi, 1958; Slobin and Welsh, 1973).

As final comment on Laurie's progress so far, it is interesting to note that Wells found 'knowledge of literacy' to be the most significant predictor of educational attainment at the age of seven (Wells, 1981).

READING AND WRITING STORIES

I have known seven or eight cases of children who have learned to write before the stage at which they were given any deliberate instruction in writing. There is one striking feature they have in common: they all wrote stories, and characteristically they wrote them in the form of story books, stitched or clipped together, with a picture on the cover, and maybe pictures inside as well. I am interested to know why there should be this common approach on the part of self-taught writers. (One of the cases I have documented elsewhere: Britton, 1982.)

Bereiter and Scardamalia (1981) make a distinction between 'open' and 'closed' schemas of discourse, the open ones being those most dependent upon interaction between speaker and listener(s). Since in writing there is no such interaction, it is the closed schemas that are more easily transferred from oral to written production. The authors suggest that oral narratives are less open than any other oral form and stories are therefore the most accessible kind of writing for inexperienced writers. Taking length of utterance as a rough measure of success, they support their view with the finding that Grade 3 and Grade 5 children produced more words both in telling and in writing stories than they did in telling and writing 'opinion essays'.

My second point of explanation also concerns the level of difficulty in writing. In his book, *The Psychology of Art*, Vygotsky (1971) refers to the difference between his response to a story and his response to a piece of informative writing. In the latter case, he says, 'I process and evaluate it according to an intellectual technique which I always use to acquaint myself with a new idea' (p.115)—a process which he does not apply in responding to a story. Applebee (1978) makes a similar point when he refers to the most characteristic feature of literary writing, including stories, as 'the release from the demands of immediate response' (p.9). In our Schools Council Writing Research (Britton, *et al.*, 1975) we referred to this difference as one of contextualization—the way we take what is on the page and make it our own. In transactional or non-literary discourse we contextualize in *piecemeal* fashion, judging as we read what to accept for further consideration and what to reject; and building relationships for ourselves between what we accept and our background of existing knowledge and opinion. There is thus a kind of running inner debate between reader and text. In poetic or literary discourse, on the other hand, contextualization is *global*—something that is postponed until the form of the 'verbal object' has been entered into and its unity reconstructed (and even then, contextualization may be slow, un-deliberate, largely unconscious—the way we gradually 'absorb' the effects of our own first-hand experience). In practice this means that beginning to read a story is like opening the gate and entering a garden and waiting to see what happens to us.

But all this reflects also on the writer's task. In transactional writing he must begin by trying to enmesh with the reader's state of knowledge, opinions, interests, and he must anticipate and play his role in the 'inner debate' with the reader. In story telling this element in the writing is missing.

Both these points concerning the difficulty of writing are relevant to the teaching and learning of writing in school. But they do not go very far towards explaining why a young child at home, when no one is taxing him with the need to write, should choose to write stories when he does not choose to write anything else.

To understand this I think we need a different order of explanation. For most children the acquisition of speech must feel something like a success story. Their evident pleasure in it, their active employment of it, alike suggest this. They may even have a sense of how well it has served them and how well it continues to meet their needs. Then why should they bother with the written language—those hieroglyphics so laborious to produce? But for some of them the advent of the picture book and the read story effect a change. The story world becomes a powerful preoccupation: the written language becomes valuable as a vehicle for stories. Story books are precious and they set about to add their own contribution to the world's stock of such treasures.

That is one way of interpreting what undoubtedly happens with the self-taught writers I have known; they arrive at a point where they *want* to write, and what they want to write is stories. And because they want to write, they learn how to. It is an interpretation consistent with Vygotsky's comments on the pedagogy of the written language. Looking at the schools of his day, he complained that, 'Instead of being founded on the needs of children as they naturally develop and on their own activity, writing is given to them from without, from the teacher's hands' (Vygotsky, 1978, p.105).

DEVELOPMENTS IN STORY WRITING

I suggest from my own observations that young children's concern with stories follows roughly the following sequence: hearing stories told and read; enacting stories in play; telling stories; dictating them, when given the opportunity; and finally writing and reading stories. Dictating stories, because it tends to be a more deliberate 'performance' sometimes reveals interesting evidence of the fact that children who have not yet learned to read have nevertheless internalized some forms of the written language. A four-year-old boy, for example, dictated a fairy story which contained the sentence, 'The king went sadly home, for he had nowhere else to go'—a use of 'for' which could not have been derived from spoken utterance in ordinary conversation. It seems likely that the early stages of progress in writing stories will rely upon the enrichment of a child's spoken resources by an increasing store of internalized written forms derived from listening and reading.

Applebee (1978), in a chapter he calls 'Narrative Form', examines the modes of organization found in the stories that children tell between the ages of two and five. He identifies two principles by which events in a story are related to each other—'centering' and 'chaining'. 'Centering' refers to the way events are related to a common core—typically, for example, in simple stories, that they are the actions of, or what happened to, a single character. 'Chaining' refers to direct links between one event and another that follows it. In the earliest stage of story telling, events may be randomly related, making use of neither principle, a form of narrative that he calls 'heaps' and which constitutes the first of his six developmental categories. The next stage, 'sequences', makes use of centering only; a later one, 'unfocused chains', employs chaining only; but his sixth and final category, 'narratives', is organized in a way that reflects both chaining and centering. What is of particular interest about this set of categories is that it does closely parallel Vygotsky's stages of concept development, on which it is based. Applebee's analysis of 30 oral narratives at each of the four age-groups two to five indicates that children are likely to be employing both modes of organizing by the time they are five years' old, i.e. at the earliest age at which they might be expected to tackle story writing.

Applebee goes on to suggest, however, that his two principles will apply recursively to longer and more complex stories and to the organization in a literary work not only of events but also of 'images, ideas or even sounds' (p.70). 'Finally when we move to fully poetic forms, both chaining and centering become all-pervasive. In a play such as *King Lear*, for example, it matters little whether the element we choose for analysis is the word, the line, the incident, the scene, the act, the character, the image, or the symbol; at each level such elements are bound in complex relationships one to another, and have an overall center or point as well. It is because these relationships are so complex, with each aspect simultaneously part of so many different chains and centers, organized at so many different levels in the structural hierarchy, that the full response to a poetic form cannot be a transactional, analytic one but must be the complex, assimilative, personal formulation that comes only in the spectator role' (pp.71–72). The term 'transactional', contrasting here with 'poetic', and the term 'spectator role' relate to a model of the functions of discourse which I shall shortly be describing. Sufficient to say here that 'language in the spectator role' would cover both the informal stories children tell or write and works of literature.

There is no doubt that a principal dimension of development in story writing will be a move from informal, casual, expressive stories to a more 'shaped' form of story. Even early story telling seems to take on more of the air of a *performance* than of a communicative exchange, demands an audience but discourages an interlocutor. The three-year-old who told the following story did so in a sing-song voice and accompanied it with a rhythmic walking to and fro. Moreover, her interpolation (in conversational tones) suggested that she regarded the utterance as an 'it' — a performance:

> There was a little girl called May
> and she had some dollies
> and the weeds were growing in the ground
> and they made a little nest out of sticks
> for another little birdie up in the tree
> and they climbed up the tree
> and the weeds were growing in the ground
> (*I can do it much better if there's some food in my tum!*)

A one-sentence story written by a seven-year-old girl seems to me to reflect a similar kind of shaping — a shaping by *sound* perhaps:

> Class 1 had Monday off and Tuesday off and all the other classes had Monday and Tuesday off and we played hide-and-seek and my big sister hid her eyes and counted up to ten and me and my brother had to hide and I went behind the dustbin and I was thinking about the summer and the buttercups and daisies all those things and fresh grass and violets and roses and lavender and the twinkling sea and the star in the night and the black sky and the moon.

The shaping of a story into 'a verbal object' will be accomplished in many different ways and by means which at present we certainly do not understand. Applebee's suggestion that chaining and centering might be traced in terms of a range of formal features as well as in his initial terms of events offers a promising field for research. Work in stylistics, notably by Henry Widdowson (1975), which attempts to specify the features that distinguish literary from non-literary discourse, will be an important source of evidence complementary to the evidence to be gained from studies of the stories children and young people write. Widdowson suggests that what is crucial to a definition of literature is 'that the language of a literary work should be fashioned into patterns over and above those required by the actual language code' (p.47) — patterns of phonology, lexis and syntax. He goes on to show that such a patterned form is necessary because, unlike other forms of discourse, a literary work is a self-contained unit, not part of a communicative exchange: 'A piece of literary discourse is in suspense from the usual process of social interaction whereby senders address messages directly to receivers. The literary message does not arise in the normal course of social activity as do other messages, it arises from no previous situation and requires no response, it does not serve as a link between people or as a means of furthering the business of ordinary social life' (p.51).

In studying the first-person narratives written by secondary school pupils from 12 to 17 years of age, Burgess (1977) was also interested in the way writers control 'the improvisation of events into a pattern'. The stories were the work of a junior and a senior class in each of five London schools on two occasions, separated by a year. They formed a part of the data collected in a four-year follow-up study by the Schools Council Writing Research Project at the London University Institute of Education.

Burgess selected for special scrutiny three aspects of story writing: (1) the improvization and sequencing of events, (2) the maintenance and development of the narrator as a character in the story, and (3) the way in which the portrayal of the narrator is integrated with the depiction of events. The least developed narratives were those which were, so to speak, at the mercy of the events themselves; *interpretation* of those events came with a focus upon persons rather than events—particularly, in a first-person narrative, upon the narrator. According to the choice of theme and persona, this would involve either self-exploration or exploration of the nature of 'the other'. Further progress then came with the development of the perspective of the narrator upon his world and, finally, in the writer's ability to represent that perspective in and through the events depicted. Thus, it was the third of his areas of concern—the integration of narrator's role with the presentation of events—that most clearly differentiated the junior writers from their seniors. He explains this in relation to what he sees as the purpose of story writing—essentially an *evaluative* purpose: 'Part of the writer's attention will remain with the shaping of events and part with the development and maintenance of the narrator, but it is in the way that these two are integrated that he has the most complex possibilities for developing a shape which will embody his own evaluation of experience' (p.367).

Dixon and Stratta (1981) have recently begun a tentative investigation into writing development by describing 'staging points' in the narratives based on personal experience produced by pupils of 16 or thereabouts. In a close study of their examples they attempt to answer four questions: (1) What kinds of ordering or re-ordering of experience occur as the writer imaginatively recovers the events of the past, and to what effect? (2) Is the writer taking for granted a reader already acquainted with the setting, the characters, the events? (3) Does the writer remain largely egocentric, or does he develop a more comprehensive perspective in which the thoughts and feelings of other participants are more fully realized? And (4) What significant uses of language indicate that the writer has at his disposal a range of choices in vocabulary and structure, and a sense of appropriate forms and rhetorical strategies? (pp.1–2).

The resulting descriptions of four examples are offered as representing 'staging points' in a developmental sequence. The first is 'an oral model', a story that relies heavily upon a reader's interpretation to give it shape; the second is 'transitional', reflecting a move towards a more formal written style; the third and fourth are 'literary models' in successive stages of 'maturity'. In evidence of this maturity Dixon and Stratta identify as key features in their fourth example (1) the pattern of events ('the dense web of inter-relationships between the events'; 'as readers perceive these complex relations they are drawn into a deeper understanding of the felt meaning of the experience for the participants'); (2) the emotional responses (which are 'explored more fully and more delicately as shifts of mood occur and the action moves forward to a climax'); (3) the social perspective ('The narrator, in taking a more comprehensive point of view and entering into the feelings of different groups, also achieves a broader social perspective, so that the reactions of the various participants are viewed from an independent and somewhat more objective standpoint'); (4) the rhetorical choices (the above effects 'can only be realised by a writer with a refined sense of the appropriate choice of word, sentence or paragraph structure') (p.20). There is interesting evidence here of the very wide range of ability in story writing on the part of students at the age of 16 + , and the idea of describing staging points in a developmental sequence is a good one; but it is the close examination of scripts and detailed commentary on them that gives value to the model.

In the works I have referred to, each of the authors is in his own way contributing to our understanding of what is meant by 'a shaped story' and hence to our understanding of a major parameter of development in story writing.

AN UNDERLYING THEORY

The account I have given of the story world and the evolution of its realization from oral to written forms rests upon a particular view of the relationship between language and experience. I hope it may serve to answer some of the questions arising from what I have said if I conclude with a brief review of that theory.

Edward Sapir (1961) gives us a starting point. Politely taking issue with the view that language is primarily a means of communication, he says: 'It is best to admit that language is primarily a vocal actualisation of the tendency to see realities symbolically . . . an actualisation in terms of vocal expression of the tendency to master reality not by direct and *ad hoc* handling of this element but by the reduction of experience to familiar form' (pp.15–14). Today, this is a widely recognized way of looking at how human beings operate: it is Cassirer's (1944) conception of man as 'the symbol-using animal' and the 'heresy' claimed by Susanne Langer (1960) as the 'new key' for modern philosophy. In order to operate in the world we cumulatively represent to ourselves our successive encounters with it, and our response to any stimulus is mediated by that 'world representation'. Thus the representation is on the one hand a storehouse of our past experience, and on the other a body of expectations as to what may yet happen to us.

To that theorem I want to add two riders. Of the many ways in which we represent the world to ourselves — what Susanne Langer (1960) has called 'the stream of symbols which constitutes a human mind' (p.42) — some have practical value to us and others are wayward, fleeting, playful, and have no practical value. Some we believe in and act upon; others, such as daydreams, in some way gratify us but the question as to how far we *believe* them is an open one, and may be left so since we are not about to test them out in action. Putting this in more general terms, we attach varying degrees of credence to the representations we make (voluntarily or involuntarily) and we accord varying degrees of credence to the representations communicated by other people. I can see no grounds for supposing that in this continuum of degrees of credence there is *any abrupt cut-off point which would divide 'the real' from 'the imaginary'*. The poles will be clearly differentiated, as for example the representations we handle if we are planning a hazardous joint enterprise, as compared with those we deal in when we exchange amusing anecdotes. The extent of our belief will be a function, not only of our judgement as to the reliability of any representation, but also of our individual purposes with respect to it.

The question as to what reasonable degree of credence we may attach to the most thoroughly grounded 'objective' statement is one, of course, that has been long debated, and still is. Michael Polanyi (1958, p.266) puts forward 'a fiduciary formulation of science' in such statements as, 'Science is a system of beliefs to which we are committed' (p.155) and 'We must now recognize belief once more as the source of all knowledge. Tacit assent and intellectual passions, the sharing of an idiom and a cultural heritage, affiliation to a like-minded community: such are the impulses which shape our vision of the nature of things on which we rely for our mastery of things. No intelligence, however critical or original, can operate outside such a fiduciary framework' (p.266). And George Kelly (1969) makes it clear that of the two choices he describes it is the second that he claims for himself: 'When a scientist propounds a theory he has two choices: he can claim that what he says has been dictated to him by the nature of things, or he can take sole responsibility for what he says and claim only that he has offered one man's hopeful construction of the realities of nature' (p.66).

If my first rider seeks to deny a dichotomy between the 'real' and the 'pretend', my second, closely related to the first, proposes an alternative categorization which would, in my view, constitute a dichotomy, at least at the theoretical level. Sapir has suggested that we operate in the real world through the medium of our world representation. If we accept that view, I think we can see that an alternative kind of behaviour is also open to us: *we may operate directly upon our world picture without seeking outcomes in actuality*. In other words, with no intention to act or decide upon action, we may improvise upon our world representation for our own satisfaction. An obvious example would (again) be daydreaming where we indulge our egos by inventing flattering visions of the future for ourselves. At other times we may improvise in order to sweeten our disappointments or recover our self-composure. Fully understood, I believe these improvisations have the effect of preserving the unity, coherence and harmony of our world picture, the conception of the world by which and in which we live.

As adults our most evident uses of language are those in which we interact with other people in the enterprises that make up our active existence, ways of participating in the world's affairs. We exchange information and store it up for future use; we argue, instruct, persuade — 'mastering reality' by interpreting every situation in the light of hypotheses drawn from past experience. It is in this mode that we solve problems, make decisions, take action. But we also take time off; in a more contemplative kind of behaviour we use language, in thought, speech or writing, to reconstruct past experiences, trying out perhaps alternative ways of construing them, and to create imagined experiences; and we listen and read in order to enter imaginatively into other people's real or imagined experiences. It is this latter mode that I have described as 'working directly upon our world representation without seeking outcomes in actuality'. I have somewhere seen a reference to a striking image offered by William James that fits the distinction I am making: it is to the effect that human consciousness, like the behaviour of birds, has alternating phases — 'flights' and 'perchings'.

We owe to Susanne Langer (1960) the recognition that this second mode of behaviour — the 'perchings', the contemplative intermissions — constitutes, in its fully developed form of expression, artistic production, works of literature. We owe to D. W. Harding (1937, 1962) the recognition that works of literature represent the formal end of a scale that includes at the informal end gossip about events, as for example the kind of chat that goes on when we go home in the evening and talk about the day's events. He saw that in both cases speakers and writers were contemplating events in which they were not participating: rather, in contemplating them they were taking up the role of *spectators* of those events. Above all we owe to him the idea that in gossip and in literature the purpose is an *evaluative* one: that the way we recount events offers an evaluation and invites corroboration of that evaluation. (If we feel we have been hardly done by, we recount the experience in such a way as to invite the sympathy of our listener.) The term 'spectator' has proved a difficult one to handle because to many people it suggests un-involvement — *mere* spectatorship; and indeed Harding defines the spectator's role as that of a 'detached evaluative response'. But the detachment is technical only — we are detached from the events because we are not participating in them: but as spectators we may be passionately involved. All this I have written about in greater detail far too often to justify my doing so here (Britton, 1970, 1977, 1979; Britton *et al.*, 1975).

These ideas, in fact, formed the basis for the set of function categories by which, in the Schools Council Writing Research Project, we proposed to describe developmental stages in learning to write. The two modes of using language I have introduced above we called 'language in the role of participant' and 'language in the role of spectator'. The former we saw as a scale from Expressive writing at the informal end to Transactional writing at the developed end; the latter as a scale from Expressive at the informal end to Poetic. We further distinguished by suggesting that in the Expressive to Transactional continuum we *do* things with language whereas in the Expressive to Poetic continuum, we *make* things with language. Expressive writing has its own particular function (that of establishing and maintaining personal relationships) but serves also as a means of carrying out — informally —

a *verbal transaction* and thus provides an approach to transactional writing; and, on the other hand, as a means of informal gossip about events and informal story telling and so provides an approach to the *verbal object* of poetic writing.

Stories come in all shapes and sizes. A deposition written for a court of law is likely to take narrative form but it will be a representation written under the injunction that, as far as may be, it is *true*. An evaluative statement — an invitation to sympathize with the writer or share his elation — would be entirely out of place. Again, what appears at first to be a 'perching' might turn out to be a 'flight': an acquaintance may begin to tell me the story of his misfortunes and I may respond by sympathizing with him, as in spectator role gossip, only to find that the hard-luck story was a prelude to raising a loan — a verbal transaction not a verbal object.

What I want to stress here is that the story world I have taken as my topic lies wholly on one side of my dividing line: it is activity in the spectator role, and is not designed to include the kind of narrative that would constitute evidence or settle an argument or supply needed information. Like play in all its forms, it occupies because it *preoccupies*, and it is in no direct sense a means to ends outside or beyond itself.

Writers who take up the spectator role are under no injunction to tell the truth; what they write may be predominantly fictional or substantially true: taken over all — a conglomerate. A great deal of autobiographical writing is, for example, writing in the spectator role, a verbal construct. In a strictly 'historical' autobiography, where the concern is not to recreate experiences but to get the historical facts right (as may happen when a politician writes to justify his actions), this would clearly not be the case. Reconstructed or remembered conversation would hardly count as evidence. [According to Julian Jaynes (1979), 'Memory is the medium of the must-have-been' (p.30).] But in the literary autobiography where the writer tries to capture the quality of past experiences we might well be justified in dissociating 'the real me' of the author from 'the pretend me' of the narrator. Louise Rosenblatt (1978) has pointed out that 'Literature especially invites confusion about its relation to reality' (p.33).

The point I am making is not so much of a quibble as it may sound: it is important, I believe, not to define spectator-role discourse in such a way as to exclude the non-fictional. Rather, we should see autobiographical and fictional narrative within spectator role as another continuum. As, on the one hand, we gossip about events or shape an autobiographical story, we shall tend to bring out aspects of the original events which heighten the evaluation we are intent upon offering — and such 'embellishments' or distortions may well grow more marked the more we repeat the telling. And, on the other hand, even the most fanciful fiction is likely to reflect to some extent the nature of our own experiences. Indeed, the unconscious motive for many of the stories children write must be that of projecting upon fictional figures problematic aspects of their own situation which they could not handle directly. This must surely be true of this story written by a six-and-a-half-year-old girl:

> There was a child of a witch who was ugly. He had pointed ears thin legs and was born in a cave. he flew in the air holding on nothing just playing games. When he saw ordinary girls and boys he hit them with his broomstick. A cat came along. he arched his back at the girls and boys and made them run away. When they had gone far away the cat meeowed softly at the witch child. the cat loved the child. the child loved the cat the cat was the onlee thing the child loved in the world.

It is the way we have characterized writing in the spectrum from Expressive to Poetic in contradistinction to the spectrum from Expressive to Transactional that constitutes a dichotomy. But, of course, it is not in practice a simple dichotomy. The distinction between the two continua is, at the informal end of each, a shadowy one. The positive function of Expressive writing, that of establishing and maintaining personal relationships, may be achieved by moving freely from spectator-role discourse into participant role and back again—from gossiping about events into exchanging views and opinions. But, shadowy though it is, the distinction can be made and the difference can be felt.

Taking then the spectator-role spectrum, it performs two useful tasks. It enables us to construe informal story telling and chatting about events as related to works of literature: i.e. it links the art-like performance in general with the work of art. The child's 'spiel' or rambling story is, like the work of literature, spectator-role discourse. (Picasso painted pictures and so do four-year-old children.) The spiel and the story are not ordinary acts of communication, such as conversation: they are performances.

But, secondly, the theory enables us to apply criteria which *differentiate* the art-like from the work of art. The child's spiel or story, our own informal gossip about events, are verbal objects only in embryo: the shaping towards a unity is at a very undeveloped stage. The sense, finally, of an 'absolute appropriateness' in every sound, word, structure, image and idea—this is the mark of a fully developed verbal object, a work of literature.

REFERENCES

Applebee, A. N. Where does Cinderella live? *The Use of English*, 1973, **25**, 136–141, 146.
Applebee, A. N. *The child's concept of story.* Chicago: University of Chicago Press, 1978.
Bereiter, C., and Scardamalia, M. From conversation to composition: The role of

instruction in a developmental process. In R. Glaser (Ed.), *Advances in Instructional Psychology* (Vol.2). Hillsdale, NJ: Lawrence Erlbaum Associates, 1981.

Berger, P. L., and Luckmann, T. *The social construction of reality*. Harmondsworth: Penguin Books, 1967.

Bower, G. H. Experiments on story comprehension and recall. In R. O. Freedle (Ed.), *New directions in discourse processing* (Vol. 1). Norwood, NJ: Ablex, 1978.

Britton, J. *Language and Learning*. Harmondsworth. Penguin Books, 1970.

Britton, J. Language and the nature of learning: An individual perspective. In J. R. Squire (Ed.), *The teaching of English*. Chicago: University of Chicago Press, 1977.

Britton, J. Learning to use language in two modes. In N. Smith and N. Franklin (Eds.), *Symbolic functioning in childhood*. Hillsdale, NJ: Lawrence Erlbaum Associates, 1979.

Britton, J. Spectator role and the beginnings of writing. In M. Nystrand (Ed.), *What Writers Know: The Language, process, and structure of written discourse*. New York: Academic Press, 1982.

Britton, J., Burgess, T., Martin, N., McLeod, A., and Rosen, H. *The development of writing abilities, 11-18*. London: Macmillan Education, 1975.

Bruner, J. S. The ontogenesis of speech acts. *Journal of Child Language*, 1975, **2**, 1-19.

Bruner, J. S., Jolly, A., and Sylva, K. (Eds.). *Play* Harmondsworth: Penguin Books, 1976.

Burgess, T. Story and teller. In M. Meek, A. Warlow, and G. Barton (Eds.), *The cool web*. London: The Bodley Head, 1977.

Cassirer, E. *An essay on man*. New Haven; CT: Yale University Press, 1944.

Dixon, J., and Stratta, L. *Achievements in writing at 16+*. Unpublished report, Faculty of Education, University of Birmingham, 1981.

Donaldson, M. *Children's minds*. Glasgow: Fontana/Collins, 1978.

Gregory, R. L. Psychology: Towards a science of fiction. In M. Meek, A. Warlow, and G. Barton (Eds.), *The cool web*. London: The Bodley Head, 1977.

Harding, D. W. The role of the onlooker. *Scrutiny*, 1937, **6**, 247-258.

Harding, D. W. Psychological processes in the reading of fiction. *British Journal of Aesthetics*, 1962, **2**, 133-147.

Jaynes, J. *The origin of consciousness in the breakdown of the bicameral mind*. Harmondsworth: Penguin Books, 1979.

Kelly, G. A. *A theory of personality*. New York: Norton, 1963.

Kelly, G. A. Man's constructions of his alternatives. In B. Maher (Ed.), *Clinical psychology and personality*. New York: Wiley, 1969.

Langer, S. K. *Philosophy in a new key* (4th ed.). Cambridge, MA: Harvard University Press, 1960.

Martin, N. C. Encounters with 'models'. *English in Education*, 1976, **10**, 9-15.

Nelson, K. Concept, word and sentence: Interrelationships in acquisition and development. *Psychological Review*, 1974, **81**, 267-285.

Newson, J. Towards a theory of infant understanding. *Bulletin of the British Psychological Society*, 1974, **27**, 251-257.

Newson, J., and Newson, E. Intersubjectivity and the transmission of culture. *Bulletin of the British Psychological Society*, 1975, **28**, 437-446.

Polanyi, M. *Personal knowledge*. London: Routledge and Kegan Paul, 1958.

Rosenblatt, L. *The reader, the text, the poem*. Carbondale, IL: Southern Illinois University Press, 1978.

Sapir, E. *Culture, language and personality*. Berkeley, CA: University of California Press, 1961.

Slobin, D. I., and Welsh, C. A. Elicited imitation as a research tool in developmental linguistics. In C. A. Ferguson and D. I. Slobin (Eds.), *Studies of child language development*. New York: Holt, Rinehart and Winston, 1973.

Vygotsky, L. S. *Thought and language*. Cambridge, MA: Massachusetts Institute of Technology Press, 1962.

Vygotsky, L. S. *The psychology of art*. Cambridge, MA: Massachusetts Institute of Technology Press, 1971.

Vygotsky, L. S. *Mind in society*. Cambridge, MA: Harvard University Press, 1978.

Wells, G. Some antecedents of early educational attainment. *British Journal of Sociology of Education*, 1981, **2**, 181–200.

Widdowson, H. G. *Stylistics and the teaching of literature*. London: Longman, 1975.

Winnicott, D. W. *Playing and reality*. London: Tavistock, 1971.

Explorations in the Development of Writing
Edited by Barry M. Kroll and Gordon Wells
© 1983 John Wiley & Sons Ltd.

2

Writing and Criticizing Texts

David R. Olson and Nancy Torrance

Writing preserves semantic structure — the very words and expressions. It does not preserve the person who generated those expressions and it does not preserve the intentions that gave rise to those expressions. Speech is preserved in writing as a fossil is preserved in resin. From the fossil some of the living forms can be imaginatively reconstructed. Primary among them are the intentions and the authority of the writer. Furthermore, skilled readers and writers know what is lost and often attempt to both compensate for that and play into what is gained by writing. Our concern in this paper is with how language users, particularly readers and writers, come to cope with these 'biases' of writing.

Historically, it has been argued that the preservation of language via writing produced important effects upon both societies and individuals. The intellectual revolution in classical Greece was, in part, related to the rise of literacy (Havelock, 1963, 1976, 1980); literacy permitted the development of large-scale political organization such as those involved in empires and national states (Innis, 1950); literacy permitted the evolution of science and philosophy in the West (Goody and Watt, 1968) and print literacy helped bring about both the Protestant Reformation and the rise of modern science (Eisenstein, 1980).

May we expect to find analogous changes in the mental life of children as they become literate? That is, is there an homology between the effects of literacy on social-cultural change and the effects of literacy on an individual? Considerable evidence has been collected to show that the effects of literacy are not always similar from one society to another. Literacy does not automatically produce modernity; social change depends upon many features of the society in addition to literacy, such as the degree to which literacy is connected with power, social advancement and the like (Heath, 1980, Scribner and Cole, 1978).

Even in a literate society such as ours, the acquisition of literate skills may not be directly associated with the cognitive and social consequences of literacy. That is, the historical consequences of literacy may be dramatic even if personal cognitive consequences of becoming literate are relatively minor. This could come about, for example, if the consequences of literacy are mediated through institutions and factors other than those school-based activities of learning to read and write. To cite a single possibility, literacy may have transformed a culture and altered its predominant modes of speech. Children growing up in that culture inherit, so to speak, the transformed culture. Their own skill in learning to read and write may be a simple continuation of life in that transformed culture rather than a dramatic transformation of themselves in the course of becoming literate. As we shall see, this appears to be the case for such conceptual categories as 'word', 'meaning' and the like; although originally associated with literacy, they are now part of the ordinary language of a literate society.

However mediated, the cognitive and social competencies involved in coping with authoritative writing, particularly those involved in learning to read and write textbook prose, what Vachek (1976) has called the 'written norm', are distinctive and important and require detailed analysis.

Although processes involved in dealing with oral utterances and written texts differ in many ways, including modality of input, degree of interaction, role of extralinguistic cues, spatial and temporal commonality of participants, specificity of audience and the like (Rubin, 1981), one factor seems to us to be central to all of the others, the one mentioned at the outset, the relation between the speaker/writer and the speech/text. Writing provides the occasion for the radical differentiation of a writer from his text. This differentiation is critical in that it may lead the linguistic form to be seen as autonomous, of having an authority different from the authority of the writer, and as having a meaning different from the meaning intended by the writer. Both of these factors, the authority and the meaning, may help to explain why school text is difficult to read, especially to read critically, and more importantly, why particular forms of writing such as expository prose are so difficult to master. Finally, they are important in justifying why it is so important that children learn to write. Let us consider each of these factors in more detail.

MEANING

In ordinary conversational language, the meaning of an utterance is usually taken as the intention of the speaker which lies behind the speaker's transparent linguistic form. Thus, in our longitudinal study we frequently come upon such expressions as the following:

Child	Adult
	What is a bicycle?
Bicycle gots two wheels, I mean, three wheels	

Notice both what the words mean and what the child means by them. The linguistic form 'two wheels' does not *mean* 'three wheels'. But of course that is not what the child is claiming. It is not the word but the child who means 'three wheels'. Because the meaning is taken to be the intentions of the speaker, it is possible to use restatements, revisions and loose paraphrases to answer such questions as 'What?' or 'What do you mean?' Here is an example from a pair of five-year-olds:

Child	Child
It's not a polite song.	
	What?
It's not polite.	
	What?
That ending isn't polite.	

The child varies the expression in the attempt to communicate an intention. Foppa and Kaserman (1979) found that four- and five-year-old children in conversation with adults, if asked 'What?', tend not simply to repeat their utterance but to attempt to make their meaning more understandable—they deleted redundant elements, added missing elements or explained missing parts and repeated only complete utterances. The same tends to be true of our children in conversation with other children. The invariant meaning, then, is the speaker's intended meaning.

Meaning in a written text may be handled in precisely the same way: one may simply treat the expressions as transparent representations of an underlying intention. Undoubtedly, that is what readers ordinarily do in casual 'assimilative' or non-critical reading (Olson and Torrance, 1981). But written language offers a new and alternative orientation to meaning. Because writing preserves the linguistic form, the meaning of the linguistic form *per se* may be taken to be the meaning intended by the speaker or writer. That is, the meaning of the linguistic form comes to be the critical meaning—the meaning is 'the meaning in the text' (Olson, 1977). Less elliptically, we may say that the meaning becomes 'the literal meaning', the meaning conventionally associated with that linguistic form in the context of a stipulated possible world. While such meanings are not 'context-free', they do depend upon context in a somewhat new way—the context is not so much the 'context of utterance' but that particular context constructed or stipulated by the text. In oral language, then, the emphasis is on the speaker's intended meaning while in written language it is upon the sentence's literal meaning.

If children's oral language has a bias towards 'intended meaning' while school texts have a bias towards 'sentence meaning', we can see one important ground for difficulty in reading and writing prose texts. But the problem is even more general; failure to make the differentiation between the meaning of what one *says* and what one means or intends by it has some important consequences. If a listener does not clearly differentiate between what one's intentions are and the linguistic forms one uses to express them, he or she will not be able to decide whether a disagreement occurs because the speaker was lying (or otherwise has faulty intentions) or whether his intentions are fine but his expression was faulty in some way. It appears that children's arguments occur for just that reason. In careful speech the two are supposed to be more or less equivalent; but when misunderstanding occurs, the problem could lie with either the intention or the expression. During the US Presidential campaign, James Lake, secretary to Ronald Reagan, was led to say: 'The governor's words do not always reflect his total meaning' (*Globe and Mail*, February 27, 1980). In other words, a listener or reader could not be sure they had recovered Reagan's intention simply on the basis of his words. In this case, the distinction is a dodge; in others, it correctly reflects the comprehension problem.

Children in the course of learning a language and in learning to read and write progressively sort out these distinctions. As we have noted, even five-year-olds realized that the question 'What?' (asked with a rising intonation) was a request for the clarification of an intention. In no case did they simply repeat a faulty or elliptical utterance but rather they corrected, amplified, or abbreviated the preceding utterance. But, of course, that is not to say that the children realized that they 'meant' something and their sentence 'meant' something and that the two might converge or diverge.

A recent study by Hildyard, Minsky and Olson (in preparation) shows that the questions 'What did X say?' and 'What does X mean?', following both direct and indirect speech acts, are differentiated by most kindergarten children, a verbatim repetition being given to the *say* question but not to the *mean* question. The *mean* questions, however, remain difficult for children and it is not until the second grade that a majority of children answer them by expressing directly the underlying intention.

Children's difficulties in managing the relations between sayings and meanings are shown most clearly in Robinson and Robinson's (1980) finding of children's tendency to 'blame the listener' for comprehension failures rather than blaming the speaker or his message. If a speaker, either the child or an adult in speaking to a child, expresses a sentence that is informationally inadequate but not wrong, and if this sentence results in an incorrect choice response on the part of the listener, the child explains the incorrect response by saying that the listener made an error or didn't try hard enough rather than blaming the speaker for producing an inadequate message. By the second grade, children correctly blame the speaker and his faulty message. While children do deal with sentences as expressions of intentions and they vary the former in the attempt to manage the latter, and while they reject those which do not match their own intentions, they fail to recognize that the sentence has a meaning and they as speakers have a meaning and that the two may or may not be congruent. When they do, they will enter the world of possibility, of fantasy, of puns, riddles, jokes and the levels of linguistic analysis that make up such an important part of early schooling.

To recapitulate, in oral language, if a listener gets the inappropriate meaning from a linguistic form it is a simple matter to reformulate the form to express the intention better—the intention is the overriding consideration. In written text, the linguistic form is the only clue to the author's intention. On one hand, that may be regarded as a loss of meaning—a reduction in access to intentionality. Socrates complains to Phaedrus: 'Written words seem to talk to you as though they were intelligent, but if you ask them anything about what they say, from a desire to be instructed, they go on telling you just the same thing forever.' But, on the other hand, this restriction has been seen as the source of advantage for writing. If the only clue to the author's intention is the words he uses, it becomes critical to use exactly those words that conventionally express (in a possible world) the author's intention. Writing becomes a vehicle for the precise expression of meaning. Writing, therefore, puts great requirements upon language. Finding the appropriate expression and revising the expression to fit the intention better are activities that are central to the processes both of writing and of critical reading. If a writer fails to recognize that he is operating with two levels of structure, expressions and intentions, and if he lacks the competence to compute both or lacks the means to bring them into congruence, he will be in no position either to revise what he is writing or to interpret and reinterpret what he is reading. As we have noted, some of these processes already occur in conversational speech—children revise their utterances when asked 'What?'—but writing and reading add one constraint—the child must serve as his own critical reader. He must detect the ambiguity or the alternative possibilities of interpretation. Empson's (1930) *Seven Types of Ambiguity* is one of the few analyses of how these ambiguities are in fact systematically employed by writers.

The procedure must be something of the order: first, the writer must construct an expression for his intention, then he must convert the intention expressed by a literal reading of his sentence, then he must compare the two and bring them into congruity either by abandoning his original intention or by revising his expression. In so doing, the writer runs off recursively a series of procedures not unlike those run off interactively in a social context. Indeed, one of our concerns is with the possibility that children who are good oral revisers are also good written revisers, but thus far we lack good data on this point. These considerations indicate the general nature of the problems of meaning in oral and written language. In conversations, if your words fail to express your intentions, listeners are quick to show their puzzlement; in writing, the writer must be his own critical reader. He or she must not only construct an expression for his intention, he or she must then attempt to determine what meaning the sentence expresses and then determine further whether that meaning corresponds to his original intention.

The relation between the meaning of sentences and the meanings intended by the speakers of those sentences is also important to the problem of 'logical reasoning'. The reasoning processes of both preliterate children and non-literate adults have sometimes been characterized as prelogical because of the apparent lack of concern for logical form. More recently this 'failure' has come to be seen as one of relative attention to the meaning in the text. When Luria's (1961) traditional, non-literate subject is told:

All the bears in Pinsk are white.
Ivan went to Pinsk and saw a bear.
What color was it?

and he replies, 'I don't know, I've never been to Pinsk', or 'You'll have to ask Ivan', he is not so much reasoning prelogically as failing to treat the question as a piece of text which expresses a meaning independently of the person who says and asks for things. This, it seems, is what schooling is all about: teaching children to treat text as an autonomous expression of meaning. It involves the transformation from the meanings of particular speakers to the expressed meanings of text. And it rests on a new awareness of the possibility of differentiating what sentences and texts mean from what speakers and writers may mean by them.

AUTHORITY

Just as the sentence meaning results from sheering off the author's intentions from his expressions, so the authority of text derives in part from dissociating the authority of the author from the authority of his words. In both cases the author is removed from the text, and the meaning and authority reside in the text rather than in the speaker *per se*. To see this point, it is necessary to note that any utterance has an authority claim as part of its meaning. If Henny Penny (or Chicken Little) runs down the street crying 'The sky is falling! The sky is falling!', the appropriate response is 'Who is she (to make such an assertion?)'. That is, the weight of an utterance depends upon the authority of the spokesman. And it is not too difficult to determine the speaker's authority as long as it is clear who the speaker is. Even in oral language, there are several devices for separating the speaker from the speech, including direct and indirect quotation, the use of spokesmen and messengers and the construction of ritualized, communal speech. *King Lear* says to his messenger:

Inform her full of my particular fear,
And thereto add such reasons of your own
As may compact it more (I, iv, 346).

When the messenger speaks, of course, it is not clear whose words will have been spoken. Archival forms including oral ritual, song, verse, prayer, proverb and the like also involve speech which originates elsewhere than in the mind of the current speaker and hence may carry much more weight of authority than if they originated solely with him. How is this authority managed in written texts? Many social commentators have pointed out that the opinions of the 'man in the street' take on a peculiar authority if they are published in a newspaper or if they are presented on television, and that the content of printed material in books is often taken by laymen as having authority, of being 'above criticism'. Esther Geva has provided an example of children's acceptance of this authority of written text: 'How do you know?' 'I read it somewhere.' 'Oh.' It is with the problem of authority that children have to learn to cope in the course of mastering the language of schooling.

Written texts, by virtue of the fact that they preserve 'the very words', foster the differentiation of the author from his words. Every written utterance becomes in a sense archival; it may be preserved across space and time, read for purposes unthought of by the writer by people unknown to the writer. Just as the words mean whatever they mean quite independently of the intentions of the author in writing them, so too the authority of the written word is also quite independent of the authority of the author. In school, the textbook is the authority; it is not even clear who the author of the book is. Indeed textbooks are not written by authorities but by 'communicators' who are presumably spokesmen for the authorities.

This social dimension of meaning in reading and writing is often addressed in theories of rhetoric through conceptions of 'awareness of audience'. Failure to be sensitive to one's audience is described as egocentrism while, at least in the sciences, meeting the requirements of one's audience is described as sociocentrism. As descriptions, these categories may be quite harmless; certainly poor writers can be described as having less sensitivity to audience. But viewed prescriptively, these categories seem to us to be somewhat misleading. They may, for example, suggest to teachers of writing that developing sensitivity to others or procedures for decentering are appropriate exercises for improving the process of writing or speaking. Let us consider the 'audience' problem rather in terms of our general principle of the differentiation of the authors from texts. From that perspective, the problem of audience is not different from the problem of meaning. The way to deal with an audience from whom no requests for clarification can arise, is to make the sentence meaning an adequate expression of the intended meaning in some stipulated possible world. That, of course, remains a somewhat lofty goal, but its pursuit marks successful explicit prose.

The central social problem is not the one of audience but the one of authority relations between writer and reader. How does one write a text so that it will have authority? And how does one critically read text which is taken to be authoritative, that is, 'above criticism'?

Consider, first, the critical reading problem. Teachers, including academics, complain that students fail to read critically or to evaluate the texts they read. They study and remember texts without recognizing the limits, weaknesses, inconsistencies in authoritative texts. Markman (1979) has found that, on a comprehension test, children fail to comment on the inconsistencies of the text, from which she has inferred that children are not 'monitoring' their comprehension. Yet, on the other hand, students are ferociously critical of works and authors they don't like and of the expressions of siblings and peers while remaining largely insensitive to the glaring inadequacies of their own and their admired set of authors. Why?

'Real talk can exist only between equals', as Farber (1977, p.155) puts it. This idea has become central to social critiques of ideologies. Ideas are seen not merely as expressions of truth but as mechanisms for defending or legitimating institutions and the exercise of power (Habermas, 1976; Skinner, 1974). As a consequence, considerations of truth and authority are conflated. To illustrate, how can one judge the truth of an idea if that idea comes backed by the weight of a person of authority? The response to accepted authority is simple deference, capitulation—not evaluation, criticism or judgement. Indeed, to challenge an authoritative idea—an idea expressed by a superior such as a teacher or a textbook—is to challenge the structure of authority itself; it constitutes insubordination. On the other hand, to challenge an idea of a peer is, at least, a contest between equals.

The problem of the social relation between people as a part of the meaning of language is an idea that is developed in both speech act theory (Searle, 1969) and in hermeneutics (Gadamer, 1975). Gadamer points out that, 'there can be no speech that does not bind the speaker and the person spoken to' (p.359). All speech is built in a social context and that context makes up part of the meaning of the utterance. Speech act theory has formalized this notion in the concepts of propositional context and illocutionary force. Austin's (1962) primary discovery was that one could not differentiate sentences that did something to the listener from those that merely communicated some proposition; all sentences did both. This interest in the social aspects of meaning has been particularly important in the understanding of the early acquisition of language by young children. Bruner (Ninio and Bruner, 1978;

Ratner and Bruner, 1978), Trevarthen (1980) and others have shown that language is learned in part by means of the mapping of language into the mutual understanding or intersubjectivity between the mother and the child (cf. Olson, 1980). Furthermore, in learning a language, the child is not only learning how to exploit the resources of a grammar but also rules or norms for social action: Who can you command? Who can command you? Who can you ask questions of? and all the other status-related issues that make up the micro-social order.

But how does that social/authority dimension affect the processes of critical reading and the processes of writing? As we have mentioned, the problem is not one simply of audience but of managing the status relations between readers and writers.

An uncritical attitude, we suggest, results not simply from a logical incapacity but rather from a lack of social authority. The reader does not believe that he or she is in a position to criticize authoritative persons or texts (except perhaps with groans and marginalia). Hence, the simple compliance with text rather than a critical attitude to it. We shall return presently to the ways in which children may acquire some status or authority and so become critical readers.

The problem for the writer is analogous. Children may feel that they cannot issue authoritative statements on any problems because they are in no position to. They lack the status or authority relative to the audiences that may read what they write, teachers among them. Yet, if a writer sinks back into an abundance of modals, the merely possible, and to the expressions of feelings and hunches, the writing will be perceived as weak and subjective.

The solution to the problems of both readers and writers is the recovery of a sense of authority, not necessarily of superiority to an audience, but of an equality to the readers who make up the writers' peer group. True discourse exists only between equals. As a reader, one must come to see the writer of a text as basically equal to oneself, and as a writer, one must come to see the audience, including the teacher as reader, as basically equal to oneself. In such cases neither the reader nor the writer can assume that the other has greater knowledge of the topic, greater mastery of the language or greater powers of interpretation and inference. Both the act of writing and the act of critical reading, then, require that the student see himself or herself as a member of a group of equals, a peer group, and as a member of that peer group as having the 'right' to assert, argue, defend and criticize the expressions of others. Much could be said about the difficulties of achieving a middle course between the expressions of a private and undefended opinion and the submissive compliance with the published views of authorities that seems to typify much of students' early writing. But part of that 'free variation' results from the student's attempts to work out the social relations between himself as student and the community of writers/readers.

But the solution to the social authority problem is precisely the key to the distinctive power of written texts generally. Once a student recognizes that the authors he reads and the audiences he writes for are equals, there is no ground for the personal authority of author or audience. Statements will not be believed simply because they originate with authoritative persons because all persons are equals. The ground of authority is free to shift, therefore, from a personal basis to a textual basis. Texts, theories, statements have authority independently of the person who generated them. They are authoritative not by virtue of the status of the writer or speaker but because they stand up to criticism within a peer group. The ground of authority therefore shifts from personal to textual base. And the way to make ideas and theories stand up to criticism is to provide evidence, valid arguments, logical cohesion and objectivity in their presentation.

It is these properties of written text that sometimes make that text seem impersonal and objective and 'above criticism'. In becoming either a critical reader or a writer, one reconnects texts to their authors and hence discovers their vulnerability but at the same time discovers the new kind of authority lodged in reasons and evidence rather than in persons. In fact, this is the ground on which Sir Karl Popper (1972) based his concept of objective knowledge—knowledge that is not simply equivalent to the personal beliefs of persons. Objective knowledge, for example, is that part of Newton's theory which did not die with Newton. Popper argued that, while both lower animals and humans hold beliefs, only humans have the capacity for the construction of objective knowledge, and that possibility rests in part on the creation of a form of discourse, tied to written prose text, which encourages the substitution of criteria of validity and evidence for those of personal authority.

The social relation between author and reader in prose text has also been noted by McLuhan (1964) in his discussion of how the form of language was 'brought into line with print'. He wrote: 'The first great change in prose style came early in the eighteenth century, when . . . . Addison and Steele discovered a new prose technique to match the form of the printed word. It was the technique of equitone. It consisted in maintaining a single level of tone and attitude to the reader throughout the entire composition. By this discovery they brought written discourse into line with the printed word and away from the variety of pitch and tone of the spoken, and of even the hand-written, word' (p.184). It is this 'tone' and the social relations maintained by tone that we have examined in this paper.

We now see why learning to write is so important. The changes in orientation to text that we have been discussing cannot simply be taught. By becoming a writer the novice gains access to the peer group of writers and with that admission the right to criticize the written expressions of others. Learning to write then not only develops competence with a new and powerful form of expression, it also alters the child's attitude to the writing of others. Critical reading, at least in part, is a byproduct of becoming a writer.

REFERENCES

Austin, J. L. In J. O. Urmson (Ed.), *How to do things with words.* New York: Oxford University Press, 1962.

Eisenstein, E. L. The emergence of print culture in the west. *Journal of Communication,* 1980, **30,** 99–106.

Empson, W. *Seven types of ambiguity.* London: Chatto and Windus, 1930.

Farber, L. He said, she said. In M. Nystrand (Ed.), *Language as a way of knowing.* Toronto: Ontario Institute for Studies in Education Press, 1977.

Foppa, K., and Kasermann, M. C. *Some determinants of modifications in child language* (mimeo, 1979).

Gadamer, H. G. *Truth and method.* New York: Seabury Press, 1975.

Goody, J., and Watt, I. The consequences of literacy. In J. Goody (Ed.), *Literacy in traditional societies.* Cambridge: Cambridge University Press, 1968.

Habermas, J. *Legitimation crisis.* (T. McCarthy, trans.). London: Heinemann, 1976.

Havelock, E. *Preface to Plato.* Cambridge, MA: Harvard University Press, 1963.

Havelock, E. *Prologue to Greek literacy.* Toronto: Ontario Institute for Studies in Education Press, 1976.

Havelock, E. The coming of literate communication. *Journal of Communication,* 1980, **30,** 90–98.

Heath, S. B. The functions and uses of literacy. *Journal of Communication,* 1980, **30,** 123–133.

Hildyard, A., Minsky, E., and Olson, D. R. *Differentiating what is said from what is meant.* In preparation.

Innis, H. *Empire and communication.* Oxford: Oxford University Press, 1950.

Luria, A. In J. Tizard (Ed.), *The role of speech in the regulation of normal and abnormal behavior.* New York: Liveright, 1961.

Markman, E. Realizing that you don't understand: Elementary school children's awareness of inconsistencies. *Child Development,* 1979, **50,** 643–655.

McLuhan, M. *Understanding media.* New York: McGraw-Hill, 1964.

Ninio, A., and Bruner, J. S. The achievement and antecedents of labelling. *Journal of Child Language,* 1978, **5,** 1–15.

Olson, D. R. From utterance to text: The bias of language in speech and writing. *Harvard Educational Review,* 1977, **47,** 257–281.

Olson, D. R. On the language and authority of textbooks. *Journal of Communication,* 1980, **30,** 186–196.

Olson, D. R., and Torrance, N. G. Learning to meet the requirements of written text: Language development in the school years. In C. H. Frederiksen and J. F. Dominic (Eds), *Writing: The nature, development and teaching of written communication.* Hillsdale, NJ: Lawrence Erlbaum, 1981.

Popper, K. *Objective knowledge: An evolutionary approach.* Oxford: Clarendon Press, 1972.

Ratner, N. K., and Bruner, J. S. Games, social exchange and the acquisition of language. *Journal of Child Language,* 1978, **5,** 391–402.

Robinson, E. J., and Robinson, W. P. *Understanding about ambiguous messages: A symptom of learning to distinguish message from meaning.* Report written for Bishop Road Infant School. University of Bristol School of Education, 1980.

Rubin, A. A framework for comparing language experiences. In R. Spiro *et al* (Eds), *Theoretical issues in natural language processing.* Hillsdale, NJ: Lawrence Erlbaum, 1981.

Searle, J. *Speech acts: An essay in the philosophy of language.* London: Cambridge University Press, 1969.

Scribner, S., and Cole, M. Literacy without schooling: Testing for intellectual effects. *Harvard Educational Review*, 1978, **48**, 448–461.

Skinner, Q. The principles and practice of opposition: The case of Bowlingbrooke vs. Walpole. In N. McKendrick (Ed.), *Historical perspectives: Studies in English thought and society.* London: Europe Publications, 1974.

Trevarthen, C. The foundations of intersubjectivity: Development of interpersonal and co-operative understanding in infants. In D. R. Olson (Ed.), *The social foundations of language and thought.* New York: Norton, 1980.

Vachek, J. *Selected writings in English and general linguistics.* The Hague: Mouton, 1976.

Explorations in the Development of Writing
Edited by Barry M. Kroll and Gordon Wells
© 1983 John Wiley & Sons Ltd.

3

Towards a Comprehensive Model of Writing Development

Andrew Wilkinson, Gillian Barnsley,
Peter Hanna and Margaret Swan

Teachers of English have always felt a particular responsibility for the personal development of their students, and writing has been considered an important instrument for this. It is argued, for example, that when the human soul possesses itself in quiet before a blank sheet of paper something special happens. And thus the literature abounds with terms like 'growth', 'fruition', 'development', 'maturity'. These terms, however, are notoriously ill-defined. And yet there are clearly differences between the language of (say) a six-year-old, a ten-year-old, and a 16-year-old. Development obviously takes place but it does not take place obviously.

There have been various attempts to come to terms with the problems of definition involved. Thus for over 70 years research workers have attempted to measure language development objectively—by classifying and counting certain language features (for summaries see Carroll, 1968; Harpin, 1973; McCarthy, 1954). The most substantial study was by Loban (1963, 1976) who followed a group of children from kindergarten over the 13 years of their schooling. On the whole, however, such studies do not take us beyond the rather obvious conclusions that, for instance, children of 12 write longer sentences and compositions, and use more complex grammar, than children of six. But as Harpin (1973) points out, the most important source of variability in all measures is the kind of language task engaged in. The severest limitation of such 'linguistic' measures as have been used is that they do not countenance meaning.

Another approach has been to investigate the cognitive aspects of language, particularly writing. Here Moffett's work in *Teaching the Universe of Discourse* (1968) is seminal. He sets a context of 'maturation' and within it sees growth as predominantly a cognitive matter: cognitive developments have linguistic correlates. Implications of this aspect of the work were developed by Britton *et al.* (1975) and a hierarchy of ('transactional') categories was devised which the team applied to adolescent writing. The purpose of the research was to 'substantiate a major hypothesis regarding the development of writing ability in school' (p.82), i.e. that it may be described as a progress from the 'expressive' to the 'poetic' on the one hand, and from the 'expressive' through the stages of the 'transactional' on the other. It is conceded that this hypothesis was not substantiated (p.187). In any case, by concentrating so predominantly on cognition, the model on which the hypothesis is based is likely to be as inadequate in its own way as the linguistic models. Even if one accepts Moffett's view that 'growth is predominantly a cognitive matter', one needs to do a good deal of explanation of how it is presented in other aspects of the personality such as the affective and moral. And in the style for that matter. It is indeed surprising that a hypothesis about writing ability should pay so little attention to the ways in which cognitive ability manifests itself.

In fact there is scarcely any work anywhere on the development of the affective, moral and stylistic aspects of language. There is more on affect than on the others, but what there is does not take us very far. In a very confusing book, *The Intelligence of Feeling*, for example, Witkin (1974) defines personal development as 'the child's progressive mastery of new and more complex levels of sensate experience' (p.49) and sees this as parallel to the Piagetian development of logical thought (p.175), but because of his insistence that they are 'not the same order' (p.177) he throws away the only structure that he has to hand and has to confess himself unable to offer 'a proper developmental sequence' for 'classifying sensate experience'. A much more promising approach occurs in the work of Harrison (1979), where cognitive and affective elements of the personality are considered in the growth of human identity as manifested in the writings of adolescents.

This then is the background against which the work at Exeter University Language in Education Centre is to be seen. What follows is largely based on the most recent project, The Crediton Project published as *Assessing Language Development* (Wilkinson, Barnsley, Hanna and Swan, 1980).[1]

THE DEVELOPMENTAL MODELS

The work at Exeter began in 1976, and, as indicated, we were faced with an almost complete absence of developmental models. Models were needed which gave a comprehensive description of human development as manifested in

1 This paper draws on findings of the Crediton Project, as described in *Assessing Language Development* by A. Wilkinson, G. Barnsley, P. Hanna and M. Swan. Permission to reprint pages 228–231 from this book, by kind permission of the publishers, Oxford University Press, is gratefully acknowledged.

language, but these necessarily needed to be supported by a hypothesis about human development. The formulation we made was as follows. Human development is a movement from a world of instances to a world organized by mind; from dependence to autonomy; from convention to uniqueness; from unconsciousness to awareness; from subjectivity to objectivity; from ignorance to understanding; from self to neighbour as self. This is, of course, a culture-bound, perhaps even a personal, definition, but it seems workable. In our description there is no 'end product' — 'maturity' is not a state which is finally attained: one does not arrive, one is continually arriving.

It seems to us that at least four models were necessary to provide evidence for such a hypothesis — a cognitive, an affective, a moral, and a stylistic. One reason for having four models is that there is not necessarily a close link in the individual between these aspects of development — that someone is highly developed intellectually is no guarantee that he is so emotionally or morally, or can write half a page of decent English. In any case our sample was not large enough to justify statistical correlations. Models cannot, of course, be devised merely from an examination of the data because one selects certain features for them as a result of one's predispositions. A way of guarding to some extent against such subjectivity is to test these predispositions against those of others. Thus on the one hand we sought help from theory and also attempted to make assumptions of the culture explicit. On the other hand we had in previous work categorized the responses of experienced teachers to students' writing (Marshall, 1978; Witcombe, 1979). In specific relation to the Crediton data we had the great benefit of working with the writers' own teachers. And of course we had the data themselves. Thus our models were devised from an interaction between all these factors; we feel, therefore, that they go some way in operationalizing development so that it can be subjected to empirical observation.

The models are detailed, so that they can be used to comment not merely on the totality of a piece of writing, but also on words, phrases and sentences. In contrast, the London Writing Research Unit was led to attempt to force any single piece into one of several procrustean categories, rather than observing the varieties of activity going on. The detail of our models makes it impossible to set them out in full here. However, we may describe the general principles on which they are based.

Cognition

The work of Piaget stands behind most recent writing on intellectual growth, seen as a movement from an undifferentiated world to one organized by mind, from a world of instances to a world related by generalities and abstractions, from the statement of specifics to the complex hypothetico-deductive argument. In our model the first two general categories, *describing* and *interpreting*, we envisage as concrete operational, and the final two, *generalizing* and *speculating*, as moving towards the formal operational. Each category is divided into subsections, which progress from word/sentence to full discourse level, so making it possible to describe quite fully the cognitive moves children make in writing. This is not a refinement present in, for example, the Moffett or Britton work.

Affective

In contrast to what occurs with cognition, there is no coherent body of theory concerned with the growth of the affect. Apparently, psychologists will not admit to even knowing what an emotion is: 'at present emotion defies definition' (Strongman, 1978, p.2). We have thus chosen to devise this model on the practicalities with which the emotions operate—as expressions of, as attitudes towards, as awareness about, as creation in terms of.

We posit three dimensions of personal development—self, others, reality. *Self* expresses emotion, becomes aware of it, analytical of it, becomes more able to tolerate complex and conflicting emotion, to recognize motives behind apparent motives. *Others* are first perceived by the individual as peripheral or as having a servicing role. Empathy develops, often manifested in writing by a greater ability to realize others as unique individuals, perhaps by characterization, and in the writer's increased awareness of the reader's needs. *Reality* is conceived on the one hand as the physical environment (more mature writers have a more complete sense of context which includes this) and, on the other, more fundamentally, as the constraints of the human condition—whether in Bruner's terms one 'defends' oneself against these, perhaps by fantasy or evasion, or 'copes' with them by understanding and interpretation as in a work of art, or personal reorientation.

Moral

Although there is some disagreement as to the number of stages a child passes through as he comes to internalize the morality of his culture, there seems to be general accord that 'anomy' or lawlessness gives way to heteronomy or rule of fear of punishment, and that to 'socionomy' or rule by a sense of reciprocity with others, and finally to 'autonomy' or self-rule. The work of Piaget (1932) and Kolberg (1963, 1964 and later) is basic here. We propose a similar model, with modifications, which is a cumulative stage model, not a discrete stage one in which the earlier forms of moral judgement are totally superseded by more mature ones.

In the empirical research we have found no studies in which the writings of children have been analysed for levels of moral thinking. Yet in the stories they write, children come to terms with notions of good and evil, right and wrong:

they read fiction in which the good are rewarded, the evil punished. They make implicit and explicit judgements which reveal moral values.

Stylistic

Confusion reigns in the meaning to be attached to 'style' in educational circles. Some major examining boards in the UK have strange assumptions; it is as though they were expecting all the candidates to be called either Addison or Steele. As for the development of style in children's writing, it seems never to have been considered in any studies we can discover. We have therefore had to offer a hypothesis which cannot be argued in detail here. Briefly it is that stylistic development is to be seen as a series of choices from a norm represented by the simple affirmative literal sentence so common in young children's writing.

Organization. Early writing contains a large number of simple sentences. Since there are only two basic sentences, those which describe ('the dog is angry') and those which narrate ('the dog bites the man'), the choice is bound to be one of these. The reason that sentences are like this is because (a) we and things exist (and therefore can be described) and (b) we and other animate beings act (and those actions can be recounted as narratives). Since we necessarily act in time, and the chronological world is so relentless, it seems that in attempting to cope with it our basic linguistic organization will be narrative. Modifications of narrative seem to us to represent developments of certain kinds.

Cohesion. Structure is supported by a cohesive system in the Halliday and Hasan (1976) sense, which gives choices of devices to establish the semantic relations of the text.

Syntax and Lexis. There will be a development from simple to complex syntax, but the furthest point will lie in the control of appropriate structures in relation to semantic needs. Associated with this is the choice of appropriate lexis. We see *lexical competence* as emerging in a movement from limited concrete vocabulary, perhaps with imprecise and general meaning, to a vocabulary which has greater precision, and uses abstraction and elaboration where necessary.

Reader awareness. For reasons which are not inevitable but likely, young children's writing tends to be self-orientated. The degree to which the writer can put himself in the place of the reader — orienting, explaining, elaborating, as necessary — is part of the decentering process. Associated with this is a growing sense of appropriateness, an increased ability to adopt the accepted style of discourse for the task in hand. Young children often write in oral modes, or mix spoken and written. At the other end of the scale a writer may be assured in a mode, and, for deliberate effect, frustrate the reader's expectation by breaking the register.

Effectiveness. This concerns the success of the writing in communicating: in a sense it is the summation of the others. There can, of course, be no final criterion of effectiveness, in that it is an interaction between writer, reader, and text. Nor can there be a single criterion. In narrative it may lie in the interest and suspense sustained, in an autobiography in the realization of the writer's feelings and motives, in a set of instructions in the successful installation of a wall bracket, and so on.

RESEARCH DESIGN

Although the summary way in which the models have had to be presented in the previous section may give the impression that they are entirely theoretical, the opposite is in fact true. We wish to repeat that a good deal of work was carried out with experienced teachers in examining children's compositions and their evaluative criteria were drawn upon in constructing the models. The research team also worked very closely with teachers in the schools used in the Crediton project and had the benefit of their insights as the work progressed.

The design of the project was to give the same four tasks to children of seven, ten and thirteen. Three classes of pupils were chosen from a secondary school and from its feeder primary school in Crediton, UK, and both the choice of schools and the guidance of the teachers suggested that these groups were fairly homogeneous in terms of background and ability.

Four different compositions—two personal, two discursive—were requested from the groups of children in the context of their normal lessons. These were a piece of autobiography on their happiest or saddest day, a narrative suggested by one of three pictures provided, an explanation (of a game), and an argument ('world it work if children came to school when they liked, and did what they liked there?'). It seemed that these four topics required differing and important uses of written language. The same four topics were given to each group so that the compositions could be more easily compared. The first two tasks were intended to give evidence primarily for our moral/affective dimensions; and the second two primarily for our cognitive dimension. The stylistic measures, of course, apply to all.

The size of the sample was small—150 students (600 scripts in all)—and no attempt was made to use the data statistically, either to compare performance on the four tasks, on the four models, or between age groups. The rating of each feature, whether above or below sentence level, was agreed by at least two members of the research team. This was a matter of economy and convenience; there is no reason to think that ratings by all four workers would have produced dissension. The ratings were used to indicate tendencies by rough summation ('over half') but were intended to be descriptive rather than normative.

Since it is not possible here to give full details of all the models, we have chosen to focus on our affective and our moral models. These two models, whilst also having the advantage of novelty, are simpler and more accessible than the cognitive and stylistic models. In the affective model, the items in each subcategory are hierarchically ordered, but the subcategories are *not* hierarchically ordered in relation to one another. The moral model is a single hierarchy.

THE AFFECTIVE MODEL

We give below the affective model from the Crediton project, and then demonstrate something of its applications.

A1 *Self*

The writer expresses his emotion and his awareness of the nature of his own feelings, or implies his emotion by describing action from which the reader can infer that the writer was in the grip of an emotion.

A1.1 The writer expresses or implies his own emotion, mechanically in some written work, explicitly in others, e.g. 'My feet were as wet as anything', 'I am afraid that day is a long, long, way away'.

A1.2 —not only expresses but evaluates emotion, e.g. 'The saddest day of my life', 'I did not like it indeed'.

A1.3 —shows awareness of self image, of how he appears or might appear, e.g. 'I looked like a fool'.

A1.4 —shows awareness of the springs and complexities of emotion, e.g. 'I got rather nervous about it and I couldn't find the way and went into another room and looked like a fool standing there asking where room one was'.

A1.5 —shows a general attitude or disposition, e.g. 'I long for the day when I can think about him without it hurting too much'.

A2 *Other people*

The writer shows an awareness of others both in relation to himself and as distinct identities.

A2.1 —records the mere existence of other people as having been present. This is the single dimension: others are present—acting, speaking— but no emotion is apparent by inference, e.g. 'The two boys went for a walk with their mother and they got lost and they came to a fence and that fence was electric and they was not lost . . .'

A2.2 —begins to indicate the separateness of others by, e.g., giving their actual words or significant actions. 'I woke up, had my breakfast' is probably not significant; 'the old man smild' may well be.

A2.3 —the thoughts and feelings of others by quotation of actual words, perhaps as a dialogue, or by description of them, or actions indicating them. More perception called for than in the previous category though it might be fairly conventional.

A2.4 Analytical, interpretative comments on aspects of character and behaviour, or insightful quotation or dialogue.

A2.5 Consistently realized presentation of another person by a variety of means, perhaps by assuming persona.

A2.6 Ability to see a person and his interactions in extended context (e.g. a character in a novel).

A3 *Reader*

It is often argued that writing to an unknown or not well-envisaged reader will be poorer in quality since it lacks focus. Certainly the imaginative leap of the writer into the minds of others so as to grasp what terms have meaning for them must characterize effective communication.

A3.1 —reader not catered for. Writing context-bound, incomplete information, links missing.

A3.2 —the reader is a person or type of person to the writer. He may not be conscious of this, but rather attempts to fulfil expectations within the situation. He may do so partially but imperfectly.

A3.3 —the writer caters specifically for the reader, e.g. by relevant information, explanation (sometimes asides), shows an empathy with him, telling him what he needs to know to be able to interpret what he is told.

A4 *Environment*

The writer shows an awareness of physical or social surroundings, a sense of time and place. On the one hand the environment may be a source of special stimulus. On the other hand a 'restricted code' may not offer the necessary context. Getting the register right is a sign of awareness of social environment.

A4.1 —assumes the environment.

A4.2 —describes or explains the environment, barely adequately giving background details, or gives enough details to clarify the background.

A4.3 —responds to the environment in a way that shows it has been especially significant and stimulating.

A4.4 —chooses environmental items to achieve an effect, thus showing a higher degree of selectivity and evaluation than that suggested by A4.3.

A5 *Reality*

This is concerned with how far a writer recognizes a distinction between the world of phenomena and the world of imagination, between magical and logical thinking; with how far the writer's own preferences or beliefs can come to an accommodation with external reality; with how far the literal-metaphorical aspects of experience can be perceived in complexity.

A5.1 Confusion of the subjective and objective world. This seems to occur with young children who believe that stories are 'true'.

A5.2 — gives a literal account without evaluation.

A5.3 — interprets reality in terms of fantasy.

A5.4 — interprets reality literally but in terms of logical possibilities.

A5.5 — interprets reality imaginatively in terms of art, perhaps symbolically or metaphorically.

AFFECTIVE ASPECTS OF WRITING

In order to illustrate the application of the affective model we may take one of our four modes — autobiography.

Autobiography — Seven-Year-Olds

The simplest piece of writing in our sample was by Peter G.:

> The saddest was when my dog got knocked down.

Peter demonstrates the literal statement as an early type of writing. The absence of 'day' indicates the difficulty he has in holding the overall sentence. Clearly there is no self-analysis (A1.0), sense of its effect on others (A2.0), no setting is given (A4.0), no explanations are offered to the reader (A3.1), there is no contextualization or distancing of the experience (A5.2). Another boy, Philip S. writes rather more:

> One day we were walking by the country side and i wanted to look in a field and my dad walked on and chased him and i fell over on my face.

He calls this his saddest day but the reason is not apparent (A1.1). The potential for emotional expression is present ('my dad walked on') but is not realized (A2.1). He assumes much about the environment, giving the reader only a vague idea of time, place, and social relations. The piece seems on the surface to be a recall of a specific experience (A5.2).

In contrast to these two pieces is that of Jean G.:

The saddest day was when my Grandad died and his wife was very
upset because she had lived for 60 years with him and me and my
sister were very very very upset to. We all had to go up to my
Grandads house to comfort my Grandmother and stop her crying
—and we stoped for two days i went with Granmar with my sister.
The End of my Story.

Jean evaluates her emotions in terms provided by the title (A1.2) and goes on
to explain the events that have brought the sadness, showing an awareness of
what causes such strong emotion in herself (A1.4). She quite remarkably
expresses an awareness of and an empathy with the feelings of her
Grandmother: 'his wife was very upset', 'we all had to go up to my Grandads
house to comfort my Grandmother and stop her crying' (A2.3). She includes
an unusually detailed description of the social relationships within the family
—the feelings of the grandmother for the grandfather, and the relationship
between the two sisters and their grandmother (A3.3). The writer is very much
aware of a real-life event and describes it literally (A5.2). Interestingly, she
does not need a large vocabulary. Under stress she uses what words she has
(e.g. the repeated 'very') and reaches out to phrases used, presumably, by the
adults ('lived for 60 years with him') to express her grief.

We may sum up some of the general characteristics of the writing.

Over half the writers evaluated the experience of the saddest or happiest day
(A1.2), not surprisingly since this was the task, but most did not state their
feelings beyond this. Two writers showed an awareness of self-image (A1.3)—
'I was so sad that I was sent to bed without any tea'. Generally speaking the
seven-year-olds did not express their own feelings explicitly no matter what
wonderful or horrendous things were happening to them.

Over half the writers mentioned others as separate identities, but gave no
indication of their attitude towards them. Some did not mention others at all;
five gave the direct speech of others (A2.2). Only two showed an awareness of
the emotions of others, one of whom was Jean G. Mothers, and to a lesser
extent fathers, appeared in half the pieces.

The writing of this age group varies from that in which there is no reader
orientation to that in which sufficient information and interpretation is
supplied to enable the reader to understand and reconstruct the situation,
though not necessarily in detail. Thus Peter G. gives us no setting or context,
whereas in other pieces, such as Jean G.'s, explanations for motivation are
offered not ostentatiously but arising naturally: 'to comfort my Grandmother'.

Some of the writers gave no indication of the setting (A3.1). Most pieces
contained a literal account of a person or persons, place, time, objects,
experience. The nature of the assignment prompted this. However, in four
pieces exaggerated behaviour indicated a less certain hold on reality. Thus in
one piece two boys are excessively punished for an unintentional offence.

On this task seven-year-olds do not explicitly state their feelings or self-awareness; most show an awareness of others as separate identities, especially their mothers; they describe the environment adequately for the reader to understand why an experience is sad or happy. The nature of the assignment results in a literal treatment in most cases.

Autobiography — Ten-Year-Olds

At this age we find that there is a tendency to make explicit the feelings of the writer in about half the scripts; the others implied their feelings by describing their experiences. Beth writes:

> The happiest day of my life was when I was on my friends pony both of us were cantering through the woods and having a lovely time. We sat down ate our picnic we had sponge cake, sandwiches, lemon juice, doughnuts, etc. It was very nice we lied down on the grass and slept for a while.
>
> Beth B.

The feelings of the writer ('having a lovely time', 'it was very nice') are clearly stated. Nothing is said about the friend — it would be irrelevant to the purpose — but there is a sense of environment — the pony, the woods, the grass (A3.2). There is considerable attention given to the reader in the amount of gastronomic information given him to enable him imaginatively to join in the picnic (A4.2). The incident has the air of slight fantasy, but is presented in self-consistent terms (A5.2).

The difficulty many ten-year-olds have in expressing direct emotions is seen in Jessica's piece. The situation is presumably fraught with strong feelings, but the potential here is unrealized in her written expression:

> One day my brother went to dartmoor and a rock fell on his leg and he broke it and he had to take him to plymouth hospital to have plaster on his leg and Mrs. Sneddon was with him and Mr. Woodford took christopher home and Mrs. Seddon and christopher was home a gen and Mr. Woodford carrying christopher in door and Mrs. Seddon took his stuf in door and mum said to me and carol go to bed to sleep good light mum.
>
> Jessica H.

Jessica tells of the incident as consecutive events and no emotion emerges. Others are mentioned in terms of their actions but do not begin to appear as people (A2.1) and even the words quoted seem rather a conventional ending than presenting a facet of personality. The details are minimal — there is no attempt at scene setting (A3.1): the problems of organization involved are so great that the writer is preoccupied with them to the exclusion of the reader (A4.1). The incident is presumably a real one, but there is no attempt at interpretation (A5.2), or pointing a non-literal significance.

Although Jessica does not realize her characters many ten-year-olds are quite capable of doing so. Sharon H.'s grandma ('She is allways making a fuss over me and I dont like it') comes to life through her supervision of Sharon and her peremptory bedtime orders.

> One day I was pick up a pot of Jam and my Graman siad oh Sharon it is to havey for you but I was still happy Sharon it is time for bed good night Sharon good night.

The writing of Francesca seems to contain a higher level of emotional awareness than many, chiefly expressed by implication, and through the environmental items selected.

> The happiest day of my life was on a Sunday when we had to go out. I don't know were the place was I don't know what it was called. It was by a little stream, and there were trees growing we could climb up to trees some were very high. There were rocks too with grasses growing on top. And a hill which had a path leading a long side the stream. You could climb up and down the hill it was a rocky hill. But it had lot of trees to catch hold of to pull yourself up. It was a long walk along the stream we walked about a quarter of the way and quater of the way was about two miles. We got tired so we thought we should turn back there was a small water fall in the river. Because of some stones stuck in the middle of the stream. There were bushes you could hide under. They were very big not many people walked on the path. There was another path on the other side of the stream. There were trees coving the path, but alot of light still came in. Then we got back we had to go because the day was over.

Details of the landscape are given to create atmosphere. Exact information ('rocks with grasses growing on top') helps here. But the landscape is not merely a backdrop—the children's actions and emotions arise in interrelationship with it—they climb up and down the rocky hill, pull themselves up with trees, get tired because of the two miles they have walked, hide under bushes (A3.3). Francesca is also able to report on her thoughts of that day, 'We got tired so we thought we should turn back' (A1.2, A2.1, A3.3, A4.3, A5.2).

In the writing of ten-year-olds as against seven-year-olds there was a tendency to state feeling at the 'I felt sad' level in about half of the 31 scripts;

in the others, as with the seven-year-olds, the feelings had to be inferred from the experiences. There is a slight development in the statement of self-awareness. Thus, Harriet C. is aware of the problem of accounting for her own feelings, 'one day I woke feeling very happy, I do not know why but I did'; but this awareness is shown only by four writers.

Many writers still refer to other people in their autobiographies in the barest terms (rather more than half as against rather less than half of the seven-year-olds) though about half of them now begin to realize other characters through what they say, feel, or do (whereas only about one in five seven-year-olds give words to others, and very few ascribe to them specific feelings).

As one would expect, partly because they are more in control of the medium, the ten-year-olds, far more than the seven-year-olds, provided information necessary for the understanding of their themes. Only perhaps two of the ten-year-olds produced context-bound writings (A4.1); most seemed to be in effect approaching a general audience (A4.3), even reassuring them that they will be taken along gently:

> The happiest day of my life happened on my holiday in july we went shopping and we made a trip to the beach this is what happened.

Perhaps the most notable development is in the use of environmental items —physical objects, spatial and temporal descriptions, social relationships. About a third of the seven-year-olds assumed an environment; none of the ten-year-olds did; and just under half of the latter responded in a way that showed that the environment had been specially significant to them, compared with about a fifth of the younger children. The sheer amount of detail often creates an atmosphere, though the danger of insufficient selection is present.

There is, as one would expect, an awareness of the real and imaginative worlds; one writer placed at the top of her piece 'half true, half fauls'. But all the writers give or purport to give a factual treatment. Nobody at this level invests incidents with a symbolic significance. The language is on the whole extremely literal, though there is an occasional (original) metaphor, as with Clare W.: 'So I slept on the floor. I woke up with the cat lying on me like I was a poofa'.

Autobiography — Thirteen-Year-Olds

The verbal information of the task was varied for the pupils in this group. It became 'The best or worst experience I have ever had'.

From a variety of points of view the most notable script is that by Nina P. Like that of Jean G. at seven it concerns a death in the family:

It was just like any other Tuesday. Normal breakfast, normal lessons, little did I know that this was going to be one of the saddest days of my life. I got off the bus as normal, walked up the hill, opened the gate, walked down the steps, pressed on the latch. Then, it was different. My Mum opened the door, her eyes were red her cheeks puffed out, she'd obviously been crying. Bewildered, I asked 'What's happened?' Thoughts flashed through my mind, who's hurt, Dad, Nana, Papa?

I was led into the sitting room, Mum held me and said,

"Theres no other way I can break this to you, Papa died this morning'.

The words were like a bombshell. I cried.

'Come and see Nana' Mum said 'Shes been very brave'.

I walked to the other room and flung my arms arond my Grand-mother. Tears fell like raindrops, until all my emotions were drained.

'How?' I asked.

'He was just sitting on the bed, getting his breath when he collapsed, he was probably dead before he fell'.

Dead, dead, dead, dead, the word ran through my mind, Papa is dead.

Memories flashed back, when he used to push me in my small pram when I was young.

His teasing, his twinkling eyes when he laughed.

I cant cry anymore, all I can do is remember, it hurts though.

The words, 'Papa died this morning', kept on in my head for days. I couldn't stop them, it was like a disease, my whole body longed for him to be back. I hoped it was just a nightmare.

I couldn't accept the fact that he was gone. I expect I will have to soon though.

I long for the day when I can think about him without it hurting too much.

I'll just put on a brave face, its all I can do.

Nina's grandfather dies, and she feels his loss very deeply. She draws a contrast between the events of a normal day and those after she gets the news of her grandfather's death. She tells of her grief not only through direct expression but also by reporting her words and actions: she is bewildered, afraid, exhausts herself with grief ('until all my emotions were drained'); she is compassionate with her grandmother, and recognizes they must live for a time with despair, waiting for the hurt to lessen. It would appear that she has a well-developed understanding of the progress of grief. She shows skill in her selection of actions and dialogue to heighten the reader's awareness of the feelings involved. She also shows an understanding of the effect of emotional shock: 'Dead, dead, dead, dead, the word ran through my mind, Papa is dead'; 'memories flashed back'. Here she appears to be going back over the cause of the shock, trying to sort it out, to come to terms with it. Nina compares her experience to a nightmare, even wishing it were, so that she could wake up and know that it did not happen in reality. In all she expresses a highly developed sense of the nature of the emotion within herself (A1.4), an awareness of that of others (A2.3), and a general disposition to be compassionate, an awareness of the way emotion works in such a situation — the recall of the past incidents for example. Particularly interesting is the attempt to find metaphorical equivalents for the emotion in order to cope with it ('like a bombshell', 'like raindrops', 'like a disease', 'just a nightmare') as well as the realistic acceptance in the later sentences — 'I'll just put on a brave face, its all I can do'. The language may seem conventional, even trite, but we must beware of thinking that therefore the emotion is not genuine (A5.2). Unique expression for unique emotion is a hard-won achievement. With writers of this age it is a virtue that they are trying on language, even if it is other people's.

Amongst the thirteen-year-olds about a third show an awareness of how they appear to others, in a way that scarcely any of the younger children do. Andrew B. looks back on himself at seven when he was given a hospital bed and comments, 'This bed was a cot which I was very put out by because I thought I had grown out of cots' (A1.3). Gordon B. gets lost in his new school and 'looked like a fool standing there asking where Room 1 was' (A1.3). In Nina's piece quoted on the previous page there is a deeper understanding of her own feelings (A1.4). As would be expected, this age group is rather more conscious of other people in its writing. The task of course does prompt introspection, but over a third ascribe emotions to others or describe their actions which imply emotions, as against a quarter of the tens and scarcely any of the sevens. The realization of others in terms of their own words or thoughts occurs in a few scripts.

Many pieces at this level are context-free, in that they contain all the information necessary for their own decoding. They sometimes contain asides for the general reader, contain information necessary for understanding or interpreting, have a careful selection of image and detail. (There is a tendency beyond A4.1 and A4.2 to A4. 3.)

One of the more significant features of the thirteen-year-olds' writing is their use of environment. Arthur M. uses skilfully selected details in order to convey a moving experience. These details are physical—the assembly, the fists, the swimming trunks—and social—the gang, the indifferent (or terrified) 'female teacher', the boy as outcast. This writer has gone past feeling the need to use language merely for scene painting (A3.4):

> . . . The first thing we did was to have assembly, when I was the only (one) able to answer the Headmaster's question, I was nick-named 'Magnus'—a bad start. I knew everything in the lessons, I could answer every question by means of a lecture, though I had not mastered the art of friendliness. As one or two fists told me.
>
> My popularity in the class was abismal. I was rated as an outcast by everyone. I was bullied perpetually and brutally by gangs. Whenever the teacher turned her back they attacked. Often when she was looking. She took little action.
>
> I hated the school. I learned absolutely nothing. I was in a back-ward class with an intelligence better than most of the top class. Just because of my age. The 'supervision' was about as effective as a catapult used in war between Russia and America. Or worse.
>
> The worst part of the day was changing back from swimming. The entire class of boys threw their wet trunks at me. At short range. Hard. Being a femal teacher no supervision could be given. This happened nearly every day . . .

A development in the expression of awareness of the environment as significant in stimulating emotions has already been noted in the ten-year-olds. About two-thirds of thirteen-year-olds, compared with less than half of the ten-year-olds, showed an ability to respond to the environment in such a way as to indicate that it had been especially significant and stimulating (A3.3). One might expect this, given the nature of the task ('my worst/best experience') but there were several examples of writing such as Arthur's that reached the A3.4 stage and illustrate the higher quality of the responses from the thirteen-year-olds.

In the pupils of this age we see a tendency not to describe but to interpret. Once again Arthur M.'s work will serve as an example. Here he obviously had a very hard experience to cope with. In retrospect he can deal with it by objectifying — by seeing himself as 'Magnus' who gave 'lectures' and as someone who 'had not mastered the art of friendliness'. He deliberately uses exaggerated imagery (the 'catapult') but the overall distancing and interpreting device is irony. It is most explicit in his apostrophized 'supervision' but it is implicit throughout, particularly in relation to the teacher, and is supported by his sense of style, particularly the laconic, grammatically incomplete comments. There is a burning resentment held under control as one of a complex of emotions by the skilled marshalling of the language. The category would be A5.5.

Discussion

Our researches indicate that it is possible to speak with some (obviously not complete) objectivity of affective development in the terms we have chosen to discuss it. (We are of course talking about such development as manifested in writing, and writing is only one of the kinds of behaviour by which individuals manifest themselves.) That our model is not completely arbitrary would seem to lie in two diverse indications. One is that in both common wisdom and psychological studies 'growing up' is attended by 'decentering' — of self, towards others, in relation to 'reality'. Of this we have said sufficient. A second indication is very different — it is concerned with the differences between the spoken and written language.

In speech a good deal of the emotion is carried in the voice, stimulated usually by face-to-face contact, whereas in writing it has to be presented by a whole range of stylistic devices — the connotations of nouns and verbs, their enrichment by adjectives and adverbs, metaphorical devices, rhythms, and so on. Thus the conveying of emotion is much harder in the written than in the spoken language. And, for young children learning to write, the difficulties are compounded by the fact that they have not yet automated a large number of complex processes — handwriting, punctuation, spelling, word choice, syntax, reader needs, and so on. Thus the tendency will be for younger writers to produce simple literal sentences, conveying fact rather than affect. In our model of style, for this and other reasons, we see the affirmative literal sentence as the norm from which choices in various directions, including the affective, are made.

THE MORAL MODEL

Attitudes/judgements about self/others and events

M1 Judging self/others by physical characteristics or consequences, e.g. 'She was ugly, so she was bad'. 'He broke fifteen cups—naughty'. Judging events by pain-pleasure to the self, e.g. 'It was a bad day. I hurt my hand'. 'It was a good birthday. I got lots of presents'. 'A bad accident—the fence was smashed up'. Principle of self-gratification—'anomy'.

M2 Judging self/others and events in terms of punishments/rewards. 'I won't do that, Mummy will hit me'. 'I'll tell Daddy on you and he will beat you up'. 'If I do the dishes, Mummy will give me a new bat'. Events judged as rewards/punishments, e.g. 'I must have been naughty last night, the fridge hit me'. Heteronomy.

M3 Judging self/others according to the status quo. Mother, father, teacher, policeman good by right of status; the wicked witch, the evil step-father bad by right of convention, e.g. 'I hated the Jerries, I used to call them stupid idiots'. Reciprocity restricted to the child's immediate circle, e.g. 'I won't do that—it will upset mummy'. Social approval/disapproval internalized in terms of whether behaviour upsets others or not. Stereotypic thinking. Events judged in terms of effects on other *people*. 'It was a bad accident. All the passengers were badly hurt'. Socionomy (internal).

M4 Judging self/others in terms of conventional norms/rules, e.g. 'It's wrong to steal. It is against the law'. Conformist orientation. Rules are applied literally on the principle of equity or fairness. 'It's not fair. We all did it, so John should be punished the same as us. We all broke the rule'. Socionomy (external).

M5 Judging self/others in terms of intention or motive, regardless of status or power, e.g. 'She didn't mean to drop those plates, so she shouldn't be punished'. 'Teacher was wrong, because she punished all of us instead of finding out who did it'.

M6 Judging self/others in terms of abstract concepts such as a universal respect for the individual rather than in terms of conventional norms of right/wrong conduct. The morality of individual conscience. Rules seen as arbitrary and changeable. Autonomy.

M7 Judgement of self/others in terms of a personally developed value *system*.

MORAL ASPECTS OF WRITING

In studying affective aspects of writing above, we took our examples from autobiographical narrative, as this gave us the widest range of responses. With the moral aspect we shall again examine autobiography and also look at argument.

Autobiography and Argument — Seven-Year-Olds

Generally speaking the seven-year-olds in the autobiographical narratives judged the best or worst events in their lives in terms of damage to physical objects they possessed or in terms of pleasure or pain to themselves. Only one child judges as bad damage to others. A few children wrote stories in which a punishment/reward orientation is discernible. On the argumentative task also this egocentrism is borne out — over half of the writers gave judgements of school as being good or bad in terms of personal pain or pleasure. A typical example of moral thinking (which we classify as M1) comes from John:

> The saddest day of my life was when we were at dartmoor I were
> feed a pony and another kicked me in the air and it hurt and I fell
> on the ground.

Most children at this age judged their worst experience as damage to self or to objects belonging to the self — broken cups, paint-stained jumpers, toes being damaged, fingers caught in doors. Happiest days were equated with birthdays or Christmas, most accounts featuring lists of presents. The same pattern appeared in the argumentative task — school was judged good or bad in terms of self-interest. For example:

> I think that there should be no school at all then I could stay home
> and watch television and eat sweets.
>
> Kathleen M.

Kathleen cannot decentre enough to realize that changes to the school system will affect others. She assesses her position in terms of what is pleasurable to the self (M1).

One of the most interesting accounts at 7 + demonstrates the upper limits of the young child's moral thinking, the shift from judgement in terms of physical consequences to a punishment orientation:

The Happiest Day of my Life

One day I was playing outside when I saw some boys and then they saw me and came up to me and called me names. So I whet in doors and when I whet out again. They were Playing with a tyre and this man had a new garig down the road and one of the boys roed the tyre down to the other boy but he mercd it and it whet right into the garig and the man told them off and then they whet home and when they whet to Sunday School when they got home a Pilceman was ther and he told them off.

Donna H.

Donna entitles this piece her *happiest* experience, happiness being equated with seeing others punished! The boys in the story have done wrong and are punished by a telling off, both by the garage owner and by the policeman. What Donna does not yet realize is the distinction between intentionally damaging property and unintentionally doing so. The tyre rolls into the garage by accident — in the light of this the punishment seems unnecessarily severe. One suspects that Donna is more upset by the boys 'calling me names' than anything else. This is close to the Piagetian notion of 'immanent justice' — punishment catches up with the boys in the end, even if not related directly to the specific offence in Donna's eyes. There is an insistence on punishment; further, it is out of proportion to the accidental offence. Taken together, these two factors put the story at M2.

Autobiography and Argument — Ten-Year-Olds

At 10 + on the autobiographical narratives we found a decline in the number of stories based on pain/pleasure to the self, an increase in the number of stories with motifs of heteronomy and the emergence of some stories in which empathy and reciprocity, judgements of others in terms of the status quo, appeared. As example of the punishment orientation comes from Tina, who judges the 'saddest' day as one in which the whole world is conspiring to punish her: 'something in the hedge' frightens her, she breaks an umbrella 'it was not mine it was my mothes'. She disobeys her father after a petulant argument with him: 'I am going for a walk, no you are not yes I am and I ran out', and parental punishment for her behaviour caps the bad day (M.2), 'You better get home to bed, you bad girl'.

The shift to judgement in terms of the status quo appears in Douglas' adventure story. Whilst an autobiographical narrative, one suspects that it is partly a fiction. It tells how he and his friend visit a Steam Rally, and continues:

We were looking at a Fowler Engine when the driver asked us if we would like a ride are quick reply was yes we both climbed up and watched as the driver took the brake off and we slowly moved around the feild. Suddenly the driver sliped of the plate that he was standing on and knocked himself out as the hit the ground. I made a grab for the wheel but slipped and went sprawling on the foot plate. The was a sudden crash and then as I got up to steer another crash knowcked me off my feet but lickily then the entine stopped and I ended up in a duck pond. We had destroyed a gate and ripped up a hedge. People came running from all directions and a newspaper reporter was soon on the scene. While we walked home I asked Snub why he hadn't tried to steer, Snub replied, 'I couldn't because my feet had got tangled in some rope and I couldn't move'. The next day I saw a paper with our photographs in and our story.

Douglas M.

Whilst the bulk of Douglas' narrative is not concerned with notions of right and wrong, but with describing accidental damage to property, the ending of the story, where the two boy heroes have their photograph published in the newspaper, is an indication that fame or respect from the local community is seen by Douglas as good. Being judged as brave in the eyes of others for preventing further damage to property or injury to people—no-one in the story is actually seriously hurt—is seen as good. Hence M3, 'social approval in terms of whether behaviour pleases others', is the final orientation of the story.

On the argumentative tasks at 10 +, judgement in terms of the status quo was the rule rather than the exception. Carol argues:

I don't think it would work in my opinion its not a very good idea to come to school when you liked and to do what you like because everyone would never come to school hardly because they wouldn't want to learn, nobody would get any qualifications.

Parents wouldn't agree either because they would want you to be educated, anyway the country would become rough with school age people lounging about everywhere. At home mothers can teach you but you can't do half the things at home as you can at school. If you wern't educated you wouldn't be able to get a job. When your younger your mother and father would make you go to school because you wouldn't understand, there would be trouble when your old enough to make up your own mind weather to go to school or not.

Personally I like school and I don't mind going. I would get fed up with doing what I liked. I think people would have a boaring life. Most people would just muck about. There are lots of oppertunitys

at school and you do things you would not be allowed to do
at home.

Carol W.

Carol's argument amounts to a defence of schooling remaining as it is. The
reasons she offers range from attributing to other children pursuit of the
pleasure principle (M1)—'everyone would never come to school hardly
because they wouldn't want to learn', 'most people would just muck about'—
to considering the effects on others in the social environment (M3)—'Parents
wouldn't agree either because they would want you to be educated'. Carol
realizes that a decision on such an issue is made by an implicit agreement
between all parties—parents as well as children, and the ultimate effects of
leaving the choice to children would be bad for society at large (M3)—'anyway
the country would become rough with school age people lounging about
everywhere'. She sees the proper exercise of parental authority as being for the
protection of the young; 'when your younger your mother and father would
make you go to school because you wouldn't understand, there would be
trouble when your old enough to make up your own mind'. Parents are right
in terms of their conventional roles in protecting children for their own good.
Carol judges the issue over-all in terms of effects on others—reciprocity is
extended in this argument to the immediate family circle; such a decision
affects others, so others' views have to be taken into account. (Hence M3 overall.) The basis on which she makes a judgement contrasts markedly with that
of Kathleen and Tania at seven years. Carol can decentre enough to realize
that other people's views must be taken into account.

Over-all on the argumentative task at 10+ only a few pieces argued for
changes to the school system in terms of 'the good is what I like and want'.
Most children explored the effects of possible changes in schooling in terms of
how they would affect others—parents, teachers, bus-drivers and other
children. Most children argued in defence of the status quo, though elements
of earlier forms of moral judgement were detected at the sentence level. The
legalistic orientation of level M4 did not make much of an appearance; only
one girl at 10+ ended her argument on the note 'But there is a law about going
to school' in the context that such a law was a good one because it protected
the rights of others. Generally, however, taking both the argumentative and autobiographical narratives into account, the trend at 10+ indicates that heteronomy
gives way to socionomy at this age. The form of socionomy is, however,
internal to the child's limited understanding of the social system; concepts of
rights or fairness and justice do not really emerge at this age with any consistency.

Autobiography and Argument—Thirteen-Year-Olds

At 13+ there is emerging the capacity to make moral judgements either in
terms of conventional norms and rules or in terms of intention regardless of

social status. Parents and teachers can now do wrong in the eyes of children; the Piagetian notion of the young child's unilateral respect for adults gives way to a notion of what is fair. On the argumentative task, most children at 13 + argue in terms of the status quo or of conventional norms/rules, looking at the implications for change in the school system in the light of how it might affect not only others within the school system, but society at large. Most children at 10 + claimed that children who didn't have to come to school would become bored; by 13 + most pupils drew the inference that such a decision would lead to an increase in crime—the legalistic orientation. The final paragraphs of Madge's argument that the school system should stay as it is begins with an exploration of the effects of optional school attendance. She writes:

> The children that didn't go to school would be out roaming the streets. They'd become bored after a while, so they might commit some petty crime, like vandalism or small shop theft. These people wouldn't get any qualifications if they stayed away from school. So they proberly wouldn't get a job with good pay so they might steal extra money.

> The system wouldn't be fair on the people who wanted to do well in school, because in the classes they would go to would be people who just wanted to muck around.
>
> Madge H.

Madge's concern here is with the welfare of the social system, that the property laws be maintained. She pinpoints a concern for law and order in her statement that children would turn to crime and vandalism if given nothing constructive to do. Further, her claim 'The system wouldn't be fair on the people who wanted to do well in school' indicates that Madge believes that justice must be based on strict equality—the principle of equity (M4). What worries her about the implications of optional school attendance is fairness to all children in the system.

In the autobiographical narratives at 13 + judgement of others in terms of intention rather than in terms of social status emerged. An example of an autobiographical anecdote which depicts this shift comes from Sally, who writes:

> My worst experience was seeing a little boy knocked down by a car.

> This little boy was standing with his mother by the main road. His mother was busy talking to another lady to see what her son was doing. The little boy saw something on the other side of the road. A car was coming, it hit the boy. The boy rolled up over the bonnet then back onto the road. The little boy was badly injured. Someone

rang for an ambulance quickly. The car wasn't travelling fast, but the boy just didn't look. The driver and his wife were very shook up. This wouldn't have happened if the mother paid a little more attention to her son, instead of to herself and a friend.

Sally M.

Obviously, underpinning Sally's direct judgement of the mother's behaviour in the incident she depicts a conception of the mother's proper social role as being for the protection of the young (M3). The incident is judged as bad because it hurts others, not only the child — 'The little boy was badly injured' — but others as well — 'The driver and his wife were very shook up'. However, blame is not attributed to the driver of the vehicle, 'The car wasn't travelling fast', but to the mother for her lack of care and concern for her child. The mother's intentions are judged as self-interest (M5) — 'This wouldn't have happened if the mother paid a little more attention to her son, instead of to herself and a friend'. Sally has a clear idea of where to apportion blame for the accident; it comes back to notions of parental responsibility, which she takes seriously. She looks beyond the obvious cause of the accident, the driver's failure to stop, to the mother's sin of omission, judging the mother in terms of her intentions.

Discussion

Generally then, our application of the moral model to the autobiographical and argumentative writing of children from seven to thirteen years illustrates that it is a useful tool for analysing the content of children's writing. We found general confirmation of Kolberg's finding that preconventional moral judgement, anomy and heteronomy, decrease with age, and that his types 3 and 4, the 'good-boy' morality of maintaining good relations, approval of others and authority maintaining morality, increase with age to thirteen years. The pleasure principle, or definition of good as 'what I want and like', dominates over half of the sample of seven years, declining to account for only a few moral judgements at $13+$. We found that heteronomy developed to ten years, then declined at $13+$. We found no evidence of 'judgement in terms of abstract principles' in children of 7–13 years. We did find, though, that whereas no children at $7+$ judged adults' actions in terms of intention, by $13+$ they were capable of doing so. As Kolberg (1964) maintains: 'Large groups of moral concepts and attitudes acquire meaning only in late childhood and adolescence, and require the extensive background of cognitive growth and experience associated with the age factor' (p.402).

CONCLUSIONS

When we began work we had good reason to believe that little had been done in the field, and it was not unexpected to have our beliefs confirmed. What did surprise us, however, was to discover how little the concepts of 'development' and 'maturity' had been considered in relation to other specific disciplines or to education in general. There were 'aims' certainly, but few procedures. However we could not allow ourselves to be side-tracked. The Exeter (and particularly the Crediton) research was designed by taking into account cognitive, affective, moral and stylistic aspects to produce a more comprehensive model of language development than has yet been devised. Clearly this is an ambitious undertaking, and we could not claim to have done more than indicate directions; but in areas where nothing has been done, that at least is something.

The models we have produced are research tools in the sense that they contain many items by which a particular piece of writing may be described in some detail. They are not intended as day-to-day marking schemes. Nevertheless the teachers who worked with us urged their publication in full, and not in summary, on the grounds that a detailed knowledge of their application even to a limited number of scripts heightened awareness of the possibilities of children's writing. Any assessment of writing, even by 'impression', is dependent on an internalized model of some kind. Our belief is that such models are frequently far too narrow, particularly those codified for examinations, and need to be modified in the light of work such as ours. Dixon and Stratta (1980, 1981) have followed up the ideas of the Crediton project in relation to the marking of external examinations (GCE and CSE) with encouraging results.

The pedagogical function of the models, however, is not primarily as testing devices but as learning devices. In the classroom we need constantly to make assessments of where students are so as to help them to develop further. In this sense the assessment process is inseparable from the teaching process.

The Crediton work was based on a sample of 150 or so children between the ages of seven and thirteen. Studies are going ahead to extend both the age range covered and the numbers in the sample, and to look at development also in the spoken mode. Nevertheless, although the sample was small, and based on schools in a remote market town in Devon, UK, there is reason to hope that our observations have some validity. Several studies in Canada and Australia, as well as in the UK begin to confirm this. The children in Crediton are not just a 'sample'; they are people. Perhaps people elsewhere are not very different.

REFERENCES

Britton, J., Burgess, T., Martin, N., McLeod, A., and Rosen, H. *The development of writing abilities (11–18)*. London: Macmillan Education, 1975.

Carroll, J. B. *Development of native language skills beyond the early years*. Princeton, NJ: Educational Testing Service, 1968.

Dixon, J., and Stratta, L. *Achievements in writing at 16+*. Unpublished report, Faculty of Education, University of Birmingham, 1980.

Dixon, J., and Stratta, L. *Criteria for writing in English.* Unpublished report, Faculty of Education, University of Birmingham, 1981.

Halliday, M. A. K., and Hasan, R. *Cohesion in English.* London: Longman, 1976.

Harpin, W. S. (and associates). *Social and educational influences on children's acquisition of grammar.* Unpublished report, School of Education, University of Nottingham, 1973.

Harrison, B. T. The learner as writer: Stages of growth. *Language for Learning,* 1979, **1,** 93–109.

Kolberg, L. The development of children's orientation towards a moral order. *Vita Humana,* 1963, **6,** 11–33.

Kolberg, L. The development of moral character and moral ideology. In M. L. Hoffman and L. W. Hoffman (Eds.), *Review of child development research* (Vol. 1). Chicago: University of Chicago Press, 1964.

Loban, W. *The language of elementary school children.* Urbana, L: National Council of Teachers of English, 1963.

Loban, W. *Language development: Kindergarten through grade twelve.* Urbana, L: National Council of Teachers of English, 1976.

Marshall, C. *Criteria internalised by impression makers.* Unpublished M. Ed. dissertation, University of Exeter, 1978.

McCarthy, D. A. Language development in children. In L. Carmichael (Ed.), *A manual of child psychology.* New York: Wiley, 1954.

Moffett, J. *Teaching the universe of discourse.* Boston: Houghton Mifflin, 1968.

Piaget, J. *The moral judgement of the child.* London: Routledge and Kegan Paul, 1932.

Strongman, K. T. *The psychology of emotion* (2nd ed.). New York: Wiley, 1978.

Wilkinson, A., Barnsley, G., Hanna, P., and Swan, M. *Assessing language development.* Oxford: Oxford University Press, 1980.

Witcombe, C. M. *Developmental aspects of children's language in junior school.* Unpublished M. Ed. dissertation, University of Exeter, 1979.

Witkin, R. W. *The intelligence of feeling.* Tadworth: Heinemann Educational, 1974.

RESEARCH

Explorations in the Development of Writing
Edited by Barry M. Kroll and Gordon Wells
© 1983 John Wiley & Sons Ltd.

4

One Child and One Genre: Developments in Letter Writing

John Collerson

The exploration of children's writing development can be carried out in various ways, each of them contributing something to our understanding. Some studies have been based on writing collected from groups of children of different ages, for example those of Britton *et al.* (1975) and Wilkinson *et al.* (1980). Studies like these usually involve writing from a lot of children and are concerned mainly with general trends of development. Other studies take account of writing done by the same children at different ages, such as the longitudinal study of King and Rentel (1981) and the work of Graves and his colleagues, which also included the intensive study of individual children's writing over a period of time (Graves, 1981). The most intensive kind of study of a child's writing development, however, is the individual case study, such as Bissex's investigation of her son's literacy development (1980a). The present chapter is based on material from a longitudinal study of one child's writing.

In order to get a comprehensive picture of the writing that a child might do in the early years of writing, I have been attempting to collect and study all the writing done by one child, namely my elder daughter Juliet. This chapter is a study of one kind of Juliet's writing covering the age range from 5 years 0 months to 9 years 6 months. During that time Juliet wrote a great deal at home as well as at school. The home writing—strictly, any writing outside the school context—included a lot of letters, and it is with these letters, written at home and elsewhere, that this chapter is concerned.

This study is limited in two ways. First, the study concerns the writing of only one child and thus its findings cannot readily be generalized to other children. However, the case-study approach makes feasible an intensive investigation of an individual child's writing, based on as complete a collection as possible of that child's writing output, together with essential information on the circumstances of each piece of writing. The study can then be compared with other similar studies and it can indicate aspects of writing development which could be pursued in a group study. As Glenda Bissex (1980b) says: 'From observing one child we have some leads—some questions to ask and patterns to look for in studying other children' (p.197).

Second, the study focuses on one particular genre: letter writing. I have assumed that there will be significant differences in the child's writing from one genre to another, and this assumption is confirmed by informal inspection of the writing. In order to get a foothold on the broad range of the child's writing development I have chosen to concentrate here on one genre in isolation from the other kinds of writing that the child was doing. Letters were chosen for the study because over the whole period there were quite a lot of examples of this genre which seemed to be fairly easy to distinguish from other writings.

The data for the study are all the letters written during the four-and-a-half-year period from age 5 years 0 months (5;0) to 9 years 6 months (9;6) (apart from a few written at school) together with the notes that have been kept on the circumstances of the writing. The numbers and average length of the letters in each year are shown in Table 1.

Table 1. Number and average length of letters at each age

Age	Number	Average length in words*
5	10	24.30
6	15	28.26
7	18	69.28
8	16	99.93
9 (to 9;6)	12	98.75
Total	71	66.17

* Based on the number of words in the body of the letter (excluding the opening and closing formulae but including any P.S.).

LANGUAGE AND WRITING DEVELOPMENT

It seems reasonable to expect that in comparing a child's letters written in the period from age 5;0 to age 9;6 we would find some changes, but if we are interested in how the child's letter-writing ability develops during that period we must decide what kind of changes we should pay attention to. Letter writing is a way of using language and as such will have something in common with all uses of language. Decisions about what features are to be investigated should therefore be based on assumptions about the nature of language and about how it develops, particularly in its written form.

Language can be regarded as a system by which people express meanings and exchange meanings with others. The particular meanings chosen in any specific instance of language use will arise from the purposes for which the language is being used. The meanings will be an expression of the purposes. The language system embodies the means by which the chosen meanings are realized as words and structures which can be expressed in speech or writing (Halliday, 1973). The purposes for which the language is being used (and thus the meanings being expressed) arise partly from the social context in which the users are involved (Halliday, 1978); there will also be factors internal to each individual user such as motivations, attitudes and emotional states.

The general approach to these letters, then, is based on the assumption that the language forms used are at least partly determined by the social context; that is to say that there is a relationship between the social context and the writer's purpose, the functions of the language used, the meanings expressed and the words and structures which realize those meanings. We will therefore be considering the letters in terms of what Juliet was trying to do in writing them and how she was using language in order to do it.

In line with this general approach there are also assumptions about language development. Halliday (1975) has argued that as a young child extends his awareness of what he can do with language, so his language system develops to allow him to realize a wider range of functions and meanings. This raises important questions for writing development and letter writing in particular. The kinds of things that a child uses writing for may be limited at first by the child's limited view of the potential of that mode of language use. With letter writing in particular we may find evidence that the child has to go through a process of discovering what letters are for and that, as her view of this widens, so will her letters develop in their range of functions, meanings and language forms.

THE LETTERS AS SOCIAL INTERACTION

Before we begin to explore the language of these letters in detail it is necessary to consider each letter in relation to its social context and to go some way towards identifying the purpose or purposes of each letter. This will be done on the basis of three categories, each of which is in principle independent of the others. This will allow us to set up a matrix in which any text can be located and to see whether there are clusters of texts in similar positions on the matrix. The three categories are initiative, occasion and audience.

Initiative is the question of whether the decision to write the letter was made by Juliet or by her parents. This is a simple dichotomy with most letters clearly classifiable as on Juliet's initiative or not; the few uncertain cases were treated as negative. Of the 71 letters, 46 were written on her own initiative while 25 were not. The fact that a parent may sometimes ask a child to write a letter to fulfil some social obligation means that letter writing is different from most other kinds of writing that children do at home, since most writing is done on their own initiative. Letter writing can thus sometimes be like school writing: required by someone other than the writer.

The *occasion* for the letter is a more diverse category, but several clear cases can be identified. Six subcategories have been identified on an ad hoc basis after informal inspection of the data; the number of letters in each group is indicated:

Reply to a letter received	15
Response to receiving a present	17
Response to a visit to the recipient	4
Response to some other specific thing	2
Temporary absence (e.g. on holidays) of writer or recipient	11
Miscellaneous	22

Replying to another letter is perhaps the most obvious occasion for a letter, though the earliest to be found among Juliet's letter experience was one of thanks for receiving a present. There were also other things which created the need for a thank-you letter or some similar response and one of these — visiting the recipient's home for a stay of a few days — is identified as a specific category. The only other specific category — temporary absence — is another obvious occasion for a letter; a few such letters were written to school friends during school holidays. For many of the letters in the miscellaneous group there was a specific occasion evident but, taken together, these occasions form a diverse group.

The final category is the kind of person to whom the letter is addressed. Four different subcategories of *audience* are identified:

Parents	10
Adult relatives and friends of the family	26
Children	30
Others	5

It might well be wondered what 'others' there could be; in this miscellaneous group are included a few letters to adults with whom no regular contact might be expected and a few letters to the fairies. No distinction was made between adult relatives and friends of the family because the distinction is not important at this level of generality. Parents were treated as a different group because, as members of the household, letters were not the normal means of communication with them.

When we look at the clustering of letters in these categories (as presented in Table 2) we find some interesting, though not surprising, results. The two biggest clusters are letters written to adults at parents' request in response to

Table 2.   The letters in social interaction categories

Audience:	Parents		Adult friends		Children		Other		Totals		
Initiative*:	+	–	+	–	+	–	+	–	+	–	T
Reply	1				12	2			13	2	15
Response to:											
present			3	13	1				3	14	17
visit				3			1		1	3	4
other			1		1				2		2
Temporary abs.	2	4			5				7	4	11
Miscellaneous	3		5	1	8	1	4		20	2	22
Totals	6	4	9	17	26	4	5		46	25	71
Audience totals	10		26		30		5		71		

* +, Juliet's initiative; –, parents' initiative.

presents received (13), and letters written to other children on Juliet's initiative in reply to another letter (12). Almost all the letters in the miscellaneous occasion group are written on Juliet's initiative, but their audience groups are quite diverse; this suggests that letters requested by parents arise from a limited and well-defined set of occasions. Letters arising from the temporary absence of the writer or the recipient can come either from Juliet's initiative or from parents' request; two audience groups are represented: children (usually Juliet's initiative) and parents (usually requested by the other parent). Some of this clustering reflects the generalization that most of the letters written to other children are on Juliet's own initiative while most written to adults (including parents) are requested by parents.

There is not much evidence of the clustering changing with age. At the ages of five and six about half the letters are written on Juliet's initiative and half at parents' request. At the ages of seven and eight the majority are written on Juliet's initiative (27 letters as against 7); yet at nine the numbers in each group are again almost equal. At age five, the letters initiated by the writer are much longer than the others (an average of 35.6 words as against 13 words), yet that great difference in length is not found in the later years. Letters to other children in reply to a letter received do not occur much before the age of seven, but that is because the need for them did not arise much before then. On the other hand, letters written in response to receiving a present are a substantial group at five and continue to be so throughout, except, surprisingly, at the age of seven.

This classification has both social and psychological implications. Letter writing—like other kinds of writing—is not an activity that occurs in a vacuum, but something that arises out of the child's way of life, involving the social interaction within the family and with networks of other people, as well as obligations which may be imposed on the writer, and her own intentions, interests and commitment to the task. From this categorization of the letters we get some indication of what the child's purposes are in writing the letters and it is to this that we must now turn our attention more closely.

WHAT IT IS TO WRITE A LETTER

If we are to consider the functions of the language in a letter, we should try to make explicit what the child might be consciously doing. How might the activity of letter writing appear to a young child? First of all, writing a letter is something that you do; it is an act which results in a physical artefact which can then be posted or given to someone. So we could say that the purpose for which language is being used is to write the letter, that is, to produce this thing called a letter. Moreover, there are certain verbal formulae for beginning and ending a letter. These conventions of letter-writing language help to establish the form of the letter and they are conventions which can be fairly readily adopted by a young writer.

The second obvious thing about letter writing is that you write a letter *to* somebody. For the young child it is generally somebody that he or she knows. Writing a letter is a bit like talking to them; it is very much a person-to-person use of language.

Thirdly, there are times when there is a specific reason for writing the letter. If the letter has a very explicit purpose, this provides at least some of the meaning that will be expressed in the body of the letter. So, a letter might be written to thank someone for something, or to reply to a letter they have sent, or to arrange something with the other person. That could provide the basis for the body of the letter; at least it could provide the writer with a start.

In any piece of writing, how to get started is one of the problems a young writer has to contend with. How to bring the writing to an end and what to put in between the beginning and the end are also problems, but as we shall see, not so much for the beginning writer as for one whose writing has developed a little. A letter has the advantage that it provides the writer with a definite conventional framework within which to operate. It offers the writer a way of starting and a way of ending the text of the letter and not much need be put in between to complete the letter. Some of Juliet's early letters have only one or two clauses in the body of the letter and one letter, written to the fairies, has no body at all (which is perhaps appropriate):

6081 (6;8) for the Fariys
To the Fariy
QUEEN Love
from Juliet
COLLERSON

It relies entirely on the meanings conveyed in the opening and closing words. However, the fact that a letter like this can be written shows that Juliet does not regard the opening and closing elements as merely formulaic; they convey some important interpersonal meaning over and above what the body of the letter can convey. Indeed, this is one of the few letters in which the opening does not follow the conventional formula.

However, the conventional opening and closing of the letter do not get the young writer very far. There still remain two problems which the letter shares with most other kinds of writing: Having said 'dear so-and-so', how do you launch into the body of the letter and then, just before you sign off, how do you bring the body of the letter to a close? In the longer letters there is also the problem, as in other types of writing, of how you get from one topic to another. The purpose that the writer has in mind in starting to write the letter often provides a way of getting going on the body of the letter. This is very obvious in Juliet's early letters thanking people for presents. How the letter develops beyond that start can depend on many things: the writer's understanding of what letters are for, the emergence of further purposes as the letter is being written, the writer's interest in the task and even things like the size of the paper.

These issues will be taken up in the ensuing sections. We shall begin by considering how Juliet began and ended her letters and with the interpersonal meanings which those parts of the letters help to convey.

The End and the Beginning

I want to consider the end of the letters first in order to examine the nature of Juliet's authorship. Almost all the letters are written entirely by Juliet, but the nature of her authorship is not always simple. At the end of most letters she just puts her own name (in 58 of the 71), usually just the Christian name (47). However, in some of the letters she has included her sister's name (5) and in some, other members of the family as well (3); even the cats are included once. It seems that she has here some notion of writing on behalf of others as well as herself, although it is not usually clear whether she begins the letter with this in mind or just adds the extra names for good measure when she gets to the end. However, in a few of these it is probably not just an afterthought, as in this letter:

6074 (6;7) Dear Auntie Olive and   them together, She also
Uncle Keith, Thank-   reads the books. I
you for all the lovely   like the dolls
presents you gave   furniture a lot.
Roslind and I. Roslind   I am sorry
likes the animals very   to say that
much. We play with   we have not got a

dolls house yet, But   (words of Christmas carol:
we will make one. I   'We wish you a merry
also like the books. We   Christmas')
are happy with all   Love from
our presents. I got a   Juliet Rosalind
scooter.   Ruth and
                                   John.

In thanking for Christmas presents, Juliet is clearly including her sister Rosalind's thanks as well as her own and seems to be consciously writing on Rosalind's behalf in the clause 'Roslind likes the animals very much' (cf. 'I like the dolls furniture a lot'). Yet at the end of the letter Juliet puts not only her own and Rosalind's name, but her parents' names as well. In another letter, written 8½ months later, we find Juliet writing for Rosalind in a different way. The letter is addressed to Kate and Anna (Juliet's friend and her younger sister) and purports to be from 'Juliet and Rosalind'. Here is the letter:

7039 (7;4)   Dear Kate and Anna,
             Are you having a lovely
             time? I went to Perth in
             the holidays. It was great fun.
             I have received your letter.
             Multi is very mischievous.
             Tiggy is not so shy as before. This is
             a message from Rosalind. (She didn't write it
             though.) Thank-you for Juliet's post-card. I read it
             too. By-by. Well what a relief to get rid of her.
             She is about a mischievous as Multi. Probably
             is to. Love
                          Juliet and
                          Rosalind.

In this letter Juliet in effect pretends to be Rosalind for a few clauses and then assumes her own identity again to make a sisterly comment. So we have something like a letter within a letter. At age 8;7 Juliet was asked to help Rosalind (aged 4;11) write a thank-you letter to a relative. The letter was supposedly dictated by Rosalind and written down by Juliet; however, it is likely that Juliet also influenced the content and wording. Juliet added a P.S. of her own, thus explicitly identifying herself with the letter.

Another aspect of authorship reveals Juliet writing in different roles. At age 7;4 Juliet wrote a letter (7038) to her aunt and uncle in Perth which finishes up thus:

> I'm sorry I have to go now, but my phone is
> ringing. (my toy phone.)
> Love From
> JULIET

As she gets to the end of the letter she slips back into the game that she has been playing before she wrote it. She was sitting up at her desk pretending to be a secretary and carrying on businesslike phone conversations with imaginary callers. She writes the sentence quoted above in that persona; it has the flavour of business conversation about it and is not really a plausible reason for ending a letter (let alone a personal letter). Yet it does provide her with a way of bringing the letter to a close and that is something Juliet is still trying to work out during this seven-year-old period.

One letter which arises entirely from the context of a game of school was written at 5;11. Juliet writes as Mrs Wadur, the teacher, to her mother cast in the role of parent of one of the children (her sister). Another letter where there is something distinctive about the authorship is 7064, which purports to be written by one of the cats (Multi), though the other cat's name (Tiggy) is added as an afterthought at the end. The letter is an invitation to the cats' birthday party; several copies were produced and addressed to various children in the neighbourhood, including Juliet and Rosalind. Almost all the letters mentioned in this section so far as having some curious feature of authorship come from the seven-year-old period.

At the age of nine Juliet collaborated with a friend in writing a letter to another friend from whom Juliet had received an anonymous letter. The collaborative reply was also sent anonymously and was written in such a way that it appeared to have been written by one person. In fact the two authors each wrote part of it, taking it in turns to add a sentence or two. They treated the whole thing as a huge joke, since they both knew the recipient would know who it was from. This jointly authored text, with the two authors pretending to try to disguise their identity, is a little out of the ordinary but quite possible given the aims of the writers.

Apart from these questions of authorship and how they are marked, Juliet uses the formulaic closing of the letter in a fairly conventional way. Twenty-four of the letters simply have 'love from' and a further 17 have either 'love' or 'from'. There is not much change in this pattern in the five- to seven-year-old period except that around the ages 7;6 to 7;8 there is a group of letters which have 'lots of love from' or 'lots of love'. These letters are mainly to school friends (3), but one is to the fairies, reminding them that the tooth fairy was overdue, and one is to the milkman. At the age of eight Juliet began to use 'yours sincerely' as a closing formula and 10 of the 28 letters written at eight and nine are thus ended. This ending makes some of the letters appear overly formal, but in language development, where a new wording or structure is being tried out, it is not unusual for it to be used inappropriately at first, or at least to be overused.

In the five- and six-year-old letters it would seem that for Juliet the question of how to end the body of the letter is not a problem. The letters are mostly quite short and their messages are simple. An elaborate coda hardly seems necessary. She just goes into the 'love from Juliet' routine straight after the business of the letter is dealt with. At the age of 6;7, in a letter to her mother, she ends with a question seeking information; the letter is perhaps seen as part of a continuing conversation. It is in the seven-year-old period that the problem of how to end the letter seems to begin to concern her. The one that ends with the toy phone ringing has already been mentioned. Another ends with the words 'Thank-you' even though it is not really a thank-you letter — it is a textual rather than an interpersonal thank-you. One letter ends with 'Good-bye for now', another 'That's all for now. By.' and one ends with this frank admission:

> I have run out of things to say now, so:
> LOTS OF LOVE FROM
> JULIET

Nearly half the seven- and eight-year-old letters have devices such as these for ending the body of the letter before the closing formula. At eight and nine 'That's all for now' is used at the end of seven letters, usually letters written to people with whom some continuing correspondence can be expected. In fact in these years (age eight and nine) all the letters to Kate, except one, end with either 'That's all for now' or 'Please write back soon'. The letters are recognized as part of a series by which a dialogue is carried on between the two writers; this is also acknowledged in the way some of these letters begin.

Unlike the problem of ending the letter, getting started is much more closely bound up with the global function of the letter, although this does not affect the opening formula 'dear so-and-so' which Juliet rarely departs from. In the five-year-old period we have noted that half the letters are written on the prompting of parents and most of these are very short thank-you letters. The only other elements are seasonal greetings like 'have a happy Christmas' or 'Happy Easter' which inevitably tend to be formulaic. Moreover, the very nature of thanking (being a performative act in the classic sense) tends towards formulaic language. Thus faced with the problem of having to write a letter, Juliet at the age of five relies heavily on a limited range of structures and conventional phrases. It is in the letters she writes by choice that she shows she can be more adventurous, but even in one of these she exploits the thanking function and the structures it offers. And even in the others written at five, Juliet moves straight into the main purpose of the letter, with openings like:

5001 Thank you for . . . .
5019 We are coming to Armidale . . . .

The letters are not long enough to allow the luxury of an introductory sentence.

The same applies to the early six-year-old letters too, but from about 6;3 onwards there is more variety. We see the first uses of two opening gambits which become much more common at the age of seven. One is the use of a question, for example:

6036 (6;3) Are you going on holiday?
7039 (7;4) Are you having a lovely time?
7044 (7;4) Are you alright?
7083 (7;8) How are you getting on?

The other feature is the use of some expressive clause:

6073 (6;7) I hope you had a Merry Christmas
7038 (7;4) It is wonderful to be back in Sydney

In some, both features are combined:

6055 (6;5) I like Anita because of her games. Do you like Anita?

Questions are used not only as opening gambits for the whole letter, but also in some of the longer letters, as ways of bringing in a new topic, as in this extract from the middle of a letter:

7005 (7;0) Kate went to North Queensland
            for the holidays. How is
            Buster? What kind of a dog is Buster.
            Uncle Greg and Auntie Lee have moved
            to New Zealand. How is Christopher.
            How old is he. I am seven now.

There are also other instances of questions either within a letter or at the end (as in the letter to her mother). All these questions contribute to the impression that Juliet perceives the letter as part of a continuing conversational interaction with the other person. It appears that she is simply transposing into writing something which would more usually occur in speech. Even though the response is not going to be immediate, the response is nevertheless invited and expected. This is particularly evident in the letter to her mother which ends with a question, but also in the letter to a school friend which includes the isolated question: 'Are you going to swimming lessons this year?' In another letter to a school friend a response to the question is invited quite explicitly: 'Wright back, if you can't ring-up'. The use of questions and the flavour of conversation are, of course, quite appropriate in personal letters; they are not in principle immature features, even though most other types of writing are further removed from the patterns of spoken language.

At the age of eight and nine, none of the letters starts with a question. Expressions of opinion, feelings or hopes are the opening gambit in eight of the letters while ten start with thanking clauses. Seven of these are thank-you letters as such and there is another thank-you letter where the opening clause refers to the gift but is not the thanking clause. However, three of the thanking clauses which open letters of this period express thanks for a letter received. These are all letters to Kate:

> 8035 thank-you for writing to me.
> 8051 Thank-you for your letter.
> 9002 thank-you for the letter you wrote me.

Other letters to Kate at this period also refer to a previous letter either explicitly ('I am writing this right on the day that your letter arrived.') or by taking up a specific point mentioned in the letter to which the reply is being written. Here again is the awareness of continuing correspondence. One letter written to me at the age of nine begins with an explicit introduction:

> 9029 In this letter I have a lot of things to tell you about.
>   I will begin with . . . .

Nevertheless there are at the age of eight and nine still some letters in which Juliet plunges straight into the heart of the letter without any special opening.

The Heart of the Matter

When you write a letter you have to have something to say. Endings and beginnings have their place, of course, but something must come in between. It is not being frivolous to suggest that in the kind of letters that Juliet writes it almost does not matter what she says as long as she says something; this even applies to thank-you letters and other specific-purpose letters once the specific purpose has been dealt with. But in order to produce something which looks like a respectable letter she does have to say something, and as time goes on Juliet apparently becomes more conscious of the need to say more, for the letters get longer. Perhaps this is evidence of her growing facility with written language and, as handwriting size decreases, her ability to fit more on the page. Thus more can be written and more needs to be written to produce a suitable finished product. Moreover, endings like 'I've run out of things to say' or 'That's all for now' show that she is aware of this need. In another letter she writes: 'I'm just about running out of things to say, but I've got a couple more.' An underlying purpose in most of her letters is maintaining friendly relations with people she knows. Merely sending the letter is enough to do that as long as something appropriate makes up the body of the letter. We shall now examine what Juliet found it appropriate to put in this part of her letters.

In order to investigate the kinds of meanings being expressed in the body of the letters it was decided to classify the clauses in terms of functional categories. Six major functional categories were used together with a number of subcategories. I have derived the major categories from several well-known descriptions of the functions or uses of language such as those of Jakobson (1973), Halliday (1969) and Britton (1971). The subcategories were devised mainly on an ad hoc basis for the study of these letters. These are set out in Table 3.

The unit to which the functions were assigned was the independent clause. For the most part these were single clauses in the traditional sense and in this chapter these independent functional units will be referred to simply as clauses, even when they incorporate lower-level clauses like restrictive relative clauses, temporal and conditional clauses and the clauses projected from verbs

Table 3.   Functional categories and subcategories in the body of the letters

1. Directive	DI	Clauses intended to influence other people's behaviour or obtain goods or services, e.g. orders, requests, etc.
2. Informative		Clauses giving or seeking the information:
		Giving information—
	IF	on future events: predictions, intentions, plans.
	IP	on past events, states of affairs.
	IN	on current events, states of affairs.
		Seeking information—
	QF, QP, QN	questions relating to IF, IP, IN.
3. Relational		Clauses concerned primarily with maintaining relationships between people:
	RG	basic greetings.
	RS	seasonal or occasional greetings.
	RT	thanking clauses.
	RA	others.
4. Expressive		Clauses expressing feelings, opinions, attitudes, etc.:
	EA	personal evaluation, opinions, attitudes, likes and dislikes
	EF	feelings towards the addressee.
	EW	hopes, wishes, etc.
5. Imaginative	MA	Clauses which help to create an imaginary situation.
6. Poetic	PO	Clauses which exploit an interest in the forms of language itself.

of saying, wishing and hoping. The identification of functions was made on the basis of my own judgement of the meaning of each independent clause.

Although instances of all six categories can be seen in Juliet's letters the majority of clauses fall under three categories: the informative (63.01% of all clauses), the expressive (22.09%), and the relational (9.49%). The following discussion will, therefore, focus on these three function categories. Over the four-and-a-half-year period several clear trends are evident in the functions of the clauses Juliet uses. The proportion of relational clauses decreases over the years, that of informative clauses increases, and that of expressive clauses remains stable. The greatest change is seen in the period from five to seven; after seven the changes are not so marked.

Relational. As already mentioned, the earliest letters contain a high proportion of clauses with a relational function. This is because so many of these early letters were letters of thanks. Those written at age five can be divided into two groups (each containing five). The first group are letters written at the prompting of parents: they are all written to adults (mainly friends of the family), they are all short (average 13 words), and the only clause functions they contain are thanking and seasonal greetings. The second group of five are all written on Juliet's own initiative and are much longer than the first group (average 35.6 words). Their clause functions are more diverse. Only one is a thank-you letter—one written to a school friend. Most of them contain informative clauses, directives and expressions of opinion or feelings.

It is not surprising to find that when parents ask a child to write a letter it is a thank-you letter that is asked for, nor is it surprising that the resulting letter is quite brief. What is worth noting is that when Juliet writes on her own initiative the resulting letters are longer and more diverse both in function and audience. Even the thank-you letter is different from the requested thank-you letters in that it is written to a school friend and it contains no less than four thanking clauses as well as an expression of personal evaluation.

In all the thank-you letters written to adults at the age of five the thanking is achieved in one clause and the only other clause is a conventional greeting. Here are some examples:

5001 (5;0) Dear Auntie Olive,
            Thank you for
            my dress and the
            cape, the book, the
            t-shirt and the
            blue slacks.
            love from Juliet

5020 (5;10) Dear Stephanie Thank
            you for letting us come
            to stay with you.
            Happy Easter. Love
            from Juliet Rosalind
            Ruth and John.

Even the letter to the school friend is a succession of separate thankings, each in a clause of its own:

> 5012 (5;7)   dear Justine thank you for coming to
> Sunday School and thank you for
> teaching me to swim. And to swim under
> water. I liked teaching you to read. And thank you
> for playing with me.
> > love from Juliet M. Collerson

Just after turning six Juliet wrote the following letter at her mother's suggestion; the first draft was as follows:

> 6008 (6;0)   Dear Aunty Olive
> and Uncle Keith,
> Thank-you for
> the card game, the
> sewing-set, the card
> and MAN AND
> HIS WORLD.
> > Love, Juliet.

Her mother then suggested that something along these lines be added:

> On my birthday I
> went to a movie. I
> had a party.

This extended Juliet's view of the possibilities of a thank-you letter. She not only took up the suggestion but followed the same pattern in another thank-you letter written on the same day. However, seven months later Juliet showed that she was capable of a much more complex and integrated thank-you letter in which the basic thanking is elaborated and supported by a series of informative and evaluative clauses. This letter (6074) is quoted earlier. Few of the subsequent thank-you letters are as elaborate as this one but they do contain the same kind of integration as well as having additional informative clauses.

At the age of seven, thanking clauses drop to a very small proportion of the total and for some reason (lack of parental prompting?) very few thank-you letters were written in that year. Whereas at five the thanking function accounted for 23.53% of all clauses and at six 12.96%, at the age of seven only 2.63% of all clauses have this function. The proportion increased slightly again after that, for at eight we find that 5.38% and at nine 3.4% of all clauses are in the thanking subcategory. In these later years there is more variety in the way the thanking is achieved. At the age of 8;3 the purpose of the letter is explicitly stated:

> 8019 I am writing this letter to thank you for my present . . .

Near the end of that year she began a thank-you letter thus:

> 8052 (8;11) Thank-you for the lovely writing
>   pad that you gave me. (I'm writing on
>   it now.) And a special thank-you for
>   the watch. Apart from the fact that
>   it is over an hour fast now, I still
>   love it!

After going on to other topics she ends this letter with a P.S.:

> P.S. And I adore the way the little second
>   hand ticks!

This is in contrast to the simple listing of presents in the one thanking clause that we find in some of the earlier thank-you letters. The following month (age 9;0) she wrote this variation on the usual clause:

> 9003 Thanks awfully for the card plus the five dollars.

However, the development of the thank-you letters is probably best seen not only in the thanking clauses alone but in what else she does in these letters. All of them include some elaboration from the basic thanking clause with either further information about the present or some evaluation. Some have associated information such as about other gifts received or what she did on her birthday. One letter thanking for a visit has a series of expressive clauses commenting on different aspects of the visit. The earliest example of this kind of elaboration is the letter written at 6;7 (number 6074) referred to earlier.

Another obvious purpose for writing a letter is to reply to one received. The act of replying gives the writer something to say; one can begin by thanking for the other letter or referring to it in a general way and one can go on by commenting on specific points the other writer has mentioned. Juliet makes use of these opportunities to some extent. A total of 15 of Juliet's letters are in this category, many of them to her friend Kate. Kate had been one of Juliet's friends since she started school and a few of Juliet's early letters were addressed to her. However, when they were both 7;3 Kate moved with her family to Nairobi, Kenya. This separation provided an ideal incentive for correspondence and in the period from age 7;4 to 9;0 Juliet wrote ten letters to Kate, eight of them in reply to letters received. Most of these were written on Juliet's own initiative and immediately after receiving one from Kate. They are all long letters, averaging 144.6 words. It must be remembered that these letters now provide the only means of contact with Kate—apart from her occasional holiday visits to Australia.

In the three replies to Kate's letters which Juliet wrote at age seven (one of them, number 7039, printed earlier) we find that Juliet does not draw on Kate's letters very specifically. She writes mainly about herself and merely thanks Kate for her letter or says she is pleased to get it. In only one does she comment on a specific point in Kate's letter, and that is an evaluative comment, expressing her own attitude ('I'm glad to hear that. . .'). However, three months later at 8;1 we find Juliet making several such comments on specific points, for example: 'It is lovely to hear that you had films at your house.') and the whole letter includes a lot of evaluative comments, wishes, hopes and so on. Nine of the 19 clauses are of this type. In one other letter she also does this to some extent. However, in the other three of these letters written at eight and nine, the clauses are mainly informative. Some of these are linked to Kate's letter by way of answering a question, though the bulk of the letters are concerned with Juliet's own activities. Quite a lot of this is reporting on past activities—to a greater extent than in most of Juliet's letters.

Informative. In Juliet's letters generally, the informative clause is a functional category that became increasingly predominant up to the age of seven and it maintained that predominance after seven. Informative clauses account for on average only 35.3% of the body of the letter at age five, 48.2% at age six and 63.2% at age seven. The letters themselves are getting longer, of course, and it seems that Juliet is learning that a letter can be fleshed out by giving people information about herself and her experiences. And whereas it generally takes only a single clause to thank someone for something or to make a request, information is an open-ended category and so it provides a basis for much longer letters. At eight and nine the position has stabilized, though a slight increase is evident (at eight 67.2% and at nine 69.4%).

Within the general informative category up to the age of seven there is a predominance of clauses concerned with current information over those concerned with previous experience. She seems to be more concerned with telling people about the current situation of her life than with recounting things that have happened to her. So present-tense verbs outnumber past-tense verbs by more than two to one in informative clauses. Moreover, there are no past experiences recounted in the five-year-old period. However, at the ages of eight and nine there is more extensive reporting of past experience, as can be seen in some of the letters written to Kate, and in this period clauses conveying information on the present are balanced by those with past information.

Expressive. Another functional category evident in the letters generally is the expressive. This includes expressions of feeling, hopes and wishes and especially expressions of attitude and opinion in which the writer makes some evaluation of what she is writing about. The proportion of these clauses in the body of the letters is more consistent from year to year, not varying much from the average of 22.1%, although there is considerable variation in individual letters. In the later letters, once the informative category has become predominant, expressive clauses are often integrated with the informative in such a way that the writer can convey some information and also evaluate it, as the following examples from letters written to friends while on holiday illustrate.

> 7083 I went exploring in the rocks yesterday. It was fun.
> 8023 While we were at Coonabarraban We climbed Nandy Hill.
>   It was a hard climb.

The same pattern applies in letters written to parents temporarily away from home.

In the letters replying to those of Kate, expressive clauses are sometimes used ostensibly to comment on information Kate has presented in hers. This may partly be just a device for responding directly to the other letter. If you comment on what someone else has written, you at least show that you have taken note of it. In any case expressive clauses lead to some grammatical complexity, since it is necessary to state what you are commenting on, express your comment and perhaps give a reason for your comment and this is often done all in the one sentence:

> 7089 (7;11) I'm very glad to hear you will be coming back soon.
> 8006 (8;1) I thought that rinho letter writing pad was very nice. I
>   hope you will keep writing to me with it till it runs out.
>   I wish you were over here so I wouldn't have to write
>   with air-mail paper because I have got nice ordanairy
>   writing paper.
> 8035 (8;7) I am very satisfied with this Christmas, because I got a
>   digital clock with an AM-FM radio attached to it.

In one or two letters written at eight or nine there is even a hint of affectation in the style of these expressive clauses — or perhaps it is simply experimentation:

> 8037 (8;7) Is Christopher growing up yet? I would apsaloutly faint
>   if you wrote back and told me he was. On the other
>   hand, I would be releved if you told me he was still
>   mischovese.

Nevertheless, in all of these uses of expressive clauses we see how the writer is concerned both to exchange information and to comment on it, to verbalize experience and to evaluate it.

Letters written in the seven- to nine-year-old period seem to differ mainly on the basis of how well Juliet knew the recipient. Some of the letters in the miscellaneous occasion group are written to people to whom Juliet wrote only once, did not know very well or expected no continuing contact. One is to the milkman requesting delivery of some flavoured milk; another was the invitation written on behalf of the cats. These tend to be the shortest letters, confined mainly to their specific purpose. Where Juliet is writing to people she knows well and writes to regularly, the letters are longer and even if Juliet begins with a specific purpose she soon moves on to the kind of reporting and commenting on experience which she uses to 'make up' the letter. Thus any specific purpose or topic is subsumed in the general idea of sending a letter to keep in contact with the person she is writing to.

FORMULATING THE WORDING

By examining a number of letters from one writer we become aware of several aspects of the wording of the letters. One issue of interest is the use of wording formulated prior to the act of writing. The formulaic features of the opening and closing of letters are obvious; these formulae are accepted conventions. In the body of the letter, any reliance on ready-made wording is not so obvious, especially once Juliet gets beyond the early stage where thanking clauses and conventional greetings form a large proportion of the short letters.

Another aspect of this is the way in which the same topic is worded for different people in letters written at about the same time. There are instances where Juliet has occasion to convey the same meaning to different people in letters written on or about the same day. In two post-cards written to friends on holidays we get the identical sentence 'Today we're going to the Big Bannana' and both letters end with 'That's all for now', but for the most part they are different, and perhaps reflect something of Juliet's sensitivity to the different audiences. They open with a similar meaning differently worded:

8039 We're having a great time in Coffs Habour.
8040 It's tops up in Coffs Habour.

The first of these reflects her everyday conversation; the second is probably derived from schoolgirl story books. Sometimes in thank-you letters written after Christmas or birthday she relies on much the same content to fill out the letter; there is some variation in how much meaning she includes in each letter, but for the same meanings the wording is often very close, as in these examples (age 9;0):

9002 (15 May)   For my party we had a steamboat tea (then follows
a 44 word explanation, with illustrations, of what
this is). For my birthday I got a watch, clutchbag,
bathcube and soap, dictonary, slippers two
necklaces, perfume, three or four books, and a lot
of other nice things.

9003 (22 May)   For my party I had a steamboat tea. I got my first
watch, too.

9004 (23 May)   I had a steamboat for my party. It was marvellous.
I received my first watch, a leather clutch bag, a
pair of fuzzy slippers, a few books, (not including
your's) and a lot of other nice things.

One wonders what the reader of the third letter would have made of the 'steamboat'.

There are a few cases of where much the same wording is used in several letters to the same person, such as these examples from letters to Kate:

7077 Justine misses you as much as I do.
8006 Justine misses you as much as I do . . . .
8020 Justine and I miss you very much.

The first two, with identical wording, were written six months apart and the third three months later. Evidently Juliet felt the idea and the wording appropriate for a letter to Kate and they came to her each time she was formulating these letters.

Another recurrent topic at one stage was the two cats. These had been acquired about a month apart in January and February 1979 (Juliet 6;8 and 6;9). In the period from then until her eighth birthday, 21 letters were written; 14 of them mentioned the cats and one purports to be written by one of the cats. Subsequently the cats are still mentioned but less frequently and more briefly. This recurrent topic does not merely reflect Juliet's interest in the cats and keenness to write about them. There is a tendency for the same phrases and clauses to recur in several letters and it seems to me that what is being written in the letters tends to reflect the talk in the home about the cats (both things that Juliet has said herself and things she has heard her parents say). Here are some extracts from the letters:

6086 We have got two cats.

7005 We have got two kittens. One is half-Burmise and she is called

Multi. One is called Tigger. She is a full tabby. They are both females . . . .

. . . . Multi's mother is called Ticky. We don't know Tigg's mother's name because we got her from the Pet Shop.

7039 Multi is very mischievous. Tiggy is not so shy as before.

7044 Multi is my kitten and she is half-burmese. Tigger is my sister's kitten and she is a full tabby, Multi just would not leave me when I came home from Perth.

7077 We love Multi and Tiggy. Have I told you about Multi and Tiggy? If not, they are our kittens. Multi is one now and Tiggy is one too.

It is also possible that the catalogues of presents received which appear in some letters have come into Juliet's conversation at that time, as well as appearing in her writing.

I think there is an important point here about the relationship between speech and writing. I have already mentioned how the use of questions in the letters seems to reflect the mode of conversational interaction. I am now suggesting that some of the content of the letters reflects the wording of actual conversations. This is a speculation, but it does lend support to the practice of encouraging children to talk about and write about their own experience. They can write about events more easily through having experienced them *in language* before they come to the writing (cf. Graves, 1979).

SUMMARY OF DEVELOPMENTS IN LETTER WRITING

Perhaps the most apparent developmental trends are toward an increase in the number and length of the letters. Up to the age of seven, there was an increase in the number of letters written from year to year, though it was not a steady increase. Most of the seven-year-old letters were written in one four-month period. An inspection of the dates shows that letter writing is to some extent a seasonal activity roughly coinciding with school holidays (December–January, May and August–September). After the age of seven the numbers of letters level off, but the average length of the letters continues to increase up to the eight-year-old period (see Table 1).

The increase in length is in itself hardly surprising. Of more significance are the things associated with this increase in length. There is the increasing proportion of informative clauses. It seems that as Juliet develops her understanding of what can be done in a personal letter and as she extends her concept of what is an adequate length of a personal letter, she relies increasingly on informative clauses. Juliet learns to extend what would have been a brief mention of a topic by adding expressive or informative clauses. Thus we find a trend away from simple and relatively formulaic letters to those which encompass a wider range of meanings requiring many independent choices of wording. There are hints in the letters that Juliet's previous language experience and conversational interaction provide sources for quite specific wordings.

Most of Juliet's letters arise from her interactions with other people, and many of the letters have features which suggest a continuing dialogue. She has learnt to use letters as a means of keeping in contact with people she knows, as well as for achieving more specific purposes. Thus, because they are still supported by social context, personal letters may serve a role in the child's transition from conversational dialogue to the monologue of written composition, bridging the gap between the kind of oral discourse which is situated in a specific context and supported by interaction and the kind of written discourse which requires a relatively autonomous text. The letters allow Juliet to extend spoken interaction into an area where written language is necessary. While her early letters were written mainly for specific purposes and thus embody specific meanings and the language forms and structures that express them, as time goes on the letters, even when they begin with a specific goal, tend to have the more general purpose of keeping in touch. Juliet learns that letters can be a means of reporting and interpreting experience, a device for exchanging information, and a method of maintaining social interaction among friends.

REFERENCES

Bissex, G. L. *GNYS AT WRK: A child learns to write and read.* Cambridge, MA: Harvard University Press, 1980. (a)

Bissex, G. L. Patterns of development in writing: A case study. *Theory into Practice*, 1980, **19**, 197–201. (b)

Britton, J. What's the use? — A schematic account of language functions. *Educational Review*, 1971, **23**, 205–219.

Britton, J., Burgess, T., Martin, N., McLeod, A., and Rosen, H. *The development of writing abilities (11–18).* London: Macmillan Education, 1975.

Graves, D. H. Let children show us how to help them write. *Visible Language*, 1979, **13**, 16–28.

Graves, D. H. Patterns of child control of the writing process. In R. D. Walshe (Ed.), *Donald Graves in Australia.* Sydney: Primary English Teaching Association, 1981.

Halliday, M. A. K. Relevant models of language. *Educational Review*, 1969, **22**, 26–37.

Halliday, M. A. K. *Explorations in the functions of language.* London: Edward Arnold, 1973.

Halliday, M. A. K. *Learning how to mean: Explorations in the development of language.* London: Edward Arnold, 1975.

Halliday, M. A. K. *Language as social semiotic: The social interpretation of language and meaning.* London: Edward Arnold, 1978.

Jakobson, R. Functions of languge. In J. P. B. Allen and S. P. Corder (Eds), *Readings for applied linguistics*. London: Oxford University Press, 1973.

King, M. L., and Rentel, V. M. *How children learn to write: A longitudinal study*. Columbus, O: Ohio State University Research Foundation, 1981.

Wilkinson, A., Barnsley, G., Hanna, P., and Swan, M. *Assessing language development*. Oxford: Oxford University Press, 1980.

5

Antecedents of Individual Differences in Children's Writing Attainment

Barry M. Kroll

As anyone who has looked closely at children's writing knows, there are large individual differences in the performance of elementary-school-age pupils. For example, below are compositions written by two nine-year-old children — compositions about a happy moment in each child's life. The first piece of writing is a loosely organized chronology of a day's events at a holiday camp.

> The happiest day of my life was the week we went to Butlins. We went to the Swimming pool. I jumped and the pool was cold. Then we went out side and the pool was warm. It warmer than the in side. We went back to the flat. We went on the helter skelter and the monorail and we went all around Butlins. We saw the pool.

The second piece of writing is also a loose chronicle of events, but it is much better elaborated than the first.

> My happiest moment in my life is when we went to the country side. It was in summer when we went.
> The squirrels we saw had very long bushy tails. They jumped about very carefully. The squirrels darted about the trees as if it were a bird going as fast as they could.
> My next thing I saw was a bird's nest. In the nest were 5 egg's 4 of them had hatched and one of them had not. I saw the nest was made by robins.
> When we had walked about a half mile more we came to a stream. It was as blue as the sky. I saw duck's quacking and diving under water for fish. I asked my mum if I could have some bread. My mum said I could. I threw it to the ducks.

Afterwards we came to a triangle of flowers they were all different. But on a notice it said do not touch. It was a pity because I wanted to pick them. But I took a picture of them. Soon we were coming back to our car our legs were weary. I said good-by to all the things and then we went back home.

The second piece of writing is obviously better than the first—more detailed, more descriptive, and more sophisticated in use of syntax, diction, and metaphor.

Why are there such striking individual differences in children's writing abilities? What are the major influences on such differences in children's attainment? Many factors could be suggested: differences in intelligence, in cognitive maturation, in social adjustment, in personality, in linguistic development, in breadth of experience, and in quality of schooling—to mention only the most obvious. Since school is the place where most children learn the skills of reading and writing, we usually focus on the last factor—on such aspects of schooling as methods, materials, and programs—as the primary influences on children's acquisition of literacy. However, while schooling is clearly a potent influence on children's learning to read and write, we need to remember that children have had a good deal of language experience before they go to school, including some exposure to the activities of reading and writing, and that they continue to learn about literacy in contexts outside of school. Children will, of course, differ in the extent and quality of their experiences with language and literacy. Some children will come from homes which have encouraged language development by providing an environment in which parents and child interact frequently in a variety of contexts, while other children will come from homes with fewer opportunities for dialogue and with a narrower range of uses of language. Some will come from homes in which reading and writing are seen as important and useful activities, while others will come from homes in which the skills of literacy play a negligible role. Thus it seems likely that these differences in experiences with language and literacy in the home will have an effect on the child's acquisition of literacy, particularly of writing, which will be the focus for this paper.

BACKGROUND: THE BRISTOL LONGITUDINAL LANGUAGE DEVELOPMENT PROJECT

The study that will be reported here drew on data collected for a much larger research project—a major longitudinal study of children's language development, based in Bristol, UK[1]. The Bristol project began in 1972, when two

1 I am indebted to Gordon Wells, not only for making data from his longitudinal project available to me, but also for support and wise counsel throughout my stay at the Centre for the Study of Language and Communication, University of Bristol, in 1979-1980. My visit to Bristol was made possible by the generous assistance of the faculty leave and foreign travel grant programs at Iowa State University. Additional support for this study was provided by the Department of English at Iowa State.

groups of 64 children, then 15 months and 39 months old, were selected as representative of the children of Bristol in terms of sex, month of birth, and class of family background. During the first phase of the project, radio-microphones were used to record samples of spontaneously occurring conversation during one day in each child's home at regular three-month intervals over a period of 2¼ years. The speech data from the recordings (approximately half a million utterances) were transcribed and coded according to a system developed specifically for the research project (Wells, 1973). From this data bank, a number of indices of the children's oral language development were derived. Data were also gathered on the children's home environment, and on the social and intellectual backgrounds of parents. In brief, findings from this first phase of the research produced evidence for a developmental sequence of acquisition for English, evidence that the relationship between measures of language development and family background is not straightfoward, and evidence that children's rate of linguistic development is associated with the quality of conversation they experience with adults (see Wells, 1974, 1977, 1979, 1981).

In a subsequent phase of the Bristol research, Wells and Raban (1978) focused on a subsample of 20 of the older children when they entered primary school in 1975. The ten boys and ten girls in this subsample were chosen to ensure a nearly equal number of subjects in four categories of social class. The principal aim of the research was to determine the extent to which four major factors—oral language ability, preschool knowledge of literacy, home environment, and schooling—contributed to successful acquisition of reading at the end of infant school (age seven). Thus, this study focused on the relative importance of various background factors and schooling on children's acquisition of literacy. Of the factors studied, the child's knowledge of literacy on entry to school was found to be the most important predictor of attainment in reading at age seven. This knowledge of literacy was, in turn, strongly predicted by differences among parents' responses to children's conversational initiations and parents' interest in literacy. Differences in schooling, by comparison, were not highly predictive of differences in reading attainment.

The plan for the present study was to investigate the relationships between selected background factors and writing attainment in the same 20 children who had participated in the reading study (Kroll et al., 1980). Since a number of the measures used in the reading project were of major importance to the present study, they will be discussed briefly here. More detailed information is available in Wells and Raban (1978).

Reading Attainment. Of the standardized tests administered when the children were seven years of age, Wells and Raban selected the Neale accuracy test as the best measure of reading attainment. In addition, a subjective assessment of the children's reading attainment at age seven was made both by a research assistant (who had worked closely with the 20 children) and by the individual class teachers. Both assessments correlated highly with the Neale test (research assistant's $r = 0.90$; teacher's, $r = 0.87$). In discussing subsequent measures, I will report the correlations which Wells and Raban found between those measures and reading attainment as measured by the Neale test.

Preschool Language Development. A number of linguistic measures were derived from spontaneous speech data recorded during the final two taping periods, when the children were 4 years 9 months, and 5 years old. Of these, three measures seem to provide the best picture of a child's oral language development before school: (1) *mean length of structured utterances* (MLU) was simply an average of the number of morphemes in all utterances with internal structures (i.e. excluding such utterances as 'yes' or 'hello'); (2) *syntactic complexity* was a weighted score derived from the number of clauses falling into each of five stage-related clause types, with utterances at the more advanced end of the scale given greater weights; (3) *functional range* was a measure of the number of different functions (control, expressive, representational, social, tutorial, etc.) performed by the utterances in a child's speech sample. The three measures were only moderately related to reading attainment (MLU with reading, $r = 0.23$; syntactic complexity with reading, $r = 0.37$; functional range with reading, $r = 0.36$; none of these correlations are statistically significant).

Parental Feedback. An index of the parents' linguistic interaction with the child was derived from transcripts of the first two recordings made in the home (at ages 3¼ and 3½ years). The index was calculated from an examination of all parental utterances in child-initiated sequences. Each parental response was scored on a scale of 0 to 5, with higher scores given to responses which extended the child's meaning. The mean score was called Parental Feedback. This measure was significantly related to reading attainment ($r = 0.58$, $p < 0.01$).

Knowledge of Literacy. The child's pre-school Knowledge of Literacy index was a combined score from two tests developed by M. Clay (1972a, 1972b), and modified slightly for use in the project: 'Concepts about Print' and 'Letter Identification'. The Concepts test consists of a book (called 'Sand') which the researcher and child look at together. The researcher asks a number of questions about the book, and the child's answers reveal his basic knowledge of the conventions of print. Raw scores on the Concepts and Letter Identification tests were combined (according to a weighted formula) to produce the Knowledge of Literacy index, an estimate of how much a preschool child knows about books and reading activities. The Knowledge of Literacy scores were strongly related to reading attainment ($r = 0.79$, $p < 0.001$).

Parental Interest in Literacy. A measure of the provisions for literacy in the home was derived from the transcripts of the first eight preschool recordings. Parental Interest in Literacy was assessed by tabulating the frequency of occurrence of a parent teaching the child about reading, answering questions about literacy (e.g. the meaning of a word), or reading aloud to the child (see Moon, 1976; Moon and Wells, 1979). This index was significantly related both to reading attainment ($r = 0.53$, $p < 0.05$) and to Knowledge of Literacy ($r = 0.07$, $p < 0.001$). Wells and Raban interpreted the strong relationship between Parental Interest in Literacy and Knowledge of Literacy to mean that certain parents were providing experiences which helped their children become aware of the purposes and conventions of literacy. And it was knowledge of these conventions which most strongly predicted reading attainment at age seven.

Class of Family Background. A measure of Social Class Background was constructed from information concerning the occupational status and terminal level of education of both parents. This measure correlated significantly with reading attainment at age seven ($r = 0.52$, $p < 0.05$). It was also strongly related to parental interest in literacy ($r = 0.71$, $p = < 0.01$).

In sum, the results of research on these children's acquisition of reading show that the home environment, particularly preschool experience with literacy in the home, plays a very important role in children's acquisition of reading. Even differences among schools in teaching materials, patterns of organization, and quality of teaching failed to alter significantly the relative level of achievement that was predicted by individual differences between children when they entered school. This does not, of course, mean that schooling made a negligible contribution to learning to read. On the contrary, Wells and Raban point out that all the children made considerable progress as the result of instruction. But schooling did not significantly affect the overall ranking of the children. Those children who came from supportive homes and who had a strong concept of literacy before entering school made good progress in learning to read, regardless of the adequacy of instruction. Children from less effective homes seemed to be more affected by the quality of schooling, but their overall attainment was still less than children from homes with support for literacy.

INDICES OF WRITING ACHIEVEMENT

The aim of the present investigation was to extend the study of some of these same antecedent factors—oral language development, preschool knowledge of literacy, parental interest in literacy, family background, and level of reading attainment—to the 20 children's writing ability at age nine. The antecedent factors included in this investigation were, for the most part, those that Wells and Raban found to be important predictors of reading ability at age seven. The one exception is preschool language development, which did not strongly predict reading ability. Wells and Raban point out that the weak predictive value of measures of language production does not mean that oral language ability is unimportant for learning to read, but rather that there is a threshold of requisite oral language ability beyond which these children had already passed. Hence, differences in oral language skills were found to be less significant predictors of reading attainment than control of those skills and knowledge more directly related to reading. A similar argument could be made for writing attainment: although a child must have reached a certain level of facility in oral language, by age nine almost all children will have reached this requisite level. Nevertheless, since one could hypothesize that early facility in producing oral language would be more strongly related to the ability to *produce* written language than to comprehend written language, the relationships between various measures of preschool language development and writing ability were investigated.

Since only 18 of the 20 children in the reading project were able to write independently by age nine, the principal subjects for this study were nine boys and nine girls (mean age 9.41 years, SD = 0.18) who, in the fall of 1979, were attending 15 different junior school classes in the city of Bristol. For the present study, the major task was to add to the earlier data from the reading project some indices of the 18 children's writing attainment. Thus, it was important to obtain an adequate sampling of each child's writing. It also seemed desirable to obtain writing from a larger number of additional children, who could serve as a 'control group' of representative nine-year-old writers. Therefore, teachers in each of the 15 classes were asked to select four children, two boys and two girls, who would represent the work of typical children of that age and class level—children who were 'average to good' writers, but definitely not markedly high or low achievers. Not all classes contained four such children, but it was possible to obtain work from a total of 56 children (25 boys and 31 girls) who seemed to constitute a sample of typical writers in the same classrooms from which the 18 principal subjects came. (Due to absences, not all of the typical writers participated in every writing task.) To avoid confusion, I will refer to the 18 principal subjects as the 'project children', and to the control subjects as the 'typical writers' group.

In order to obtain comparable scripts from all subjects it was necessary to exercise some control over the topics and the conditions for writing. Thus, the writing was done in response to specific 'tasks', so that each child produced samples of writing in response to the same instructions during the same five-week period. Four tasks were used so that the writing samples would represent various writing 'aims': to write about a *personal experience*—a happy moment in the writer's life (an expressive aim), to write a *story* based on a picture (a narrative aim), to write *letters* seeking a home for a puppy (a persuasive aim), and to write an *explanation* of how to play a new game (an instructional aim). The entire class of which the subjects were members participated in the writing tasks, which were introduced by the class teachers as if they were a normal part of class work. Teachers received a handbook detailing procedures to follow in assigning the tasks. They were given guidelines on such matters as providing assistance with spelling, controlling the extent of collaboration among pupils, and so forth. In general, the procedures were designed to be as close as possible to typical school practices while assuring some control of the conditions under which the writing was done.

The compositions obtained from the subjects were analysed to yield two kinds of indices: *linguistic* indices of syntax and vocabulary, and indices of the adequacy or overall *quality* of the compositions.

Linguistic indices. Three measures of linguistic structures were used in this study: an index of syntactic complexity, an index of subordination, and an index of vocabulary diversity. The index of syntactic complexity was mean T-unit length (MTUL), a measure introduced by Hunt (1965) and widely used in research on written language development (e.g. O'Donnell *et al.*, 1967; Richardson *et al.*, 1976). The index of subordination was mean number of clauses per T-unit (MCTU). Vocabulary diversity for compositions written by the 18 children was assessed by using a formula suggested by Carroll (1964) to obtain an index approximately independent of sample size: types/$\sqrt{(2 \times \text{tokens})}$; indices were computed separately for each of the five pieces of writing and these were averaged to produce an index of overall vocabulary diversity for each child.

Indices of writing quality. Since the four writing tasks involved different discourse aims, they could not all be adequately assessed with the same scoring procedure. Nevertheless, the scoring procedures used were related in that each assessed the overall effectiveness of the composition in achieving its central aim. The personal experience and story compositions were both scored using a 'holistic' assessment procedure. The persuasive letters were scored by assessing the adequacy with which the writer created a context for the transaction and by identifying specific appeals used to persuade someone to accept the puppy. And the explanation of the game was scored by assessing the extent to which the rules for playing the game were adequately communicated.

The four tasks and the procedures used to assess them are discussed in more detail below.

Personal-experience Writing

In the first writing task, the children were encouraged to write freely about an aspect of their personal experience: the 'happiest moment' they could remember. Teachers prepared the classes for writing by asking children to close their eyes and picture this happy moment. Children were told to 'make a picture of it in your mind. Try to remember exactly how you felt and why you were so happy.' After the children had been given time to gather some ideas, they were asked to write about their happiest moment as if telling the experience to a close friend.

The compositions were assessed using a version of the 'holistic scoring' procedure (following many of the suggestions given by Myers, 1980). Fourteen college seniors specializing in English education served as raters. These raters were given approximately 1½ hours of training and practice in using the scoring system. Practice papers came from classmates of the children in the study. All papers were typed, but original spelling and punctuation were retained. In the first part of the training session, the raters were told about the writing topic and then given a common set of six papers to rank from worst (1) to best (6). These six papers had been selected because they seemed to be clear examples of the six categories of performance. After the raters had ordered the papers they compared rankings and discussed the criteria used to make judgements. Then, using the six papers as 'anchors' for the categories, all raters judged a common set of nine papers. In the discussion which followed, raters were encouraged to focus on those features of the writing which were relevant to the aim of the piece (i.e. the success of the composition in recreating the feeling of the happiest moment). Specific features of successful or unsuccessful compositions were listed on a blackboard. Thus, while the raters' attention was directed to the central aim of the task, the specific criteria for assigning scripts to categories were arrived at inductively, by the raters themselves. The effect of this procedure, however, was that the raters were not simply marking an essay according to a general impression, but rather were considering how a number of features of a piece of writing contributed to its overall effectiveness in achieving a particular aim. Finally, a second common set of nine papers was rated and discussed. By the end of this training and practice, raters were largely in agreement on their scoring judgements.

After the training session, three copies of compositions from each of 54 typical writers and the 18 project children were distributed so that each rater had a random selection of papers, but no duplicates. Thus, each composition was scored by three different raters. An analysis of variance procedure was used to estimate the reliability of these ratings (Winer, 1967). The reliability was $r = 0.85$. The sum of the ratings became the final score for the piece (scores could thus range from 3 to 18). The two compositions printed at the opening of this paper illustrate a weak and strong response to the topic. The first paper received a score of 6, while the second received a score of 17.

Story Writing

In the second writing task, each child was given a copy of a humorous cartoon depicting a hunter being cornered at the edge of a cliff by a group of animals (figure 1). Along the side of the picture was a list of the animals' names, provided as an aid to spelling. In preparing the children for writing, teachers led a discussion about what was shown in the picture, keeping this discussion descriptive and not permitting children to begin telling stories about the picture. After the picture had been explored, the teacher asked each pupil in

Figure 1

the class to write a story to go along with the picture, making it 'a story that somebody else your own age would like to read'. The stories were evaluated through the same process of 'holistic' evaluation as that outlined above. The reliability of the ratings was $r = 0.95$. Two example stories are printed below: the first a strong piece (score = 18) and the second a weak piece (score = 5).

> (1) I drew back three steps. Nearer the cliff edge I got. The lion moved closer. My dog frightened hid behind me. The animals looked feirce and angry. Closer and closer the animals came. The rhinoceros snorting, the snake hissing. 'Wuff, wuff,' my dog said. 'Be quiet Tod.' Closer I came to the cliff, edge. Afraid I picked up a stone and was just about to throw it. Will they go away or come closer.' Putting the stone back I drew back some steps. I reached

and picked up Tod in my hands 'You'll be safer in my arms'. Whine, Whine, 'Be quiet.' The giraffe reached out his long neck. The lion roared. A cold feeling came to me. I looked down at the cliff edge. It seemed a long way down. 'I can't stand,' I said out aloud. I hugged Tod. The parrot screeched. The ground as the elephant thudded. I stepped back. My left foot slid of the edge. 'Oh, no.' I moved forward. The sun was shining hard. I grew hot and tired. The snake slid off the elephant's back. 'Go, away,' I shouted. The monkey's chatterd. A little bird flew to-wards me. 'Help I'm falling.' The big bird caught hold of my coat and dragged me up. By this time the crowd of animals had moved closer. I could not breed. I had no idea. I lay down the animals came closer. Not breathing I lay still the animals smelt me. They turned to go away. The snake slid away to a shade. The rhinoceros snorted again and went thumping away. The elephant trihumphed and moved away. Chattering the monkey's went away. Turning his neck the giraffe stepped back and went away. The big bird scheeched and flew off. Every thing was gone I got up and ran away with Tod.

(2) Once there was a man. He was falling off the cliff. A dog was holding his leg I think the dog was frightened. There was lots of animals looking at him. He was wisaling. He had a gun behind his back. Next he looked at the animals. There was a giraffe a snake an elephant birds monkeys and rhinoceros a lion and tortoises. The man nearly fell of the cliff. The sun was out. The snake had his tounge out. The next day I went to the zoo. There was a zebara liying on the ground. A zebara was having babies.

Persuasive Letters

In the next task, children wrote two letters to strangers, asking them to provide a home for a puppy. Subjects wrote two letters because a single letter tended to be shorter than the other pieces of writing. Thus two letters ensured that the quantity of persuasive writing would be roughly equal to the quantity of writing in the other modes.

The children were asked to pretend that they were in the following dilemma: their family dog had had puppies, but there was not room to keep them. Therefore the children had to find good homes for the puppies. Although they had been successful so far, one puppy still did not have a home. Children were given a sheet containing pictures of this puppy and of a person to whom they were to write a letter, seeking a home for the dog. About a week later, children were asked to pretend that this first person had replied that he could not take the dog. Therefore, the children were asked to write a second letter to a different person. They again were given a picture of the addressee and the puppy. The two target addressees were a nine-year-old boy, David Moore, who lived in London (name, address, and age of target person were on the sheet), and a 55-year-old farmer from Somerset, Mr. Fisher. Subjects were given a plausible reason for writing to these two individuals (e.g. they had heard about Mr. Fisher from their grandfather, who lived in the same community). In both letters, children were asked to persuade the addressee to take the puppy. They were encouraged 'to mention as many things as you can' to make the person want to take the puppy, and to write the letter in such a way that the person 'will want to take your puppy and give him a good home'. Children were told that they would send the picture of the puppy with the letter. This procedure was adopted to counter tendencies to produce elaborate descriptions of the puppy, thereby threatening to make the letter a descriptive rather than a persuasive piece.

Successful letters both supplied a *context* in which the reader could understand and respond to the request and presented *appeals* to make the addressee want to take the puppy. Context was scored by rating the adequacy of four types of information: (1) introduction of the writer, particularly information establishing a relationship with the addressee; (2) explanation of the problem; (3) request to take the puppy; and (4) statement of how the addressee should respond to the request. The adequacy with which the letter presented each of these four kinds of information was rated on a scale of 0 to 2. Thus, for the two letters combined, context scores could range from 0 to 16. Appeals were simply statements designed to make the addressee want to accept the puppy. Seven categories of appeals were defined: Types I to III were based on characteristics of the dog; Type IV included appeals for sympathy ('if you don't take him, he won't have a home'); Type V involved special enticements for accepting the dog (free food or a reasonable price); Type VI involved flattery of the addressee; and Type VII was a statement of the match-up between dog and new owner. For purposes of the present study, the total appeals score was simply the sum of the appeals across both letters.

The total score for performance on the persuasive-letters task was the sum of context and appeals scores. Rating of context adequacy and scoring of the number of appeals was done independently both by a rater unfamiliar with the details of the study and by the researcher. Interrater agreement on total scores was high, $r = 0.96$ (Pearson product–moment correlation). The two raters compared scoring judgements for each category on every letter, discussed disagreements, and decided on a final score to be used in subsequent analyses. Example letters from two children are printed below. The first pair of letters received an overall score of 42; the second pair received a score of 11.

(1) Dear David,

I am writing to tell you about a puppy you might like you see my female dog Lucy had four puppy's about three weeks ago. I have sold three puppy's but I haven't been able to sale this last puppy and I thought you might like it. I know you liked dogs because my Aunty Pat lives down the road from you. The puppy is a Jack Russell. His coat is soft and white. On his left eye he has got a black patch. His nose and ears are black he is a very cuddly dog and loves being tickled. Also he is very friendly and likes meeting new people. He likes being taken for walks. Most of all he likes children and he eats any kind of food. I am selling him for ten pounds. I enclose a photograph of him. If you would like him please phone me.

Dear Mr. Fisher,

My name is Nicola. I am writing to ask you if you would like a Jack Russell puppy. You see my grandfather lives in the cottage next to you and he said you keep sheep and I thought you could train him to look after the sheep. I call my puppy William but you can change it. He is very quick at training. I have already trained him to sit and to come. One day my uncle was going in for a sheep dog contest but his sheep dog fell ill. So he asked me if he could take William in the contest as his dog was unwell. I said yes because you didn't really have to have a sheep dog for this contest and William got all the sheep in the pen in two minutes. But best of all he won third prize. He is about ten weeks old. But if you don't want him to look after the sheep maybe your children would like him. I know you got children because my grandfather told me. You would spend about one pound fifty on food each week if you would like him please tell my grandfather and will tell me and I will deliver him I am selling him for ten pounds. But if you buy him a brown lead he will chew it. So what ever you buy him make sure its blue. I enclose a phothgrath.

(2) Dear David

I have heard about you because my anty has told me I have a dog and she has just had puppies and all the puppies have gone to homes and I have one left and his name is James. He is white and black and he has blue eyes.

Dear Mr. Fisher,

My grandfather has told me about your farm and you needed a dog well I have a dog a she has just had puppies and I would like to give one of the puppies to you the puppies name is Jovis.

Game Explanation

In the final task, children were taught to play a two-person board game and were then asked to write a set of instructions for it. Pupils first watched a silent, color film which showed two people playing through the game twice. Use of the film ensured that all subjects viewed the same game sequences, in which all the rules of the game were demonstrated. However, for nine-year-olds, it also seemed desirable to have some 'hands-on' experience with this game. Since it was not feasible to play individually with each child (as had been done in some previous research using this game; see Kroll, 1978; Kroll and Lempers, 1981), the class participated in a 'team' version, using an enlarged playing board placed at the front of the room so that the whole class could view it. One person from each of two teams came, alternately, to the front of the room, rolled a die, and made the appropriate move. After the game ended, the children again viewed the film of the 'first round', to remind them of the normal, two-person version of the game. Pupils were then given standard instructions: 'Now that you understand how to play this game, what I want you to do next is to write an explanation of how to play it. Right now the game doesn't have any written instructions to go with it. Imagine that your explanation will go along with the game to tell another child how to play. Be sure to write your instructions so that another child your age could read your explanation and then know how to play perfectly.' Children were given a 3 × 5 inch color photograph of the game materials to refer to while writing.

The advantage of using this game as an explanation task is that it has a specifiable number of elements that need to be included in a good explanation. It is therefore possible to judge the explanations according to the adequacy with which these elements are conveyed. In brief, the game is a race in which each player tries to be the first to move a rubber bird from a starting point to the finishing point. Moves are made by rolling a die with colored faces and advancing to the closest stripe of a corresponding color, with players alternating turns. Several complications can arise in the course of this race along the board. If a white face turns up on the die, the player cannot advance, since there are no white stripes on the board. If a player rolls a color which would land him on the stripe already occupied by the opponent's bird, the player cannot advance—he loses a turn. Players must roll the color of the goal circle to advance to the end and win the game. Other game elements involve the details of properly setting up the board and initiating the game.

Scoring involved rating the adequacy with which children conveyed ten 'elements' of the game, for a possible total of 30 points. Scoring procedures for the game are discussed in detail elsewhere (Kroll, 1977). Both a rater unfamiliar with the study and the researcher scored all the explanations from 59 subjects. Interrater reliability was high, $r = 0.95$. Disagreements in scoring were examined and a final set of scores agreed upon.

One difficulty with the scoring procedure for this task is the possibility that a child might receive a low score on the explanation because he didn't adequately understand how to play the game, rather than because he was unable to present his knowledge in a written explanation. To attempt to control for this possibility, all subjects were given a multiple-choice test over the ten elements involved in the game. This test was administered individually to each child by a research assistant. The test item stem and three alternatives for completing the stem were printed on a 3×5 card, which the assistant helped the child read aloud (some subjects had difficulty reading the items). The child then chose the response which accurately completed the stem. In general, children found this testing procedure unfamiliar, stressful, and difficult. For the typical writers group, a score of 8 correct responses was accepted as evidence that the child understood the game. Only explanations from those subjects with test scores of 8 or above were included in the analysis (41 children scored 8 or above; 11 scored below 8). However, explanations from all of the project children were analyzed, even though three children scored below 8 on the test. Two example explanations are printed below. The first received a score of 23; the second received a score of 7 (30 points were possible).

(1)   This is how you play the bird game. You should have a counter, cup, dice, board, and two birds one yellow and one blue. The game is for two players. One person takes the two birds and hides them behind their backs and changes the birds to one hand to the other. Then close your hand up tight with the one bird in each hand. Then show your hand to the other player without him or she seeing the birds then him or she tochs a hand the other person opens that hand and lets just say him or she picked the hand with the yellow bird in. Now the game can start. One person throws the conter and say it landed on blue then the person with the blue bird goes first. So then the person who can go first throws the dice and if the dice landed on red, blue, yellow, or green they may move their bird on two the colour the dice landed on. If the dice lands on green, red, blue, or yellow. If theres a green or any other colour near the bottom of the board you may not move to green or any other colour on the bottom. You go to the nearest blue, or green or whatever colour the dice says. But if you land on white you may not go. You just pass the dice over to the other person. If you land on green and the other bird was there before you stay where you are. You start where the black squares are you should know which is yellow and which blue because at the bottom of the board there are blue and yellow circles. You finish on the circles but you must land on blue or yellow to win the game.

(2)   First you put the birds on the board and then you throw the
counter to see which side you are on then you ues the dice and cup
if you have white you can not go and if you have two the same you
go back to wher you was. This game is esay to play and it is also a
good game.

The mean 'overall quality' scores on the four writing tasks for the project
children and typical writers group are displayed in Table 1. Mean scores for

Table 1.   Mean scores on writing measures for
project children and typical writers groups

	Personal experience	Story	Persuasive letters	Game explanation	Syntactic complexity (MTUL)	Subordination index (MCTU)
Project children	8.28 (SD = 3.03)	8.00 (SD = 3.36)	23.11 (SD = 5.56)	11.50 (SD = 4.71)	8.43 (SD = 1.14)	1.27 (SD = 0.11)
Typical writers	9.44 (SD = 3.60)	9.22 (SD = 4.12)	25.55 (SD = 8.60)	12.83 (SD = 5.00)	9.11 (SD = 1.23)	1.34 (SD = 0.11)

syntactic complexity and subordination are also shown (lexical diversity was
not calculated for the typical writers because this index is time-consuming to
compute and of only peripheral interest in this study). On all measures, the
mean scores for typical writers are higher than mean scores for the project
children, although the differences in mean scores for the two groups reach
statistical significance only for the two linguistic measures (MTUL, $t = -2.05$,
$p < 0.05$; MCTU, $t = -2.45, p < 0.05$).

Composite Index of Writing Quality

The scoring procedures outlined above yielded four 'overall quality' scores
appropriate to the central aim of each of the writing tasks. However, it seemed
desirable to combine these four scores into a composite measure, if the
individual scores were strongly interrelated. Such a composite measure would
provide a convenient index of writing ability, which could then be used in
subsequent correlational analyses.

The scores for the four tasks were, in fact, significantly interrelated. For all
subjects (typical writers and project children combined), correlations were as
follows: personal experience with story, $r = 0.62$; personal experience with
persuasive letters, $r = 0.55$; personal experience with game explanation, $r = 0.55$;
story with persuasive letters, $r = 0.48$; story with game explanation, $r = 0.54$;
game explanation with persuasive letters, $r = 0.42$. Thus, a composite index of
writing quality was constructed by first converting the project children's raw
scores for each task to z scores. These four z scores were then averaged, and

the average score converted to T scores (with a mean of 50 and standard deviation of 10) to eliminate negative numbers. The composite scores correlated highly with raw scores for each of the four tasks: with personal experience, $r = 0.65$; with story, $r = 0.72$; with persuasive letters, $r = 0.84$; with game explanation, $r = 0.71$.

RESULTS AND DISCUSSION

From previous work in the Bristol Longitudinal Project, eight key measures were obtained for the 18 subjects: the Neale test of reading accuracy (at age seven); the preschool Knowledge of Literacy index (at age five); three indices of preschool language development—MLU, Syntactic Complexity, and Functional Range (at age five); a Parental Feedback score; a measure of Class of Family Background; and the Parental Interest in Literacy index. To these were added four measures of writing development at age nine: Composite Index of Writing Quality; Syntactic Complexity (MTUL); Subordination Index (MTUL); and Vocabulary Diversity index. Pearson product–moment correlations between all measures were calculated and are shown in Table 2. Given the small size of the sample, these results must be treated with considerable caution. Nevertheless, the results do reveal some interesting and quite reasonable relationships among the measures.

A major focus for this study was the relationship between writing attainment and potential preschool antecedents of writing skill. Wells and Raban found that measures of preschool language development were only weakly related to reading attainment, and thus it is not surprising that the language development measures, while they correlate somewhat more highly with writing than reading attainment, are not strongly related to composite writing quality. Moreover, the measures of oral syntactic development are quite weakly related to measures of written syntactic development. These findings suggest that, beyond an essential threshold, facility in oral language in the preschool years is not strongly related to later developments in written language ability. However, a concurrent measure of oral syntax (or other measures of oral language) might be more strongly related to writing. Development of written language can, in fact, feed back to spoken language (Kroll, 1981; Yerrill, 1977).

The Parental Feedback measure is also only very weakly related to writing attainment. Thus, the quality of parents' preschool linguistic interaction with their children, while it has been found to be a powerful factor in oral language development and was also related to reading attainment, appears not to be directly related to writing ability. One might suggest that it is parents' responses to their children's efforts to read and write—rather than responses to children's efforts to talk—that are most relevant for the development of literacy. In fact, the major finding of this study strongly supports such an

Table 2.   Correlation Matrix of Assessment Indices

	1	2	3	4	5	6	7	8	9	10	11
WRITING (Age 9)											
1. Composite Index of Writing Quality	—										
2. Written Syntactic Complexity (MTUL)	0.50	—									
3. Subordination Index (MCTU)	0.66	0.71	—								
4. Vocabulary Diversity	0.79	0.47	0.60	—							
READING (Age 7)											
5. Neale Reading Test	0.54	0.06	0.26	0.33	—						
PRE-SCHOOL LANGUAGE DEVELOPMENT (Age 5)											
6. Mean Length of Structured Utterances (MLU)	0.42	0.06	0.30	0.42	-0.02	—					
7. Syntactic Complexity	0.47	0.21	0.26	0.27	0.30	0.51	—				
8. Functional Range	0.21	0.13	0.21	0.00	0.31	0.18	0.33	—			
KNOWLEDGE OF LITERACY (Age 5)											
9. Preschool Knowledge of Literacy	0.64	0.25	0.51	0.46	0.76	0.03	0.30	0.27	—		
PARENTAL INFLUENCES											
10. Class of Family Background	0.59	0.11	0.43	0.64	0.50	0.53	0.42	0.18	0.64	—	
11. Parental Feedback (Ages 3¼–3½)	0.17	-0.10	0.06	0.14	0.51	0.07	0.49	0.10	0.44	0.53	—
12. Parental Interest in Literacy (Ages 3¼–5)	0.73	0.41	0.52	0.66	0.56	0.16	0.35	0.10	0.72	0.71	0.47

Significance levels: 0.47 $p = 0.05$,   0.59 $p = 0.01$,   0.71 $p = 0.001$

interpretation. The most powerful predictors of writing attainment are Parental Interest in Literacy ($r = 0.73$) and the Knowledge of Literacy index ($r = 0.64$). It appears, therefore, that those children whose parents demonstrate an interest in literacy are the children who not only develop a grasp of the meaning of literacy before they enter school (and become the better readers at age seven), but who also go on to become the most successful writers at age nine.

The Class of Family Background index is also significantly related to writing achievement ($r = 0.59$). The meaning of this relationship needs to be considered rather carefully, however. The Family Background index, since it is based on occupational and educational criteria, provides a 'status' measure of social class. Although status measures are generally predictive of educational success, Kifer (1977) points out that such measures 'are of limited utility in explaining how homes actually operate to provide either effective or ineffective educational settings for children' (pp.6-7). In contrast to status measures, 'process' measures indicate what parents actually *do* to influence the educational achievement of their children. The major process measure in this project is Parental Interest in Literacy, a measure based on such parental behaviors as teaching about reading, answering questions about words, and reading aloud to the child. The process and status measures are strongly correlated for this group of children ($r = 0.71$)—as one would expect, since parents whose levels of educational attainment are high and whose occupations place a value on literacy skills would tend to take an active interest in their children's acquisition of literacy. Nevertheless, the process measure (Parental Interest) not only provides a better predictor of children's writing attainment than does the status measure (Family Background), but the process measure is of more utility, educationally, because it provides 'clues about how optimal learning environments can be structured' (Kifer, 1977, p.7).

Finally, the measure of reading attainment at age seven (Neale) is significantly related to writing quality, although the relationship is only moderately strong ($r = 0.54$). On the one hand, a stronger relationship might have been expected, since, for most children, reading constitutes an introduction to the conventions of literacy, and thus early success in reading should put a child at an advantage for the development of writing ability. On the other hand, two years intervened between the measures of reading and writing attainment, and one would expect that some children who were slow in developing reading skills might make considerable progress in reading and writing during that period, and might even overtake those children who had a good start on literacy but did not maintain this rate of progress in the acquisition of writing skills and vice versa. An examination of the rank orders of the 18 children in reading and writing attainment helps clarify this matter (see Table 3). To simplify the analysis, the ranks in the table have been divided into thirds, producing high, middle, and low groupings for attainment in reading and writing. Within each of these groups, two-thirds of the children remain in (or very near) the same group in writing as they were in reading attainment. But in each group there are also children who rise or fall quite dramatically from their grouping on reading attainment when we examine their writing attainment two years later. Of those children in Group III in reading attainment, all but two remain in Group III in writing—but the two exceptions, Phillip and Allan, rise

Table 3.   Rank order of project children on reading and writing attainment

		Reading attainment at age 7 (Neale)		Writing attainment at age 9 (Composite)	
		Child	Score	Child	Score
GROUP I	1	Susan	44	Sandra	65.12
	2	John	33	David	59.92
	3	James	26	Susan	59.73
	4	Sandra	23	John	56.96
	5	Elizabeth	23	Philip	56.65
	6	Wendy	21	Judy	52.61
GROUP II	7	Judy	17	Allan	50.38
	8	Derek	15	Ann	50.17
	9	David	13	Elizabeth	49.66
	10	Ann	13	Peter	49.47
	11	Peter	13	Mary	48.08
	12	Mary	12	James	46.19
GROUP III	13	Janet	10	Wendy	44.95
	14	Philip	9	Paul	44.30
	15	Allan	8	Derek	43.69
	16	Kathleen	2	Kathleen	42.53
	17	Paul	0	Andrew	41.84
	18	Andrew	0	Janet	37.74

impressively in writing attainment. The picture is much the same in Group I: of those children in the top third in reading attainment, four remain in Group I in writing, but two—James and Wendy—drop to the border between the lower two groups. In Group II, of those children in the middle third for reading, three remain in the same grouping for writing attainment, and one (Judy) has risen only slightly into the higher grouping. But David rises dramatically to near the top of Group I in writing, while Derek falls to the bottom group in writing attainment. Thus, while most of the children remain in the same broad groupings for writing as they were for reading attainment, there are notable exceptions. Early reading success seems to be important for later success in writing, but a relatively slow start in reading does not necessarily preclude a child from becoming a successful writer a few years later.

In sum, the findings of this research are very much in harmony with the results of previous studies of the Bristol children, in that the findings point to the home—specifically, the kind of environment for literacy which parents provide—as a major influence on the development of reading and writing abilities. The comments of Wells and Raban, summing up their research on reading attainment, are worth quoting at length here.

> What emerges is a major dimension, on which homes can be rated, concerning the extent to which parents manifest their interest in their children's personal and cognitive development through the context and manner of their interaction with them, of which an interest in books and reading is one particular example . . . . For the more fortunate children, this means being treated as an autonomous individual with valid purposes and interests that can be shared with adults . . . . Looking at books with a parent or being read to, often at bedtime, forms part of the regular experience of such children, with the result that an introduction to literacy occurs as part of a complex of enjoyable and meaningful, shared activities, which the child is ready, both motivationally and intellectually, to develop in the more formal context of the classroom.
>
> For the less fortunate children, by contrast, adults have been less consistently responsive to their purposes and interests and their efforts to understand and control have been less fruitful, frequently because the parents themselves have never acquired a sense of their own power to control their environment through rational understanding and planned activity. Typically, though not always, such parents have, themselves, never fully discovered the role that literacy plays in extending this sense of control. However it is important to reiterate that such parents are, for the most part, equally interested in their children and keen to see them succeed. What they lack is an intuitive understanding, stemming from their own experience, of how their own behaviour can enhance the chances of their children's success. (p.115)

If we look at the backgrounds of the children in the project—using the case-study data in Moon (1976)—we find corroboration for the proposed link between parental attitudes toward and provisions for literacy and subsequent success in reading and writing. For example, the two children with the highest and lowest levels of attainment in writing, Sandra and Janet, afford an interesting comparison. They are almost exactly the same age (Sandra is two days older) and thus entered school at the same time. Both have one sibling, a brother two years older. However, the differences between their home backgrounds with respect to literacy are striking.

Sandra comes from a modern home in a middle-class suburb of north Bristol. Her father is a well-educated quantity surveyor. Most important, however, is the fact that Sandra is growing up in a home filled with books and a high regard for reading. Sandra's brother could read and write before he went to school, and Sandra was anxious to emulate him. With her mother's help, Sandra learned some reading skills before going to school. She also pretended to write, scribbling in imitation of her brother. She watched little television and often preferred to scribble while the television set was on. Sandra liked being read to. She was curious about words on billboards and asked questions about words in the books that were read to her. She was taken regularly to the public library, where she enjoyed selecting books for her parents to read to her. When Moon examined the first eight recordings of spontaneous speech in the home (recorded between ages 3¼ and five years)— tabulating the frequency of occurrence of activities in which parents teach, answer questions, or provide experiences related to literacy—he found that Sandra attained the highest score for parental interest in literacy. Thus there is considerable evidence that Sandra's home environment was strongly supportive of her efforts to learn to read and write.

Janet comes from a predominantly working-class area of east Bristol. Her father is a skilled laborer in a printing firm, and, since he is a shift worker, is often home during the day. Moon reports that the family relationships seemed excellent. The father, in particular, was very interested in and knowledgeable about both children. Nevertheless, Janet's home environment was not strongly supportive of literacy. She was read to only about once a week, an activity which started after her brother began going to school, as a means of giving Janet increased attention. In the preschool years, Janet was not very interested in looking at books or in writing activities. She could not read or write before going to school, although she could recognize her own name by seeing it written by her parents. Her favourite activity was playing with dolls, as well as a great deal of 'make-believe' play. Although her parents read a newspaper daily and her father regularly read books, Janet was taken to the library only four times before entering school—twice by her mother and twice by teachers at the nursery school she attended. Moon's examination of preschool recordings revealed little evidence for literacy-related activities in Janet's home. Janet's score placed her in the bottom quarter for parental interest in literacy.

Thus, an examination of background information available for these two children seems to support the notion that children's homes differ considerably in the support they lend to literacy-related activities. And the measure of parental interest in literacy during the pre-school years correlates strongly with writing attainment. The results from this study and the reading project suggest some tentative interpretations of what this correlation might mean. One interpretation would be that parental interest is related to writing attainment through a hierarchy of intervening relationships. Thus, parental interest in the preschool years leads to a well-developed knowledge of literacy, and such knowledge is critical for learning to read in the primary school, perhaps because it provides children with 'cognitive clarity' about the task of reading (Downing, 1979). Those children with knowledge of literacy get a head-start on reading, attain higher levels of reading proficiency by age seven, and are then, because of their strong reading skills, at an advantage in learning to express themselves in writing. The significant correlation between reading and writing attainment would support such an interpretation.

But there may be a more direct relationship between parental interest in literacy and writing attainment. Parents who demonstrate an interest in their children's early efforts to read are, almost certainly, parents who continue to provide support and a source of motivation when their children confront the demands of school tasks. It is therefore plausible that the parental interest index, although assessed from preschool recordings of parent–child interactions, actually reflects the extent to which parents support the child throughout the process of learning to read and write. Thus, it may not simply be the case that parental interest gives the child a head-start on reading by enhancing knowledge of literacy, but also that continued interest and support at home is important for the development of writing ability.

However, this picture of parental influence is complicated by the role of the school in the child's acquisition of literacy. Like homes, schools differ in the quality of their provisions for and support of literacy. The strong influences of home and school can therefore be variously matched or mismatched: a child from a literacy-oriented home may have either an effective or ineffective school experience, and a child from a materially and intellectually impoverished home may experience successful or unsuccessful schooling. Although no information is available concerning the quality of schooling that the 18 project children received during the period from ages seven to nine, my informal classroom observations at age nine provide some tentative insights into what can happen when home and school provide complementary environments for the development of literacy. Let me focus again on Janet and Sandra. Although both girls were the same age, entered school at the same time, and were therefore both classified as second-year junior school pupils, their classrooms differed markedly.

Janet, whose home was relatively unsupportive of literacy, was in a mixed class of first- and second-year juniors. Thus, many of the children in the class were younger than Janet. Perhaps because of these younger children, the teacher tended to 'mother' her pupils—that is, to provide an informal atmosphere in which they would feel comfortable and protected. The classroom procedures and expectations for work were much like those one would expect to find in an infant school. For example, during the writing sessions the teacher had pupils bring their finished pieces (which were uniformly quite short) to her desk, where she read the writing quickly, wrote a brief, laudatory comment, and pasted colored stars on successful pieces. This teacher's methods may have been well-suited to a number of the younger pupils in her class. And Janet seemed to be quite comfortable in the classroom setting. Nevertheless, it was difficult to escape the impression that, placed in a class with many younger children and taught by a teacher who tended to be protective, Janet was not being challenged to extend her writing skills. Unfortunately, Janet's home did not provide an alternative environment for stimulating her growth into literacy.

In contrast, Sandra was in a class with a number of older children — a mixed class of second- and third-year juniors — and she was taught by a teacher who emphasized individual achievement and who provided challenging activities for writing. This teacher's methods, expectations for behavior, and standards for work were more like those one would find in a secondary school. For some nine-year-old children, this classroom environment would have been too formal, the demands too rigorous. However, even though she was younger than many children in her classroom, Sandra was very bright, was confident of her abilities, and was therefore challenged by her teacher's demands. Moreover, Sandra came from a home with very strong parental interest in and support for reading and writing. For Sandra, then, home and school environments worked harmoniously to encourage her growth in literacy.

In sum, both home and school are complex and powerful influences on a child's achievement in writing. The emphasis in this project has been on the influence of the home environment. However, this emphasis is not meant to minimize the importance of the school in providing a meaningful and challenging environment for learning to write. Although parents may, through their interest in literacy, make their children more ready for and receptive to instruction, the school is still the place where the vast majority of children learn how to read and write. It is important, therefore, to explore what conditions best support writing development, as well as to research the merits of various methods, materials, and instructional programs. Nevertheless, the effects of the home environment on the acquisition of literacy need to be considered more carefully than they have in the past. It is not enough to talk in generalities about 'good' or 'bad' homes, or to focus on status indices of social class. We need to know much more about what specific kinds of parental practices facilitate children's reading and writing attainment. We may then be better able to enlist the support of the home in the critical task of teaching children to read and write. As Kifer (1977) reminds us, 'in the best of all educational worlds . . . the home and the school are not vying to be the major influences on the learning of children. Rather they are two institutions, or better, two sets of competent persons, operating simultaneously and cooperatively to influence and direct the growth of children. Educationally, a child deserves no less and could hope for no more' (p.13).

REFERENCES
Carroll, J. B. *Language and thought.* Englewood Cliffs, NJ: Prentice-Hall, 1964.

Clay, M. M. *The early detection of reading difficulties.* London: Heinemann Educational, 1972. (a)

Clay, M. M. *Reading: The patterning of complex behaviour.* London: Heinemann Educational, 1972. (b)

Downing, J. *Reading and reasoning.* Bath: W. R. Chambers, 1979.

Hunt, K. W. *Grammatical structures written at three grade levels.* Research Report No. 3. Champaign, IL: National Council of Teachers of English, 1965.

Kifer, E. The relationship between the home and school in influencing the learning of children. *Research in the Teaching of English,* 1977, **11,** 5–16.

Kroll, B. M. *Cognitive egocentrism and written discourse.* (Doctoral dissertation, University of Michigan, 1977.) Dissertation Abstracts International, 1977, 38, 3439A. (University Microfilm No. 77–26, 284.)

Kroll, B. M. Cognitive egocentrism and the problem of audience awareness in written discourse. *Research in the Teaching of English,* 1978, **12,** 269–281.

Kroll, B. M. Developmental relationships between speaking and writing. In B. M. Kroll and R. J. Vann (Eds.), *Exploring speaking–writing relationships: Connections and contrasts.* Urbana, IL: National Council of Teachers of English, 1981.

Kroll, B. M., Kroll, D. L., and Wells, C. G. Assessing children's writing development: The 'children learning to write' project. *Language for Learning,* 1980, **2,** 53–80.

Kroll, B. M. and Lempers, J. D. Effect of mode of communication on the informational adequacy of children's explanations. *The Journal of Genetic Psychology,* 1981, **138,** 27–35.

Moon, C. *Pre-school reading experience and learning to read.* Unpublished M. Ed. thesis, University of Bristol, 1976.

Moon, C., and Wells, C. G. The influence of the home on learning to read. *Journal of Research in Reading,* 1979, **2,** 53–62.

Myers, M. *A procedure for writing assessment and holistic scoring.* Urbana, IL: National Council of Teachers of English, 1980.

O'Donnell, R. C., Griffin, W. J., and Norris, R. C. *Syntax of kindergarten and elementary school children: A transformational analysis.* Research Report No. 8. Champaign, IL: National Council of Teachers of English, 1967.

Richardson, K., Calnan, M., Essen, J., and Lambert, L. The linguistic maturity of 11-year olds: Some analyses of the written compositions of children in the National Child Development Study. *Journal of Child Language,* 1976, **3,** 99–115.

Wells, C. G. *Coding manual for the description of child speech in its conversational context.* University of Bristol School of Education, 1973. (Revised edition, 1975).

Wells, C. G. Learning to code experience through language. *Journal of Child Language,* 1974, **1,** 243–269.

Wells, C. G. Language use and educational success: An empirical response to Joan Tough's 'The Development of Meaning'. *Research in Education,* 1977, **18,** 9–34.

Wells, C. G. Describing children's linguistic development at home and at school. *British Educational Research Journal,* 1979, **5,** 75–98.

Wells, C. G. *Learning through interaction: The study of language development.* Cambridge: Cambridge University Press, 1981.

Wells, C. G., and Raban, B. *Children learning to read.* Final Report to Social Science Research Council, 1978.

Winer, B. J. *Statistical principles in experimental design.* New York: McGraw-Hill, 1967.

Yerrill, K. A. J. *A consideration of the later development of children's syntax in speech and writing: A study of parenthetical, appositional, and related items.* Unpublished doctoral dissertation, University of Newcastle on Tyne, 1977.

6

Who Writes What, and Why

Morwenna Griffiths and Gordon Wells

Very few people in England manage to live without doing writing of some kind; nor would they want to. The same is true for the inhabitants of most other industrial countries. Yet writing is not a natural activity for human beings in the way that talking is, or making music. There are no human societies without speech or music, but there are many without writing. Historically, it is clear that many generations of people have managed their lives quite successfully without being able to write, or even to read. There has also been some speculation that, in the future, writing will become an irrelevance to most people as we move into a post-literate age made possible by other means of recording language and transmitting it across distances.

In the present, however, our society is still characterized by a high degree of literacy. The written word is highly regarded, and the skills of reading and writing are often taken for granted. Writing is an activity that is so common that many people say it is difficult to imagine life without it. When asked about the value writing has and the difference it makes, many people give answers like 'It's another sense like sight or hearing', or 'It's a necessary general skill', or 'You can get by with it'.

This high degree of literacy is also evident in the education system. Children in school spend a large proportion of time writing and this practice is rarely questioned. If justification is called for, the answer is likely to be that writing is necessary in education because it helps to develop certain kinds of mental attitudes and abilities, or because some kinds of learning would be impossible without it. But by itself, this argument could not account for the large amount of time children in school spend writing. Other reasons are connected with teachers, pupil and parental perceptions of the skills needed to get and keep jobs. Yet others are connected with views about the skills needed for a satisfying adult life. There may also be historical reasons of inertia. Suspicions have been voiced, too, that writing looks reassuringly like real schoolwork, and that it may be used as a good way of keeping the children quiet.

119

However, there is very little factual evidence to bring to bear on these matters, and so the arguments tend to rely on speculation. We do not know, for example, whether writing is more or less needed than it was in different types of employment, or about its relationship to mental development. Nor do we know if or how adult life is enhanced by it.

Some of these facts are extremely hard to discover. Evidence about the facilitating relationship between writing and mental abilities is an example. On the other hand, many of the facts that are needed are to do with the writing that adults do in relation to the lives they lead. These should not be so difficult to obtain.

For example, we should be able to find out what kinds of writing adults engage in and how often, and what their attitudes are to different kinds of writing. We should also be able to find out how much variation there is in the population in these respects. Such information would provide evidence about writing and employment, and about how writing affects other aspects of the ways in which people manage their lives. Also, apart from the purely practical reasons for writing, there are others of a more personal or affective nature which could be discovered. It cannot be assumed that everyone is alike in this, nor that teachers (or any other single group of people) are particularly well equipped to judge the needs of their pupils here. Since education is universal, and is collectively paid for, the opinions and values of all sections of the population need to be taken into account.

Furthermore, evidence of this kind is not only necessary to inform debate about writing needs and wants. It is also necessary for any study of writing development and, hence, for any curriculum planning that is intended to be based on a developmental model, since such a model necessarily implies a view of what developed writing ability is. The influential report of the Bullock Committee, *A Language for Life* (Bullock, 1975), which offers guidelines for the language curriculum in Britain, adopts the developmental model proposed by Britton *et al.* (1975) in *The Development of Writing Abilities (11–18)* (hereafter referred to as DWA). Yet, as the authors readily admit, knowledge of the 'end-point' of development was not available when they were constructing their model:

> A developmental model, however, presupposes some sort of end-point, presumably a model covering all kinds of adult writing (or to put it another way, covering the completion of the socialisation process with regard to writing), and since no adequate description of the kinds of adult writing existed we needed to produce such a model and to relate a developmental account of children's writing abilities to it. (DWA: 12)

In the absence of information about adults' writing, the model that they developed was, in fact, based largely on theoretical discussions of the functions of speech. But, as is now beginning to be more clearly recognized, the way language functions in the two modes of speaking and writing is systematically different (cf. Chafe, 1982; Olson, 1977) and it may be that the model proposed in DWA will need to be reconsidered when data about what adults write and why they do so become available.

The same arguments apply, of course, to any curriculum model for writing that adopts a developmental perspective. If the DWA model is singled out for critical attention here it is because it is probably the most fully developed and because it has achieved very considerable influence amongst teachers in Britain.

In short, the general point we wish to make is that all discussions about what writing people need to be able to do, what they should learn and how they should be taught would benefit from information about what writing adults actually do and what they feel about writing.

AN EMPIRICAL INVESTIGATION

This chapter reports the results of a small-scale investigation intended to answer some of these questions. The subjects of the investigation are not a uniform group of people. They vary, for instance, in age, sex, occupation and marital status. They also vary in what they write and how often, ranging from those who are reluctant to write anything at all to aspiring authors of stories and poems and an academic regularly publishing articles. The investigation was designed to find out more about such differences in writing habits and to discover the attitudes and values that the subjects held with respect to the various types of writing.

In carrying out the project, there were two problems which had to be faced immediately. These were, first, finding a system for categorizing the different kinds of writing, and, second, finding a method of eliciting from the subjects information about what writing they did. These problems are not independent of each other. As we wished to investigate the whole range of adult writing, we could not collect scripts and construct categories on the basis of what we found in them. People do not keep their shopping lists and would be unlikely to hand over their personal diaries. Nor could we have handed out questionnaires and asked the subjects to answer questions about their own writing in writing. Subjects might have been unwilling or unable to cooperate in this way. So we had to rely on asking questions. As a result, we had to specify our theoretical categories in advance and the difference between categories had to be expressed in such a way that the subjects would easily recognize them.

Classifying the Writing

Constructing a system of classification for any form of human activity is always a difficult undertaking. On the one hand, there is the theoretical problem of how many parameters to recognize in the description and how many and what kind of distinctions to draw within them. And, on the other hand, there is the danger that the distinctions one arrives at as an analyst will not correspond to those that non-analysts make between the different activities in which they engage. If this is true for human activity in general, it is particularly so for language activities. Not only may apparently similar activities be engaged in to achieve quite different purposes, but the same purpose may be achieved by different means on different occasions and in different contexts. Furthermore, it is not at all unusual for one activity to be aimed at achieving several different purposes simultaneously. We were already familiar with this problem as it applies to the classification of 'speech acts' in oral language (cf. Labov and Fanshel, 1977; Searle, 1977; Wells, 1981a), so it was no surprise to find that the same problem had bedevilled attempts to categorize types of writing.

Most systems for classifying writing have focused on a single parameter: either subject matter, or form, or writer–audience relationship, or function. DWA is one of the few exceptions in taking account of both audience and function in its scheme of classification.

Classifications by subject matter are familiar to every library user—as are their complexity. Classification by form can be effected by drawing simple distinctions like that between prose and poetry, or it can pick out certain well-known writing forms such as memo, novel or thesis.

Of the classifications by writer–audience relationship, the best known are probably those of Joos in *The Five Clocks* (Joos, 1961) and of Moffett in *Teaching the Universe of Discourse* (Moffett, 1968). Joos makes a fivefold classification. His categories range from an audience of intimates, where the speaker pays the addressee 'the compliment of implying that she knows him inside and out', to people who are to remain social strangers. Moffett's classification is only fourfold, but it ranges more widely. It includes a category of 'reflection' in which the audience and speaker are the same person. The classification by audience in DWA is similar to that of Moffett, but the categories are adjusted to suit the special purpose of investigating children writing in school. For example, Moffett's second most intimate category, 'conversation—interpersonal communication between two people in vocal range' has been subdivided into 'teacher' and 'known wider audience'. The systems of classification by audience are not enough by themselves, though, because they have such wide categories. For instance, in all the systems, messages left for the family on the kitchen table come into the same category as love poems.

Classification by function (or its close relatives of intention, aim or purpose) is also common. This basis for classification dates back to antiquity and the study of oratory. The traditional division was into literary, theoretical and dialetical. Recent exponents of this basis for classification of language have, by and large, followed this ancient division, but have modified it.

Roman Jakobson used this idea in his influential paper 'Linguistics and Poetics' (Jakobson, 1967). In his analysis of language he identified as basic factors the addresser, the addressee, the context, the message itself, the contact between the people and the code used. These determine the following six functions: emotive, conative, referential, poetic, phatic and metalingual. In Jakobson's model, all the functions are potentially relevant for the description of any piece of speech or writing. Although in some kinds of writing one function may be dominant, other functions will almost always be relevant as well; there will thus be a hierarchical order of functions. What is important about this suggestion, in our view, is the emphasis on the multifunctionality of messages, different messages being distinguished by the relative importance of each of the functions in determining the meaning that is intended or understood.

The notion of a hierarchy of functions is the basis of the model proposed by DWA but in practice it is the dominant function only that is given weight in the scheme of classification. Jakobson's six functions are regrouped into three superordinate categories: poetic, transactional and expressive. Poetic writing is not confined to poetry:

> Poetic writing uses language as an art medium. A piece of poetic writing is a verbal construct, an 'object' made out of language.
> (DWA: 90)

Transactional writing brings together both the conative and the referential functions in 'Language to get things done' (DWA: 88); it also incorporates the metalingual function. The expressive function, with its emphasis on the addresser; self-revelation, combines Jakobson's emotive and phatic functions.

The expressive function differs from the other two in that it is seen as the matrix from which the writer moves in either of two directions: towards the poetic or towards the transactional. That is to say, the poetic and transactional functions are the fully differentiated extremes of the dimensions that bear those names. The other extreme in each case is the undifferentiated expressive. However, the meaning of the term is shifting and unclear. It is defined as follows:

> Firstly, expressive language is language close to the self. It has the functions of revealing the speaker, verbalising his consciousness, and displaying his close relation with a listener or reader. Secondly much expressive writing is not made explicit because the speaker/writer relies upon his listener/reader to interpret what is said in the light of a common understanding . . . . Thirdly, since expressive language submits itself to the free flow of ideas and feelings, it is relatively unstructured. (DWA: 90).

Also:

> Expressive writing is relaxed . . . the demands made on the writer (demands made from *outside*, by the reader, by the nature of the task) are at a minimum. (DWA: 93)

None of these criteria are always present in the examples cited, which range from diary entries to 'interest' articles in specialist journals and some editorials. In fact, they have to be thought of as a disjunctive set, with any one of them being sufficient to identify a text as expressive.

There is a further problem for the DWA model. Because the two dimensions of poetic and transactional are treated as mutually exclusive alternatives, there is no place within the model for texts, or types of text, in which both dimensions are apparent. Satire is one type of writing where this is the case, and another is the philosophical novel, a kind of writing associated, for example, with Camus and Voltaire. Britton *et al.*'s response to this is as follows:

> It is easy to find examples of literature which have, as part of their function, the influencing of the judgement, beliefs and attitudes of the reader . . . . Satire functions as satire only because the poetic function is clearly established beyond all doubt . . . this writing is not necessarily less conative because its poetic function is clearly established, but we would classify it as poetic. (DWA: 100)

This is difficult to understand. The poetic function has been defined as 'an immediate end in itself, and not a means'. It is contrasted with the transactional, which is a means to an end:

> The form it takes, the way it is organised is dictated primarily by the desire to achieve the end efficiently. (DWA: 93)

But satire functions as satire largely because the 'poetic' structure is not just an immediate end in itself. It is often the best way of getting opinions across, and is chosen for that reason.

Literature is not the only kind of writing that can achieve transactional ends while being at the same time an end in itself. Neither philosophic arguments nor scientific reports are purely transactional in this sense. Moreover, like 'poetic' writing, they are highly structured and unified and are meant to be read as a whole—though you can quote from them as you can from Shakespeare.

More generally, since there are many types of writing that fulfil more than one function simultaneously, it follows that any classification scheme that

requires texts to be assigned uniquely to one of two or three contrasted superordinate function categories, such as 'poetic', 'expressive', and 'transactional',
will fail to do justice to the functional diversity of actual writing. Britton
and his colleagues do recognize this problem but the solution that they felt was
appropriate for their study of writing assignments in school—to assign a text
to the 'dominant' function [i.e. 'the function to which other functions seem to
be subservient (DWA: 108)]—effectively cuts off further consideration of
texts which realize, for example, both poetic and transactional functions
simultaneously. For the present investigation, such a solution does not seem
acceptable. We therefore prefer to retain Jakobson's notion of multifunctionality and to leave hierarchies of function to emerge from an analysis of the data.

However, none of the existing systems entirely suited our purposes. As well
as having a theoretical interest in devising appropriate ways of classifying
writing, we were constrained in our investigation by the kind of question that
can be asked in an interview. Whilst categories of 'audience' and 'form', we
felt would be fairly readily understood by our subjects, we were less confident
that this would be true of 'function' categories. We decided, therefore, to
construct a two-dimensional matrix with audience and form and to ask about
the resulting combinations quite directly, but to adopt a more indirect
approach to the investigation of function.

Audience is not difficult to ask about. We found that it was convenient to
use the following categories: 'universal—available to anybody', 'strangers
identified by their role in society', 'colleagues and acquaintances', 'family and
friends' and 'self'. People generally have a clear idea about who they are
writing for, and we found there were few difficulties in assigning items to these
categories.

Form is rather more complex than audience. A simple division such as
poetry and prose, or formal and casual, seemed too broad, while detailed lists
of all the various kinds of writing from shopping lists to sonnets would be too
long and unwieldy. However, it is easy to distinguish certain broad categories
intuitively and we think than the criteria which enable us to recognize them
consist of a number of independent dimensions, each of which may be,
somewhat arbitrarily, divided into two or three segments. These are not
theoretical di- or trichotomies because they do not mark differences in kind
but, like 'hot' and 'cold', or like portions of the colour spectrum, mark
differences in degree. The dimensions which we distinguish are short to long,
prose to poetry, fact to fiction, and casual to formal. However, in some cases
making all these contrasts produced such small categories that we did not think
it worthwhile to include them. The categories we found to be convenient were:
formal and casual prose, stories, poetry, witticisms (i.e. epigrams, graffiti),
notes, (i.e. a sentence or two) and jottings (of less than a sentence).

There is a problem in asking about form. The writer and her audience (or a
researcher) might classify the same piece of writing differently. What was

intended as casual by the writer might seem to the reader stiff and formal, or vice versa. Since we were not assessing actual scripts, we classified types of writing according to the conventionally expected form.

Function, however it is defined, has a close connection with intention and perception, or, in other words, with the reasons people have for writing. We prefer to deal with 'reasons' as being a more transparent term than 'functions' (cf. p.144 below). We did not assume, and did not expect, that a classification of writing on the basis of reasons for which it was carried out would coincide with a classification by audience and form. It is therefore treated as a further independent dimension. However, we did not include it in the classification matrix with audience and form, because asking about reasons involved asking questions which were more ambiguous, and which called for more judgement on the part of both the subject and the researcher.

The final classification thus used the two independent variables of audience and form, and we examined reasons separately. The advantage of this classification system over the others that have been discussed is its simplicity, comprehensiveness and adaptability. Clearly, it has borrowed from other systems, but it relies on as few technical distinctions as possible, which makes it easier to use than any of the other systems we considered.

Figure 1 shows the matrix with examples of types of writing in the different categories. The simplicity of the system is apparent. It could, in principle, be filled out directly by the subject. This means that the interviewer's questions could be directly related to the classification system. Since the distinctions among the categories only depend on such ordinary language conceptions as length, formality, fiction, and poetry, it is not, as it stands, highly theory-impregnated. On the other hand, it is easy to pick out statistics for the more theory-laden concerns like writer–audience relationships, so it can be used to compare results with those of other theorists.

The system has proved to be comprehensive. There was no new item of writing which came up during the investigation which would not fit unambiguously into the grid. This is in contrast to experiences with some of the other systems. Moreover, the comprehensiveness has not been achieved at the expense of what is intuitively acceptable. There is not a great disparity among the items in any of the categories.

It could also be adapted in various ways. For example, it would be easy to increase or decrease the fineness of the distinctions. We remarked how in DWA an audience category had been added for teachers. In our classification this would be inserted between 'strangers identified by role' and 'colleagues and acquaintances'. Bosses and others in positions of power could appear here too, being socially more distant than most colleagues. The number of forms could also be extended. For instance, the variable of length could be divided into more segments, distinguishing writing of a page or two from more extended writing.

	Casual prose	Formal prose	Stories/Drama	Poetry
Universal	Gossip column	Letters Articles Theses	Novels } for publication Plays }	Poems for publication
Strangers	Newsletter	Letters Reports Newsletter		
Colleagues		Letters Reports Essays Minutes	Play for school by teacher	Poems for colleagues
Family Friends	Letters		Stories for family	Poems, Rhymes
Self	Diary		Stories for own pleasure	Poems for own pleasure

	Jottings	Notes	Witticisms
Universal	Signatures	Slogans Notices	Graffiti
Strangers	Forms	Notices	Comments on notice boards
Colleagues	Case notes Engagement diary	Messages Memos	Comments on notice boards
Family Friends	Lists Wall calendar	Messages Postcards	Humorous messages
Self	Lists Engagement diary	Plans Notes	

Figure 1.   Matrix of Audience × Form categories, with examples

The Questionnaire Used in the Investigation

As well as asking direct questions about the categories in which writing is done, we included questions about satisfaction, enjoyment and competence and about values and reasons for writing. We also included questions about the background and experience of the subjects. We asked about age, education, occupation, previous occupation, number of children, and reading habits. We also included questions about frequency of writing. Many kinds of writing are done periodically. The tax form is filled in annually, and some people only write letters at Christmas. School reports occur termly and minutes of meetings may be written up monthly. Other writing is sporadic. Writing applications for jobs is one example, and writing to an MP is another. We gave people a choice of frequency categories for each item we asked about. These were 'never since leaving school', 'at least once since leaving school', 'at least once a year', 'at least once a month' and 'at least once a week'.

Having established what questions we wanted to ask, the questionnaire had to be designed so as to encourage complete and honest answers. This was not, of course, easy. There are several reasons for there being difficulties here. One of these is unease felt about writing. Many people feel inadequate in some way about their ability, or obscurely ashamed that they do not write more. A second is the fact that most people do not normally feel the need to introspect and remember what writing they do, or to consider what they feel about it.

The interview began:

> People seem to agree that both writing and reading are valuable, and should be taught, and taught well at school. And, in fact, children in school do spend a lot of time reading and writing. It is easy to see why people need to read. But teachers wonder if they are teaching the right sort of writing, writing suited to a world full of telephones, tape-recorders and dictaphones. So we want to know what people actually do write, both at work and at home. We've tried to get into contact with all kinds of ordinary people so as to get a true picture, so, of course, not all the questions will apply to everyone.

Then followed the questions about the person's background, job, education and social circumstances. We tried not to make these questions impertinent or threatening to their self-esteem. Since we already had some information about the qualifications and ages of all the subjects we did not need to be too intrusive. We did not probe about qualifications and neither did we ask about exact ages. Obtaining this information was considered to be less important than retaining a cooperative and relaxed interviewee.

We then asked some questions about reading newspapers, magazines and books (including reference books) to obtain a picture of the person's reading habits. This was useful from the point of view of the research; it also meant that nobody had to give the interviewer an impression of illiteracy, even if they did practically no writing. Since some people are sensitive about the extent of their skills in literacy, this was important.

The interviewer then went on to ask about types of writing. These questions began with what was likely to be written by most people (forms and messages to the family) and ended with the less likely (stories and articles intended for publication). These questions were nearly all closed, and not hard to answer. However, we also included some more open ones. In some of these we asked for reasons: 'If you prefer phoning, why do you ever write?', and 'Why do you write a diary?' were examples. We began with closed rather than with open questions because they had the effect of allowing the person time to think about her writing habits, and so when questions were asked that needed introspection, she was ready.

The last section was more general. Here we used questions that were open. They were designed to see what personal involvement people have in writing and how much satisfaction people derive from it and how far they felt it was a good means of expression for them.

As we have said, we also wanted to know the values and opinions people held about writing or, in other words, what meaning and uses writing had for them. Although it had been relatively easy to run a small pilot investigation to establish a list of items that people write, it would have been difficult to do this with values and opinions. The list of possible items that people can write is not very different among different sections of the population; on the other hand, the values attached to the different types of writing are likely to vary. To have asked a list of closed questions would almost certainly have biased the range of ideas expressed. We would have been inviting people to express opinions where they had none and, moreover, to have suggested ways of thinking other than their own. This would not have given us a fair indication of their ideas. Without open questions in the pilot study we would never have realized how important many people consider it simply to be literate. We assumed that there would be other values mentioned that were equally unexpected by us.

We put two open questions at the end of the interview. They were: 'Do you yourself value being able to write? Why in particular?', and 'What difference does it make to your life?'. These two questions are not really very different in intent. We felt that by asking both of them we encouraged the subjects to think more about writing and to express themselves fully. We also included a catch-all question, just before the end, in case there were aspects or types of writing we had missed: 'Have I left anything out that you think I should have asked about?'

The Sample of People Interviewed

The investigation was carried out with very limited resources both of time and money, and this affected the samples of people we chose to interview. We interviewed two sets of people, but they were smaller and less randomly distributed than we would have liked. On the other hand, they included a range of social class and occupation, and were not drawn from a group with any special interest in common. The first set of people had already taken part in another research project concerned with children's language development nine years before (see Wells, 1981a, for a summary). Since that was an investigation involving young children, all the people in the sample were similar in that they were parents of nine- or ten-year-old children. All of them were in their late twenties or older. In order to balance this we also interviewed a sample of people who were all between the ages of 26 and 30. For convenience we refer to the first set as 'parents' although, of course, some of the younger ones are also parents.

The sample of parents was chosen from an initial 902 families who had babies in Bristol within a certain timespan. Of the initial 902, 10% refused to be interviewed at all and a further 26% were excluded on various grounds, or proved impossible to contact. Of the remainder, about half were chosen at random for detailed interview. Each of the families was assigned a rating on a family background scale calculated from a combination of occupational and educational factors. The scale was divided into four roughly equal segments and an equal number of families was selected from each segment. This meant that the sample of parents, as it stood, was not representative of Bristol parents, as the two extremes of the population were over-represented. However, since the selection for interviews had been made on a well-understood basis, it was possible to correct the bias when assessing the results.

The sample of younger people was chosen by approaching all those who had left a Bristol comprehensive school in 1971–1972. We judged this school to be 'comprehensive' also in the sense of having a social and academic mix of pupils. Data collection on this part of the investigation is still in progress; so far we have interviewed 27 of this younger sample, 9 male and 18 female.

We attempted to contact all of the 192 parents and actually managed to interview 133, 63 male and 70 female. Those who refused all came from the working class (Registrar General Classes III, IV, V) although only half of the interviewed were working class. Refusals were also more numerous among men than among women. One of these men is thought to be nearly illiterate, but, on the other hand, another near illiterate agreed to take part.

THE RESULTS OF THE INVESTIGATION

The Frequency of Writing

We counted the total number of people who reported ever having written in each category since leaving school; and how many of them reported doing so at least once a year, month or week. In the same way, we also counted the number in each of the five audience categories, and in each of the seven forms. Figures 2 and 3 show the results from the parents for audience and form, corrected to allow for the way these people were chosen from the original sample of parents. We made the same count for the younger sample. The figures for the two groups are remarkably similar and, in fact, we found no significant differences between them. This is not to say, however, that there is no difference at all. In almost every category of writing, and for each audience

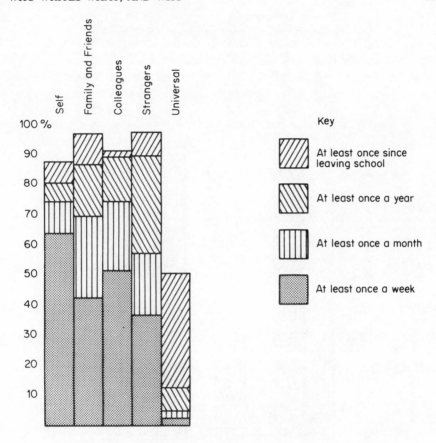

Figure 2.   Distribution of frequency of writing by audience addressed

and form, the figures for the younger sample are higher. The exceptions are pieces written at least weekly either for publication or addressed to strangers. This result suggests that, if anything, the younger group are writing more than the parents. No firm conclusions can be drawn about it at this stage, since only a small number of the younger sample have so far been interviewed.

Several things are immediately evident from these histograms. Most people have found at least some occasions both to jot things down, and to write at more length. Most have also addressed themselves at least annually to every audience category, with the exception of the universal; even here 50% have attempted to write at least once for a universal audience. The figure of 50% includes writers of public graffiti, and hopeful poets, as well as people writing formally and factually. However, only 25% have attempted the latter type of writing and only 5% do it at all regularly, that is, at least once a year.

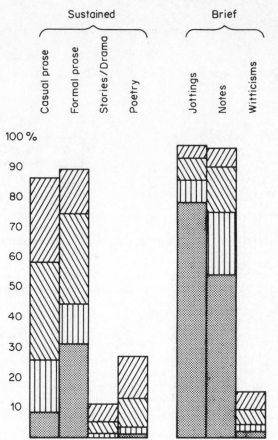

Figure 3.   Distribution of frequency of writing by form

The most frequent writing is for the self. Only 13% reported never having done this, and nearly 75% do it at least once a month. Most of this writing is lists, notes and plans. Extended writing is something much rarer. For instance, 80% said that they had never written diaries or other forms of journal for themselves.

Although jotting things down for the self is done so frequently, an even higher proportion write at least sometimes to their family and friends. Only 3% have never found occasion to do it at all. A high proportion of this is writing in the form of messages; 50% reported doing this at least every month. A remarkably high proportion have also found the need to write personal letters. Only 13% said that they had never done so. On the other hand this is something that few people do frequently. While 60% said that they wrote to their family or friends more than once a year, only 7% said that they wrote every week.

Where there is little social pressure or practical requirement to write, very little writing occurs. Of the 20% who have had occasion to write diaries, few do so regularly. Only 6% said that they did so more than annually. A few more than this write poetry or verse of some kind; 27% said they had done so at some time, and 13% said they did so at least once a year. About 10% as regularly chalk up odd sentences to amuse or annoy on walls, blackboards or other convenient surfaces.

Several questions were raised by these figures. They show that there are great differences within the sample in both frequency and type of writing. We were interested in investigating what kind of thing influences what is written. Is it a function of age, occupation, sex, socioeconomic class, education or, perhaps, the possession of a telephone. We also wanted to know what opinions people expressed about writing and how those opinions related to what they actually did.

Differences Related to Background

We began by looking at what differences the varying backgrounds of the people in the sample might make to their writing habits. For this we considered both samples together. Some factors which we had thought might make a difference turned out not to vary very much within the sample. For example, almost everyone had a telephone or access to one. Numbers and ages of children were also so uniform that it would have been unwise to draw conclusions from the few exceptions who had large families or young babies. Other differences among them were more widely spread. Of these, we thought that occupation must make a difference, since so much writing is done at work. We also wondered if sex, age, or education would make a difference.

Many of these variables interact with each other. For instance, while the Registrar General's classification is socioeconomic and generally thought to be of class, it is based on occupation. Occupation, in turn, is affected by education and vice versa, as some people study at night as a result of the job they are doing by day. Neither social class nor occupation is independent of sex or age. In 1971, according to the Census, there were about four times as many Class I men as women, and about four and a half times as many women as men in clerical occupations. Also, people have had more time for study or for promotion as they get older. We did not attempt to sort out these inter-relationships as it would have been impossible, given the size and composition of the samples. On the other hand, it was possible to get an idea of which factors were most related to writing habits, whatever the underlying pattern of cause and effect might be.

We classified the variables as follows.

Age. We assigned people to one of four age bands: less than 27, 27–34, 34–45 and 45–55. There are more women in the younger age bands, but this is not surprising given that most of the people are married couples.

Class. Subjects were assigned to one of five class groups on the basis of the Registrar General's classification. Everyone was classified according to the highest-rated job held. Only one woman proved impossible to rate in this way. Possibly because the sample included many parents of rather young children, there was not one Class I woman in it.

Occupation. For this variable we adapted the finer classification of the standardized 1971 Census. Since it only deals with the 'economically active', we added a category for housewives. One unemployed man, one blind man and one full-time student were left unclassified. The categories are: housewives; self-employed and higher-grade professionals; employers and proprietors; administrators and managers; lower-grade salaried professionals; inspectors, supervisors and foremen; clerical workers; sales personnel and shop assistants; skilled manual workers; semiskilled manual workers; and unskilled manual workers.

Education proved more difficult to classify. We wanted to be able to assess whether people who had studied arts wrote differently from those who had studied technical subjects—where diagrams and formulae often replace written words. We also wanted to assess whether absolute level of qualification makes a difference. In the end we decided to use three distinct systems. Firstly, we looked at the types of education: arts or sciences, college or sixth form, practical or academic. Secondly, we took account of the level of qualification, although we still distinguished vocational courses that were science-based such as nursing, from vocational courses which were arts-based, such as social sciences. We had some problems with assessing the level of qualification. It was rare for the younger group not to have passed some public examination at school, whereas the parents had hardly ever passed such an examination unless they had then gone on to gain further qualifications. We made no assumptions that one category was higher than another except were one leads directly to another. In the odd case where there was conflict or ambiguity, we took the person's subsequent career as a guide to which qualification to count as the significant one. Thirdly, we used a simple dichotomization of educational qualifications: minimal level of school-leaving qualification or less (GCE 'O' Level, CSE, City and Guilds) versus additional qualifications (GCE 'A' Level, University degree, etc.).

Relationships between these variables and frequency of writing in the various categories were investigated using the chi-square test for independent samples. None of the variables were related to the writing of stories, poems or witticisms. Of course, this was partly because there was so few who wrote in these categories anyway. There was some evidence that occupation was related to those who wrote graffiti or chalked up comments for their colleagues. Both unskilled workers or housewives were unlikely to do so, or at least to admit to it. On the other hand, both lower- and higher-grade professionals were rather more likely to do so than might be expected by chance.

Sex, class, education (when dichotomized) and occupation all showed high degrees of connection with writing frequencies in at least some categories. However, as might be expected from the similarity between the two samples already noted (p.130), age was quite unrelated to either audience or form.

There was a difference between the sexes over writing to family and friends. Women were much more likely to do this ($p < 0.01$). There was also a difference between the sexes over the amount of writing they did in both casual and formal prose. Men were much less likely to write in casual prose than women ($p < 0.001$). However, they were both more likely to write often in the formal form and also more likely never to do so ($p < 0.01$).

There were strong class differences over which audience was addressed and which forms were used, in the case of notes, casual and formal prose. Class also showed this high degree of connection when dichotomized into middle (I and II) and working class (III, IV and V).

When educational qualifications attained were dichotomized, the results were very similar to those obtained for social class. Those with higher educational qualifications were more likely to write notes, casual prose and formal prose. They were also more likely to have written at least once for a universal audience and to write more frequently for strangers and colleagues. Perhaps surprisingly, neither of the first two methods of classification of education showed a clear relationship between education and writing habits. The only exception was in formal writing and, possibly, writing for colleagues.

The relationship between writing habits and occupation is much harder to interpret because with only some of the data so far available, many of the cell sizes are too small to give a reliable result. Nevertheless, there seems to be no relationship between occupation and frequency of writing for the family audience; nor between occupation and writing either casual prose or notes or jottings.

We examined all the variables that were highly correlated with writing frequencies in more detail, to see how each of them was related to individual cells in the matrix of types of writing. The results are shown in figure 4. The relationship with occupation was still too difficult to interpret with any conviction, probably again because of the large number of categories of occupation relative to the total size of the sample. The relatively small size of the sample also means that we are unable to detect differences which we still believe to exist among age groups and among those with different educational experience. For instance, we think that there may be important differences in the types of writing undertaken by those, for example, with science-based as opposed to arts-based education, which would show up if the sample investigated were large enough for all the relevant types of education to be adequately represented.

However, there are some interesting sex, class and education results. Most of the class and educational qualification differences are work-related–writing

	Jottings	Notes	Casual prose	Formal prose
Universal	Not investigated			Class: H > L, $p < 0.001$ Education: A > M, $p < 0.001$
Strangers		Class: H > L, $p < 0.01$ Education: A > M, $p < 0.02$		Sex: M > F, $p < 0.02$ Class: H > L, $p < 0.001$ Education: A > M, $p < 0.001$
Colleagues	Class: H > L, $p < 0.001$ Education: A > M, $p < 0.05$	Class: H > L, $p < 0.001$ Education: A > M, $p < 0.01$		Sex: M > F, $p < 0.05$ Class: H > L, $p < 0.001$ Education: A > M, $p < 0.001$
Family and Friends		Sex: F > M, $p < 0.001$ Education: A > M, $p < 0.01$	Sex: F > M, $p < 0.001$ Class: H > L, $p < 0.05$ Education: A > M, $p < 0.01$	
Self	Class: H > L, $p < 0.01$ Education: A > M, $p < 0.01$	Class: H > L, $p < 0.001$ Education: A > M, $p < 0.01$	Sex: F > M, $p < 0.05$ Class: H > L, $p < 0.01$ Education: A > M, $p < 0.01$	

Sex: F = female   *Class:* H = higher   *Education:* A = additional
M = male   L = lower   M = minimal

(Note: only significant differences are reported)

Figure 4. Relationships between amount of writing in different categories and sex, social class and education

done for colleagues and reports. However, it seems that the habit of using a pen to think with also carries over into home life, in that the more educated middle-class subjects are more likely to jot things down for themselves. They are also more likely to use writing in their relationships with family and friends.

So far, we have drawn no conclusions about causal relationships. All we have done is report the significance of the differences between groups in the population. In doing so, we have tried to keep speculation to a minimum.

Significant relationships do not necessarily imply causality. Also, of course, which differences were discovered to be significant to some extent depends on which variables we were able to measure.

However, causes are extremely interesting and, naturally, we have beliefs about the correct explanations for the patterns we have discovered. For instance, the fact that middle-class people are more likely to use pens at home, and to see writing as an essential part of their occupations, means that preschool children in these homes are more likely than others to perceive and experience language in the written as well as the spoken mode. More evidence in support of this is provided by Wells (1981b). He notes that the best single predictor of attainment after two years' schooling is the extent of the children's own understanding of the purposes and mechanics of literacy at the time when they started school.

On the other hand we do not want to strike a deterministic note, preferring to confine our remarks to the probable influence of social factors and their relative persistence over the course of a person's lifetime. Sex and — in the case of certain sections of the population — class seem to be attributes which have a continuing influence in a way that age, occupation and educational experience do not. This does not mean that any attribute is causally determinant of writing habits. On the contrary, the evidence does not support such a view. Some men, rather than their wives, take on the responsibility for writing to their families, just as some people with few educational qualifications frequently write formal reports. Some working-class people often write formal letters, and some middle-class people never do so. There are people for all groups who at least occasionally use pen and paper to work things out for themselves, just as there are those in all groups who do not.

Enjoyment and Competence

We asked our subjects which kinds of writing gave them a sense of satisfaction or pride, and which ones they enjoyed. They were also asked:

> I wonder how competent you feel as a writer? I don't mean: do you think you're brilliant at it but simply: do you feel you cope quite well, or do you worry about it when you have to write or do you feel you have any particular difficulties?

Many people expressed generalized dislike or liking, hatred or enjoyment of writing. Not surprisingly, this valuation was linked to whether doubts were expressed about competence. Which way cause and effect run between enjoyment and competence is very difficult to assess, even in individuals known personally. Someone with an eye for the ball is more likely to enjoy ball games, and the cack-handed are unlikely to enjoy inlay work or fine embroidery. However, some of the doubts expressed about writing competence were about handwriting, spelling or the phrasing of formal letters, none of which are special talents. With proper teaching they can all be learnt by anyone, as is demonstrated by the success of adult literacy schemes with people who have failed at school.

Among the variables we examined, class and sex differences were the most strikingly related to differences of writing habits. So when we looked at the comments that had been made we divided them into four sets by class and sex. We looked at the comments made by working-class men and women, and by middle-class men and women.

Extreme dislike of writing was expressed by about 8% of the middle-class men and women, 13% of working-class women, and 25% of working-class men. In each set, about three-quarters of those who hated writing also expressed worries about their competence. Apart from problems with spelling, handwriting and grammar, there were also difficulties with expression.

> I get tongue-tied when it comes to writing—I prefer to see a person. (Postal office worker)

A catering worker said that she couldn't think coherently when writing.

Quite a high proportion of the sample usually disliked writing; 25% of each class of men, 30% of working-class women and 15% of middle-class women expressed either mild or extreme dislike. Of these, about half the middle-class and three-quarters of the working-class subjects expressed doubts about their capability. Only about 1% of those who did not dislike writing expressed such doubts. In the whole sample about 30% of the working-class subjects were unhappy about their competence in some way, as were about 10% of middle-class women and 15% of middle-class men.

It was difficult to assess the answers expressing positive enjoyment and satisfaction. Apart from the direct question about it, we also asked about the writing that they did for their job, such as report writing or articles written for publication:

> Are they a trial to you or do you like (did you choose) the job because it involves that sort of writing?

On the whole we were unable to get any clear information from these questions. Many people did not really think of writing in terms of enjoyment or satisfaction, and we were doubtful whether the terms were being used consistently enough by everyone throughout the sample to allow us to make generalizations.

The answers about writing at work were a little clearer. A few people wished they could do more:

I always wanted to be a writer but the system got me. (English teacher)

I'd like a job that involves more writing—I think there is the possibility of more interesting jobs that involve writing. (telephonist)

Few people were positive about report writing, though a couple of people were nostalgic now that they no longer had to write them:

I did enjoy it. I now miss not having so much to do. (sales assistant)

Most saw them as essential and did them more or less willingly:

Quite an interesting part of the job. (instructor of mentally handicapped adults)

Difficult—but I enjoy them. (insurance broker)

The writing is incidental—there's some satisfaction if I've clearly described what I'm trying to get across. (technical engineer)

A change from usual work. (engineering planner)

Simply part of the job. (general foreman)

It has to be done—I don't like paperwork. (mechanic)

Time consuming and annoying. (residential social worker)

I changed jobs because I disliked paperwork. (master baker/lecturer)

Some people also mentioned that they valued writing just because of the enjoyment it gives. Middle-class women mentioned this more than others, while working-class men hardly did so at all. The pleasure was not necessarily in the actual writing; you have to write letters if you want the pleasure of receiving them. You may enjoy being on a committee even if you do not much like writing up the minutes.

The Value of Writing in Everyday Life

The two questions at the end of the interview asked about the value that writing had for the subjects and the difference it made to their lives. Few people found it easy to answer these questions about the value of writing.

Literacy usually means reading, and people found it difficult to focus just on writing. Also, literacy is something society approves of, usually uncritically. If standards fall, it is an occasion for national alarm. So people found it difficult suddenly to question or justify the value of writing. A few people simply said that it was a good thing. Others justified it in vague terms like 'valuable as a means of communication'. On the other hand, some were able to be more precise. A part-time cleaner said she thought writing was valuable for personal communication and she appreciated it more because of being able to write personal messages to her husband.

When we looked at all the answers given to these two questions we noticed that some points appeared again and again, while others were quite idiosyncratic. An example of the latter was the sharp observation made by a distribution clerk that 'writing improves your understanding of what you read'.

We made a list of the most commonly given observations. These were: its importance for employment; the value of self-expression and recording ideas; general remarks about communication; pleasure in being literate, and in the independence it gives you; convenience, especially as a memory aid; help in dealing with the practicalities of life like the Social Security and tax; the importance of helping children; how it increases choice in lifestyle and leisure activities; the enjoyment it brings; that it is an asset in general; and wishes that it was done better or more. However, there were several who thought that it really made very little difference to their lives.

As with the comments on enjoyment and competence, we divided the subjects up into four sets by class and sex in order to examine the results. We recorded how often each point was made, but if someone had said more than one thing about one of the headings on our list, emphasizing different aspects of it, we only recorded it as one observation. The results are tabulated in figure 5.

Evidently the method of arriving at the results depends very much on the judgement of the researcher and the interviewer, and so the results can only be treated as indicative. A further difficulty is that the interviewer cannot be considered neutral. Everyone knew that she came from a Faculty of Education. This may have affected the number of people expressing educational concerns, and the desire to help the children. Moreover, the interview was directly about writing and was conducted by a highly literate interviewer, which must have had an effect on the opinions ventured.

Examining the results, it is possible to concentrate on differences. It is also important to point out similarities. As can be seen there is a widespread emphasis on the importance of writing for getting jobs and then doing them. There is a general belief that being able to write enhances employability. Some of this importance is not integral to carrying out the job, as some people remarked. A foreman commented:

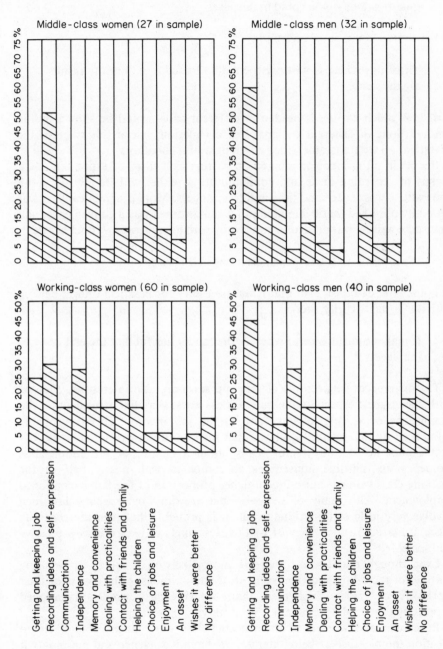

Figure 5. The value of writing: class and sex differences

> Tradesmen don't need it, but you can't get jobs now without
> qualifications — you could in the past.

A hairdresser commented on training:

> These days there is writing: there didn't used to be but the results
> are the same.

Just how much writing is needed in different cases would be shown by the amount done in different categories of occupation, but at this stage of the investigation we are unable to say anything useful about this.

People in all groups commented on writing as a form of expression, as a means of recording ideas and communicating, either with family, or more generally, across space and time and to strangers. More pragmatically, it was generally observed that being able to jot things down was a convenience, and that some writing was needed to cope easily with bureaucracy. A docker said:

> It's useful — to fill in forms, get along in the world.

A housewife, ex-typist, said that it was necessary for practical things, dealing with the Social Security, etc:

> It makes a difference to whether the family has food at the end of
> the week.

The differences between the classes and sexes are also interesting. Men of both classes, and especially the middle-class ones, were likely to mention the importance of writing at work and in the job market. This is probably influenced by the greater likelihood that men are using writing at work, but that cannot be the only factor. Only about a quarter of the middle-class women were full-time housewives as compared with nearly half of the working-class women; but a much higher proportion of the latter mentioned employment. Also many of the jobs that are done by working-class men involve very little or no writing at all. It is probable that men are generally more utilitarian in their view of writing, less likely to regard it as expressive and sociable.

Even though middle-class men are more likely than others to be using writing for recording and expressing ideas and opinions in the course of their work, fewer middle-class men than working-class women mentioned expressing or recording ideas as a reason for valuing writing.

Both men and women of the working-class were much more likely to mention the pleasure of being literate, or the independence and autonomy it gave them. A lorry driver said he would feel ignorant if he could not write. A dinner assistant said it made a difference to her that she was not dependent on other people to do her writing for her. Hardly anybody from the middle-class groups mentioned this sort of thing. Neither did they express a generalized wish to write more or better. This is a wish that appears to be more about self-confidence than usefulness. An engineering worker said that writing was an asset, that he wished he was more inclined to write, that he considered it a loss that he was not so inclined. He also said that writing makes no difference to his life. Not everyone who has difficulty writing loses confidence as a result. A mechanic who said that he depended on his wife for most of it added:

> If I had to do it, I would apply myself, overcome laziness and write
> more.

The beliefs and opinions that people expressed have some relation to the kinds of writing that they reported doing, but not a close one. It is unlikely that anyone is quite consistent about how they behave in relation to what they say they think, but it is also unlikely that the one has no effect on the other. The strong class differences that we observed in job-related writing and in writing for the self (p.135) are not really reflected in the expressed opinions, except possibly in the number of working-class people who do not feel that writing makes much of a difference to their lives. Also middle-class women, though not middle-class men, are more likely than any other group to mention the convenience of writing and to say things like:

> I don't have to retain so much in the memory. I can write down
> things like shopping lists, etc., for reference.

or

> I would be lost without it — writing lists, it makes me more orderly,
> like when giving a party for instance.

The sex differences we observed in writing messages to the family and in writing letters are more obviously related to the opinions stated. Many fewer men than women mentioned personal letter writing, and none mentioned children.

We feel that the number of comments by women on self-expression and communication do not really reflect a difference in practice. There are only a few differences between the sexes as regards writing habits. Few people do any of the kinds of writing which could be called purely expressive and, in so far as other writing such as writing reports at work is expressive and communicative of self (as some feel it is), men do as much as women.

It may be that women were expressing a general frustration because of their relative inability to influence their world, and express themselves in it. Many more women than men were doing less interesting jobs than they were qualified for, or than their spouses were. When we asked if people had any wishes to do more writing, more women said they had. Some remembered the pleasure of work or school. A housewife, who used to write reports at work, said that she had enjoyed them because of the satisfaction of seeing her arguments proved right. Another housewife said:

> I'd like to write more stories because I used to enjoy doing it at school.

More women, and especially middle-class women, said they had a wish to do imaginative or self-expressive writing.

It seems to us that a belief is being expressed that writing is a good means of self-expression. Actual practice and the structure of society belies this. There were a variety of reasons why women did not do more, some of them related to the kind of society we live in.

> If there were a purpose—I couldn't do it just for myself. I don't know who to contact, where to start. (housewife)

> There's a lack of need, enough motivation to do it, no practical point. (unemployed youth leader)

> No need or opportunity for it. (nursing auxiliary)

Others were less perceptive about the gap between belief and practice. A housewife said she valued writing as a way to express herself, and also said she wished she wrote more letters. However, she wrote letters less than once a month, and then only if they were addressed abroad, or the person was not on the phone. A part-time librarian, who disliked all forms of writing, said she valued it because 'you can express yourself, communicate with people'. But the only extended writing she did was the occasional letter when phoning was too expensive.

Reasons for Writing

As well as obtaining a general idea of how people feel about the value of writing, we wanted to discover more about the reasons for which people write. As noted above (p.126), there is obviously considerable overlap between the notions of 'reason for writing' and 'function of writing'. But there are also important differences. Generally speaking, a description of function is carried out with reference to linguistic products, the classificatory decisions being made on the basis of features of the actual messages produced. Although there is not an exact one-to-one match between features of form and the function of a message, the relationship is systematic and, to a large extent, governed by convention. This is particularly true of written productions, the meanings of which (including functional meanings) are, as Olson (1977) argues, to be found very largely in the realization of the message in the text. The relationship between reasons for writing and the finished text is not so straightforward: whilst the function(s) conventionally recognized in the text almost always constitute one reason for putting pen to paper on any particular occasion, there are often other reasons which are not overtly realized in the finished product but which are, nevertheless, important in accounting for the impulse to write at all. To be complete, therefore, a description of reasons for writing requires an examination both of the texts produced and of the writers' reports of their subjective states at the time of writing.

In this particular investigation, we were only able to obtain generalized reports from subjects concerning the reasons for which they engaged in different types of writing; we were not able to relate these reports to the actual texts. As a result, the reasons associated with the conventional functions of different types of writing tended to be assumed, with subjects' answers to questions tending to emphasize the more personal and subjective reasons for writing. The information we were able to collect is far from complete, therefore. Nevertheless, within these limitations we think it is of considerable interest.

In carrying out this part of the study we looked at all the comments that subjects had made during the interview which cast light on the reasons they had for writing. People sometimes remarked on their reasons when we asked them about audience. We also asked directly for reasons in the case of letters, jokes and diaries. We wanted to consider all the idiosyncratic comments as well as the ones that kept recurring. We were more careful to distinguish shades of meaning than when we had looked at what had been said about value.

We wrote down every comment that we judged to be a separate point — 200 in all. Reasons ranged from pure enjoyment to convenience, from the privacy and secrecy of writing to the pleasure of sharing jokes with friends, from the satisfaction of clarifying ideas to the chore of social duty. Some of the comments were very specific, while others were abstract or vague. Some referred to special circumstances, as in the case of someone who preferred to write letters because he was rather deaf. Others were more widely applicable. For example, a lot of people mentioned the pleasure of looking back on past events. It was clear to us that writing is used flexibly for various and complex reasons.

We wanted to find a way of classifying all these disparate comments. We found that Jakobson's classification of function (p.123 above) was a useful starting point, although we made some adjustments and changes to it in the light of the comments we had elicited. Although he uses his classification to discuss written language, it is predominantly orientated to speech, and certain aspects of writing have been neglected.

For example, writing is useful for making permanent records in a way that speech is not. Both can be recorded, but written things can be scanned, skimmed, taken in at a glance, and edited in a way that tape-recordings, as yet, cannot. Moreover, writing is handy and cheap; no bulky or expensive technical equipment is required. Recording is a very ordinary use of writing, but it does not seem to be covered by any of Jakobson's categories. We have added it to them.

A further aspect of writing which needs to be emphasized is the effect of the reader on the writer. This is not just a question of writer–audience relationship but one of expectations. Orientation to the reader is too often taken to be a matter of persuasion or of wanting some action to ensue. It is not often mentioned that the expectations that are attributed to the reader or that are current in society exert a powerful influence on why a person chooses to write at all. For example, people expect to send postcards on holiday, and there is a belief that condolences and congratulations expressed in writing have 'a built-in sincerity factor'. The reader can exert an influence through what the writer believes about her individual expectations and pleasures. One person said that she wrote letters to her old aunt because:

> She looks forward to them — a pleasure that couldn't be given by phone.

Another person said that he wrote a letter to his mother when he had not been to see her for a few weeks 'to avoid the backlash'.

The effect of the reader on the writer is also important when they are the same person. It is a distinguishing feature of writing that the writer is routinely also the reader. She is sometimes the only reader. This is not just a question of monitoring at the time of writing. Writing can be reread and this makes it very different from talking to oneself. Few people have the habit of talking into a tape-recorder. That writing is reflexive in this way is important in a consideration of the reasons for which people write. Many people do so to reflect on their ideas and problems.

Focus on the message is not the only aesthetic possibility when the message is a written one. Calligraphy can also be a source of artistic pleasure and several of the interviewees referred to it as such. This was something of a surprise to us, since neither of us have this interest. However, we included calligraphy among the categories. On the other hand, we could find no clear analogue of Jakobson's 'metalingual' in written language, so we left it out.

In our revised scheme, the focus can be on the writer, the context, the message, the appearance, the record, the contact, the writer-as-reader, and the other-as-reader. The respective reasons or functions are expression, reference, literature, calligraphy, memory, phatic, reflection, and communication, influence and social duty (depending on the nature of the perceived other).

The full analysis of the data on reasons for writing in terms of this scheme of classification still has to be completed and so will not be reported in this chapter. However we can already say with confidence that any idea that most pieces of writing—particularly sustained writing—are performed for one of a small number of mutually exclusive reasons is simply not correct. Many of the subjects in our sample commented in ways that suggested that their approach to writing was much more flexible than such an account would imply and that, more often than not, a complex of reasons motivated the different types of writing that they undertook.

CONCLUSION

We began by giving two reasons for carrying out this investigation. We wanted to assemble some evidence about the importance of writing for the adult population. We also wanted to look critically at models of writing development, particularly that proposed in DWA. We can now say something more about both these matters.

The Model of Writing Proposed in DWA

The model of writing in DWA depends on a dichotomous distinction drawn between the transactional and the poetic with hierarchies of function being further distinguished within each of the major functions. It seems to us, looking at the reasons people gave for writing, that the model of two continua, with expressive at the centre and poetic and transactional functions at the two extremes (DWA: 83) misrepresents the case. Even using the more elaborate classification with eight major categories that was outlined above, we found that multiple reasons were expressed so routinely that to have a single dominant reason as Jakobson and DWA suggest, was the exception rather than the rule. There were a few cases where we could distinguish a dominant reason. For instance, 'an emotional release', 'a social duty' and 'keeping in contact with the family' seemed to be orientated to self, other and contact, respectively. More often, remarks suggested a more complex stance.

You can put more heart into a letter. (writer, reader, context)

Personal letters are more creative than conversation. (writer, message)

A chance to reconsider and refine—to come to your own consensus
before communication. (context, reader-as-self)

We argued against the use of the category 'expressive' in DWA. It seems to
us that in it are conflated several functions that it is more helpful to keep
separate. Not only does the category include orientation to the self as writer,
but also contact with the reader. At other times the self-as-reader becomes
important and, where writing is used to think round problems, the orientation
is to context. Not all these forms of writing were found to be relaxed, even
when they were enjoyable. One relaxed form of writing we found was the
writing of sarcastic or satirical comments in fairly public places or on forms.
On the other hand, the expression of feeling in personal letters was reported by
some subjects to cause them considerable difficulty.

These are matters of more than theoretical importance. There are
consequences for education. Since DWA emphasizes only the dominant
categories of transactional expressive and poetic functions, it is easy to read it
as suggesting that transactional writing does not include a component which is
non-utilitarian and expressive of the self. That part of the value of transactional writing derives from the emotional involvement of the writer and his
self-expression is consistent with DWA, but it would be unfortunate if the
contrary implication were draw.

Another implication for education is concerned with the quantities of
expressive writing in the secondary school. The authors of DWA believe that
expressive writing, close as it is to the spoken form, is accessible and relaxed.
They were disappointed to find very little expressive writing in the scripts they
collected. This disappointment arose from the belief that:

expressive writing . . . may be at any stage the kind of writing best
adapted to exploration and discovery. It is language which extern-
alises our first stages in tackling a problem or coming to grips with
experience (p.85).

We found that people varied considerably in how likely they would be to use
informal writing to aid thinking, or whether they found it easy to express
feelings in writing rather than in talk or in other ways. Planning, thinking or
recording in writing does not seem to be either unstrained or universal. For
instance, many people prefer diagrams, pictures or discussion. An absence of
non-formal writing does not mean that the writer is not involved in the first
stage of tackling a problem or in coming to grips with experience. We share
with DWA a concern that children should be involved with these matters and a
worry lest examinations pressurize teachers and pupils away from independent
thinking. Nevertheless, we are less certain that such initial involvement should
take the form of non-formal writing.

Our classification has some similarity to that proposed in DWA. The audience categories are not very different. Also within our system, the forms can be seen as closer to one or other of DWA's major functions. For example, the poetic function would be most evident in writing in our forms 'poetry', 'stories' and 'witticisms'. We agree, therefore, that the distinction between transactional and poetic does have some intuitive basis in experience, but we do not consider the two categories to be mutually exclusive, nor are we persuaded that the criteria used in DWA to define them are the most appropriate. However, our data do offer two kinds of support for a distinction of this kind. In the first place, there was much less writing in the three forms that can be broadly considered as poetic and, in the second, its occurrence was unrelated to any of the independent variables that we investigated.

The Importance of Writing for Adults

We do not wish to claim too much for our findings. The investigation is small-scale and it would be unwise to infer too much about the rest of the population from information about comparatively few Bristolians. Moreover, the investigation is not yet complete. We still have data to collect, and we still have to analyse some that are already available to us.

Before going on to draw what conclusions we think are warranted, we will summarize the results obtained so far. First, variety of types of writing. In the classification matrix shown in figure 1, 29 cells contain plausible examples. All but three of these were undertaken at some time by at least one of the subjects in our sample. The range performed by individuals at least once since leaving school varied from 0 to 18, with more than 50% of the sample having undertaken at least nine different kinds of writing. Even when the criterion of frequency is increased to at least once a month, more than 50% of the sample still engage in at least five different kinds of writing.

However, not all of the kinds of writing mentioned are engaged in with equal frequency. Sustained writing is less common than short notes or lists, and fictional writing less common than factual. Very few people write at all regularly for a universal audience; however, all the other categories of audience are each addressed at least once a week by between 35% and 60% of the sample. Lists and notes for self are the most common individual categories. Nevertheless, it is worth remarking that more than 25% had attempted to write stories or poems at least once and almost 90% had attempted a sustained piece of formal non-fictional writing at some time.

Sex differences were noted in a number of categories, particularly in correspondence with family and friends, which is more likely to be carried out by women than men. Because of the complex interrelationship between education, occupation and social class, it is difficult to separate out the relative contribution of each of these variables. As a group, they are related to differences in all the categories of both formal and casual non-fictional writing and to most of the categories of notes. In all cases it is the middle-class subjects, who have higher-status occupations and, in general, more education, who write more in these categories.

None of these results is surprising. Taken as a whole, they suggest that writing plays a significant part in the lives of the majority of people. However, there are also some individuals for whom it is clearly not a frequent activity. With a skill that is possessed and taken for granted by such a large proportion of the people we interviewed, it is difficult to be certain how important it actually is to be able to write. And, in any case, this will depend upon personal circumstances, particularly occupation. On the basis of the replies of those who do not write at all frequently, it can probably be concluded that literacy is not essential for a happy and comfortable life. Married couples and lovers helped each other with their writing needs and often enjoyed doing so. But it was disturbing how many people said that they were uncomfortable about their basic capabilities, and that they wished they could write better. There were also many remarks about the embarrassment or lack of confidence that people could feel if they were not competent. It seems that, where a society expects literacy, self-image, self-respect and self-confidence can be damaged by the lack of competence in writing. This is borne out by Charnley and Jones (1979). They found that gains in confidence and self-image were of primary importance as criteria of success in adult literacy programmes.

It is also obvious that choices of employment and of leisure are affected by literacy. What evidence we have points to the conclusion that, if anything, people are writing more than in the past. Many jobs involve some. Even the family could be said to be becoming bureaucratized. Members leave each other memos, and files are kept of dealings with the authorities. The level of literacy required is mostly a basic fluency in handwriting, spelling and expressing oneself in formal written language. Some people commented that they had learnt a lot since leaving school. Sometimes this was said accusingly, as if they should have been taught at school whatever writing skill it was that they had since learnt. However, it was clear that they had in fact left school with the basic skills to enable them to learn the new ones, which is all they had needed.

How far education should be related to the requirements of employers is always a difficult matter to decide. We agree with the authors of the 1976 UNESCO report on literacy that, while the idea of functional purpose should be kept in education, narrowly productivity-centred functionality is not the answer. It is not the purpose of public education to supply the economy with individuals tailor-made to fit specific job requirements.

Ability to write also affects the capabilities that people have to influence events. Many people felt that information and opinions expressed in writing were taken more seriously than when communicated face-to-face or by telephone. Some also felt that they could express themselves more powerfully and persuasively in a formal letter. Two housewives said that it was easier to get complaints across in writing, and several people had experienced the need to approach various government authorities in writing. Telephone conversations can achieve much but written confirmation is often needed, especially if the matter is a legal or financial one.

Open society can only operate if there is a free flow of ideas. Opinions and ideas are disseminated through leaflets, broadsheets, minutes, reports, and formal letters. Everyone needs the means to approach and challenge the authorities. Some people commented on the pleasure of this. A company secretary said how he enjoyed scoring a point over the authorities. Others had evidently experienced a great deal of frustration. A diesel fitter said:

> It has made a difference not being able to write well. I could have
> gone much further with my union work if I had been better at it.
> It has been an obstacle and disappointment, a handicap.

We have so far discussed the need for competent formal writing, but we have said little about fictional writing. The frustration that is felt there is less one of capability than of opportunity. The reasons for this are complex and probably stem from the pervasive influence of a centralized market economy. Nor have we said anything about the value of writing as a learning aid, although we believe that it can have an important role in this respect. We have ventured no opinions about the relative merits of training in literacy, as opposed to oracy, from the point of view of encouraging clear and critical thought. Although these are important issues, our investigation did not obtain any evidence that bears on them at all directly and so they must remain outside the scope of this report.

What is clear is that teachers need to think carefully about why they are teaching any particular skill. The justifications that are given for making children write are many and various: we listed some of them at the start of the report. Although some of these justifications refer to the lives that pupils will lead after they leave school, they are rarely based on anything more than hunch or personal experience. We hope that the kind of information we have collected will inform the judgements that teachers make about the kinds of writing that they require pupils to undertake.

It is also clear that we have failed pupils if they leave school after ten years unable to write fluently and confidently. It may be that they will hardly use these skills again—though it is more likely that they will. They may prefer to express themselves by making music or creating gardens. But if they want to tell their experience in their own written words, if they need to battle with bureaucracy, or if they mean to change the world, they will need to be able to write.

152   EXPLORATIONS IN THE DEVELOPMENT OF WRITING

ACKNOWLEDGEMENT

We should like to thank Sheron Tyminski and Lynne Houlton for helping us to carry out the interviews, and we should also like to thank all the people who were interviewed for giving up their time to supply the answers that are reported here.

REFERENCES

Britton, J., Burgess, T., Martin, N., McLeod, A., and Rosen, H. *The development of writing abilities (11-18)*. London: Macmillan Education, 1975.

Bullock, A. *A language for life*. London: HMSO, 1975.

Chafe, W. L. Integration and involvement in speaking, writing and oral literature. In D. Tannen (Ed.), *Coherence in Spoken and written language: Exploring orality and literacy*. Norwood, NJ: Ablex, 1982.

Charnley, A. H., and Jones, H. A. *The concept of success in adult literacy*. Cambridge: Huntington, 1979.

Jakobson, R. Linguistics and poetics, In S. B. Chatman and S. R. Levin (Eds), *Essays on the language of literature*. Boston: Houghton Mifflin, 1967.

Joos, M. *The five clocks*. New York: Harcourt, Brace and World, 1961.

Labov, W., and Fanshel, D. *Therapeutic discourse: Psychotherapy as conversation*. New York: Academic Press, 1977.

Moffett, J. *Teaching the universe of discourse*. Boston: Houghton Mifflin, 1968.

Olson, D. R. From utterance to text: The bias of language in speech and writing. *Harvard Educational Review*. 1977, **47**, 257-281.

Searle, J. K. A classification of illocutionary acts. *Language in Society*, 1977, **5**, 1-23.

UNESCO. *The experimental world literacy program: A critical assessment*. Paris and London: UNESCO, 1976.

Wells, C. G. *Learning through interaction: The study of language development*. Cambridge: Cambridge University Press, 1981. (a)

Wells, C. G. Some antecedents of early educational attainment. *British Journal of Sociology of Education*, 1981, **2**, 181-200. (b)

Explorations in the Development of Writing
Edited by Barry M. Kroll and Gordon Wells
© 1983 John Wiley & Sons Ltd.

7

The Development of Planning in Writing[1]

P. J. Burtis, Carl Bereiter,
Marlene Scardamalia and Jacqueline Tetroe

Writing permits and sometimes requires deliberate planning. Unlike the speaker, who must maintain a certain pace of discourse in order to hold the attention of an audience, the writer is usually free to give extended periods of time to reflection, both before and during writing. Also, because of the freedom that writing allows for revision, plans may alter or grow over successive drafts of a composition. On the other hand, speakers can use the rapid give-and-take of conversation to compensate for a lack of planning. A speaker can produce a hastily constructed utterance and rely on the ensuing interchange to clarify, alter, or enlarge upon the message. In written composition more is at stake in the document as it first reaches the reader. Consequently there is a greater need for the writer to plan a message so that it is understood and achieves its desired ends without further cycles of communication. Planning is also called for in order to handle the complexity and the quantity of ideas that go into a long composition. Flower and Hayes (1980) recommend planning as a way of reducing the cognitive strain of writing without sacrificing attention to requirements of the task.

We do not wish to overstate the distinction between speaking and writing as far as planning is concerned. Certainly there are times in conversation when one must think out a statement carefully before uttering it. But such circumstances occur much more often with written communication. Similarly, there are times in writing when spontaneity has preference over deliberation — as in 'expressive' writing, for instance (Britton *et al.*, 1975), or in chatty correspondence with a friend — but these are more common in conversation.

1 The research presented in this chapter is supported by grants from the Social Sciences and Humanities Research Council of Canada, the Alfred P. Sloan Foundation, and the Ontario Institute for Studies in Education. We would like to thank Lilita Ezergaile and Larry Turkish for collecting the data presented here, and Earl Woodruff for help in the data analysis.

It would be foolish to maintain that all writing must be planned. But it does not seem unreasonable to assert that good writers must be able to plan. Flower and Hayes (1980) find, in fact, that expert writers can be distinguished from inexpert ones not only by the compositions they produce but by the amount and kind of planning they carry out.

Our own research is concerned with the development of writing abilities, and in this paper we address the question of how the planning process evolves. The available data might be examined for answers to questions such as Do young children plan?, How well?, How much?, and so forth. Questions of this type, though, are apt to turn on one's definition of planning, and hence to be ultimately unresolvable and not worthwhile. The approach we will take instead is to construct a developmental scenario, based on trying to understand what is actually going on in the minds of writers, which may be summarized as follows:

In the course of writing development, planning becomes gradually differentiated from text production. This differentiation involves at least the following two steps that we can identify. In the beginning years of composition, children's mental activity is so closely tied to producing the written composition that it is difficult to identify much in the way of separate thinking that can be called planning. Gradually, as writing ability develops, there is a separation of the problem of finding content for a composition from the problem of actually writing the composition. At this point, clearly identifiable planning can be seen, but the planning remains at the same time tied to the content needs of text production, so that the plan that is generated consists of a listing of content possibilities. In adolescence, planning starts to become sufficiently differentiated from production that we begin to see the plan as having properties and containing elements that have only an indirect bearing on the content of the text. This emergence of the plan as an object of contemplation in its own right marks, we believe, a major advance in the student's development. For able writers, the plan comes to include the consideration of organizational possibilities for the content and becomes a medium in which goals and strategies may be formulated that shape the emerging composition but are not themselves part of it.

PRELIMINARY OBSERVATIONS

The term *planning* has a variety of meanings in current usage, and one can find it applied to almost any kind of constructive mental activity. We use planning here in the sense defined by Hayes-Roth and Hayes-Roth (1979) as 'the predetermination of a course of action aimed at achieving a goal'. That defines the ultimate or ideal form of planning activity, however. Most of our attention will be directed toward the rudimentary forms of goal-directed planning. At what point in development activities begin to merit the label 'planning' is a matter of judgement not in itself crucial to understanding the course of development.

The earliest glimmerings of 'predetermination of a course of action' are revealed in children's vocalizations or lip movements when they write (Scardamalia et al., 1982; Simon, 1973). In the first two years of writing, children almost all show some indications of vocalizing or subvocalizing as they write, and these vocal movements appear to be synchronized with their writing. Children are spelling or sounding words as they write them. By the fourth year (around age 10), however, this type of mouthing of words had largely disappeared among the children we studied and was replaced by a process of constructing a segment of language subvocally, then writing it, constructing another segment, writing it, and so on. This type of activity was found to be more pronounced in the students judged to be better writers. Hence there is reason to suppose that it represents a cognitively more advanced way of composing. When we call this preformation of language 'planning', however, we must be aware that it is still very closely tied to the immediate needs of text production.

Elementary school children tend to start writing almost immediately when given a writing assignment. The delay in starting, although usually less than a minute, nevertheless varies with the task, which suggests that some kind of task-relevant thinking is going on during this brief period. The delay in starting to write an argument to parents on a familiar household issue is less than the delay in starting to write an opinion essay on a similar issue (Scardamalia and Bereiter, 1980). The delay in starting to write an opinion essay that starts with a statement of belief is shorter than the delay in starting with a less conventional opening (Paris, 1980).

These delays are far too short, however, to allow much in the way of goal-setting or explicit planning with respect to the text as a whole. More likely, the time spent is that required to find an appropriate first thing to say. Still, the criterion of appropriateness implies that the first item must be judged against some more global intention, and this is certainly a kind of implicit planning. Bereiter and Scardamalia (in press) have proposed a model of text composition called the 'knowledge-telling strategy', which they attribute to novice writers. In this model, items of text content are retrieved by the use of topical words as probes and are judged for their fit to a selected text grammar function. 'Appropriateness' in this model, accordingly, consists of topical relevance and conformity to text grammar requirements. The amount of planning required to discover a content item appropriate in this way could plausibly be carried out in half a minute or less in most cases.

A fourth-grade student once related to us an incident that was remarkable to her because it involved the whole class being stumped for several minutes before starting a writing assignment. The assignment given by the teacher was to write a story on the theme, 'The Christmas That Almost Wasn't'. The class, according to our informant, sat in puzzlement until one child whispered to the others, 'Santa was sick!' Immediately all the children started writing.

The story is believable, even if not well authenticated. Children evidently have readily available schemata to handle the form of narratives, but in this case the assignment did not give sufficient clue to a topic to guide a search for relevant content. The phrase 'Santa was sick', however, did provide necessary topical information, and accordingly the knowledge-telling strategy could be set into motion.

The fact that children do little planning in advance of starting to write does not mean that they do not plan during other phases of composition, of course. It is by now well known that expert writers often do much of their planning while they write rather than before they start writing. Nevertheless, planning in expert writers stands out as a distinct mental activity, concentrated largely though not exclusively in the early phases of producing a composition (Hayes and Flower, 1980).

In their studies of adult writers thinking aloud while they compose, Hayes and Flower (1980) identified three kinds of planning episodes: generating (which means retrieving information relevant to the writing task), organizing, and goal setting. Together these comprise about 80% of the thinking-aloud content statements produced early in the process of composing. In the latter portions of work on a composition, translating (the actual production of written language) and editing come to predominate.

As part of a larger study conducted by the York/OISE Writing Research Group, thinking-aloud protocols were gathered from 20 students writing one-page essays on the topic, 'Do you think that women should have jobs that take them away from their homes?' There were five students at each of grades 4, 6, 10, and 12 (approximate ages 10, 12, 16, and 18). Table 1 presents frequencies of different kinds of protocol statements. Dictating and rereading include the

Table 1. Analysis of thinking aloud protocols collected during the writing of an argument essay. Percentage of total protocol devoted to each type of statement

Age	Dictate and reread	Language	Content	Organi- zation	Goals	Reader	Diffi- culties
10	54	9	37	0	0	0	0
12	53	9	35	1	0	0	2
16	31	17	49	0	3	0	0
18	23	20	45	2	3	1	7

verbatim recitation of text as it was being written or read over; Content includes statements of information that provide content for the text; Language includes statements concerned with spelling, grammar, punctuation and the like; and Organization, Goals, Reader, and Difficulties include statements that indicate planning of four specific kinds: organization of the text, setting goals, considering the reader, and dealing with expository problems. Among ten-year-olds the majority of protocol segments consist of dictating or rereading text, and almost all the rest is taken up with content generation. Content generation remains the predominant kind of planning at all ages, but by age 18 other types of planning have begun to appear with sufficient frequency to account for 13% of protocol segments.

Eighteen-year-old performance does not appear to be out of line with that observed in expert writers. Hayes and Flower's experts devoted much more thought to organizing, but they were writing longer compositions. The youngest students, however, do not look much like the experts at all. They are primarily engaged in thinking of content and writing it down.

Several problems with studying the development of planning are suggested with this investigation. First there is a problem of the method possibly interacting with age. Perhaps children think of all the same kinds of things that adults do, but they don't report certain kinds of thoughts—possibly because they don't think they are appropriate, possibly because things like goal setting are carried out at not quite so conscious a level in children. Both possibilities are plausible.

A further difficulty is that, even if thinking-aloud protocols give us a realistic picture of what goes on in children's minds when they write, they may not tell us anything about children's competence. Given a short essay-writing assignment, young writers tend to start writing almost immediately and to write down additional items of content as they think of them. This 'what next' or 'knowledge-telling' strategy has little place in it for conscious goal setting or organizational planning. But perhaps this is just the way students are in the habit of going about school writing tasks. What would happen if students were induced to plan for a while before starting to write and to think about such things as what they were trying to accomplish, how they might present their ideas, and what a reader might think of them? Perhaps students would then exhibit the same kinds of planning that adults show, and thereby demonstrate that they have the competence to plan even if they don't routinely use it. Or perhaps they would be at a loss and have no idea how to fill the time designated for planning.

The study to be reported in the next section was an attempt to find out. The study, accordingly, involved students in planning and note-taking activities taking place in advance of their actually producing a text. In this study we also looked at notes taken during planning and at the texts produced afterwards, in order to avoid complete dependence on thinking-aloud protocols as a source of data on planning.

AN EXPERIMENT IN ADVANCE PLANNING

The research considered in the preceding section leaves the impression that planning by young students is dominated by concerns of producing content in sequential order—of what to write next in a composition. We have suggested, however, that this research may only be telling us about the habitual behaviour of younger students in assigned writing tasks and may not be telling us about their abilities to plan.

In the experiment to be reported here we took a direct approach to inducing students to put their planning abilities to work. We made it clear to students that we wanted them to plan, and we introduced a variety of increasingly explicit guides as to what was expected—guides designed to encourage a range of planning activities, including goal setting and problem identification as well as figuring out how to attain goals and solve problems.

Students were asked to carry on planning, making notes as they proceeded, but not to begin actually writing their text until they had done as much planning as they could. This approach was taken because of our finding that under ordinary circumstances children tended to plan only one point at a time. Although mature writers do not typically plan very extensively in advance of starting to write (Emig, 1971; Gould, 1980), we have found that they have no difficulty doing so on request. Some data from adult advance-planning protocols will be discussed later in this chapter. Advance planning seems to involve a relatively minor adjustment of adult composing strategies. In asking children to do advance planning, our thought was that by removing them from the think–write–think–write pattern we might give them an opportunity to reveal a greater range and depth of planning capabilities.

When, in exploratory interviews, we told children that adults sometimes think for 15 minutes or more before starting to write, many children were incredulous. They could not imagine what there was to think about for that length of time. They were inclined, in fact, to think that such a slow start was a sign of incompetence and that expert writers, being smarter, should be quicker off the mark. In order to overcome misconceptions of this kind, we built into the experiment several different ways of suggesting the kinds of mental activities that might go on in advance planning. The result, of course, is that the planning behaviors observed in this experiment may to some unmeasured extent be attributable to the suggestions given. But, conversely, when certain planning behaviors fail to appear even though they were directly suggested, this may be taken as an indication that such behaviors were not readily available to the students.

The study was conducted with 72 students, 24 from each of grades 4, 6, and 8. The approximate ages of the three groups were 10, 12, and 14 years. At each grade the students were divided equally into four groups which differed in the kinds of guidance given. Each student was seen individually, in a session lasting on the order of 45 minutes to an hour.

All students were assigned to write a brief essay on the topic, 'Should children be able to choose the subjects they study in school?' They were asked to plan aloud for as long as they could before actually beginning to write. Paper and pencil were provided, and they were encouraged to take notes as they planned. All students received the following general instructions, suggesting five things they might think about in their planning. Italicized phrases indicate the five points that were suggested as planning focuses.

> . . . Just plan out loud the kinds of things you usually plan when you're going to write something. You may think of things like what *difficulties* might come up while you're writing, you know, what problems you might have and how you'll handle those problems. And you might want to think about the topic, trying to *remember what you know* about it and what kinds of things you want to put in your paragraph. Also, you might want to think about *what your goal is* in writing this—what you're trying for in what you write. There are also things to think about like *how the people who read this will react* to it, what they'll think and what that means for how you should do things in the paragraph. Then, of course, you need to figure out *how to put everything you've thought about together* to come up with a really good paragraph. So really, I just want you to think about the kinds of things you and other writers usually think about when they're planning to write something . . .

Students in the Control condition received only these general instructions. Students in the Card condition were in addition provided with five cards to serve as reminders of the five kinds of planning. Each card contained a short phrase: Thinking about difficulties and how you will handle them; Remembering what you know about the topic; Thinking about your goal— thinking about what you're trying for; Thinking about the reader; and Putting your plan together. No particular way of using the cards was prescribed; they were simply made available to students with the suggestion that they might be helpful if they got stuck in planning.

Students in the remaining two conditions viewed a specially made videotape in which an adult writer planned an essay (not on the assigned topic) and modeled thinking aloud about each of the five areas of planning referred to in the general instructions. Each area was represented in a short segment of three or four minutes. The tape was stopped after each segment and the student was asked to indicate, by referring to the five cards described above, which kind of thing the planner was mainly thinking about during that segment. The reason for adding this discrimination task was to direct attention to relevant aspects of the videotape demonstration. However, it also provided supplementary data on students' metacognitive knowledge of planning—that is, conceptual knowledge of the cognitive process, as compared to tacit 'know-how' (see

Flavell, 1979). Students in the Modeling Only condition then planned their own compositions without having cards available as reminders, whereas students in the Modeling Plus Card condition retained the cards and were invited to use them, as in the Card condition.

Finally, all subjects were told to keep planning for as long as possible before starting to write. It was mentioned that writers often plan for 20 minutes or even longer. During the actual planning aloud, each student was prompted once to continue planning after he or she indicated being finished planning.

RESULTS

Among the kinds of data to be considered here are accuracy in identifying planning behaviors on the part of those students who viewed the model videotape, the relation between notes taken during planning and texts written afterward, and the appearance of different kinds of planning in the thinking-aloud protocols. There were pronounced age differences in each kind of data, but each highlights a somewhat different aspect of the overall developmental process. We had expected that there would also be pronounced differences between experimental conditions, but this proved not to be the case. There were some differences, which will be noted, but they are overshadowed by and also linked to the age differences, which will be the main object of our attention.

Identification of Videotape Planning Segments

In the videotape produced to model advance planning, the focus of the different segments on audience, organization, content, etc., was intentionally made very obvious and consistent. Adults on whom we pretested the videotape had no difficulty identifying the five segments according to their intended focuses. The mean number of segments correctly identified by students in the experiment was 2.17 at grade 4, 4.00 at grade 6, and 3.83 at grade 8. The large jump in accuracy between grades 4 and 6 suggests that during this period students are making a major advance in their *conceptual* grasp of text planning. This could come about either through gaining an understanding of the abstract notions involved or through becoming able to view cognitive behavior more analytically. In either case, however, it remains to search in the other data for indications of whether a change in actual planning behavior is linked with this conceptual advance.

Notes and Text

The way in which the notes are used to generate text was found to change considerably in the age-range studied.

Let us begin at the most advanced level, with an example of notes written during the planning phase and the subsequent text produced by one of the better planners in the group:

NOTES

— opinion (mine)
— responsibility of the children — their goal in life
— parents — their understanding of their children
— what will happen with what they take
— examples
— what rights do they have
— what I think about it
— the grade (if they chose) should be 7 and up
— school subjects should be made more interesting
— now future will be

TEXT

I personally think that students should be able to choose which subjects they want to study in school. In grade 9 students are allowed to choose certain subjects which they want to but even then the students aren't sure. Many don't know because they don't know what they want to be when they get older. If they choose the subjects they wanted most students would of course pick easier subjects such as art, gym, music, etc. I think that this doing is partly the schools fault. If the school made math classes more interesting students would more likely pick that. Their parents should be able to discuss with the children what they should take. The parents of course have more responsibility and of course want the best for their children. Many children (if they could pick their own subjects) would pick something their parents didn't approve of if their parents were mean to them. Then the children would be ruining their own life. This would probably go around in circles. The world is a very mixed up place but it would be even worse if there wasn't any control. Control must begin with children of today because they will become the adults of tomorrow.

Although the composition itself is not particularly distinguished, this 14-year-old student has gone about producing it in a relatively mature fashion. Her notes represent gists of ideas that are expanded into complete thoughts when the text is written. Some of them (e.g. 'my opinion') indicate her intention without giving the contents of it. When the notes are used in the text, they are used in a rearranged order, and a single note may be expanded into two sentences or two notes collapsed into one. Some notes are not used, and some new material is added. Thus a large variety of transformations are made in passing from the notes to the text.

For contrast, here are the notes and text of a 10-year-old:

NOTES

I don't like language and art is a bore.
I don't like novel study.
And I think 4s and 3s should be split up.
I think we should do math.
I don't think we should do diary.
I think we should do French.

TEXT

I think children should be able to choose what subjects they want in school.

I don't think we should have to do language, and art is a bore a lot. I don't think we should do novel study every week. I really think 4s and 3s should be split up for gym. I think we should do a lot of math. I don't think we should do diary. I think we should do French.

In contrast to the age 14 protocol, the age 10 example shows very little transformation taking place between the notes and the text. The notes are already complete sentences, and they are used in the text with minor modifications, and in the same order as they were listed. Only the first sentence of the text is new, and forms a sort of title for the essay. (The space between the first sentence and the rest of the text appears in the original.) For the rest, the notes themselves are copied as if they already constituted a complete first draft of the essay.

These examples highlight the main developmental trend that we find in the notes-to-text data. For the older students the notes represent ideas that are later worked into a composition. For the younger students the notes represent a first draft of a composition, which is then edited into a final draft. In order to quantify this age trend, we counted the number of transformations of different kinds between notes and text for the three age groups. Table 2 shows the resulting frequencies. There is a clear increase from age to age in the amount of transformation done on notes to convert them into text.

These findings do not tell us anything directly about the process of planning but they tell us something quite remarkable about the product of planning. In younger children the product of planning is text. There does not seem to be any intermediate product. For the more mature students, however, the product of planning is a plan. It is not just a stripped-down text, for it contains elements texts do not contain — notes to oneself, as it were — and it bears little structural or stylistic resemblance to the subsequent text.

Table 2. Changes made in passing from notes to text. Percentage of notes undergoing each type of transformation. (Transformations are not mutually exclusive.)

Age	Minor changes only	Major changes					
		Elabora-tion	Reorder-ing	Division	Combi-nation	Omission	Addition
10	31	42	5	5	5	29	15
12	4	65	9	3	11	32	7
14	0	73	18	11	11	25	15

In effect, the younger students subverted our effort experimentally to separate planning from production. Asked to plan before writing, they simply used note-taking as a way of producing text and so were able to go about composing in their accustomed way. This binding of planning to production is not a phenomenon that can be easily attributed to motivational factors or to some residual confusion about what was expected. In clinical work with a small group of children, sustained over a period of weeks, Robert Sandieson tried to initiate the children into the planning strategy that we find older students using spontaneously—the strategy of jotting down ideas in tele-graphic form that are later used as raw material in a composition. In spite of modeling and close face-to-face coaching and monitoring, the children showed a persisting inclination to produce continuous text (even though it was superficially in list form), thus losing the advantages of brainstorming because of having to deal with all the travail of text production from the beginning. Only by introducing formal procedures such as a list of questions to be answered—procedures that effectively disrupted the continuity of production—was it possible to get idea generation to take place apart from text production. It is interesting in this regard that a variety of current methods for enhancing the thought content of students' writing have this property (e.g. Jones and Amiran, 1980; Robinson *et al.*, 1972; Young *et al.*, 1970). A prevalent form in all these approaches is the matrix, which introduces a geometric framework not easily assimilated to the continuous production of linear text.

Use of Conceptual Planning Cues

Inasmuch as all the forward-looking thought involved in composition can be called planning, we need a special term to distinguish those kinds of forethought that deal with goals, strategies, organization, and the like, from those that amount to the actual mental generation of text. We will refer to the first kind as *conceptual planning*. The outcome of conceptual planning is not text content or language; rather it is knowledge that guides or interprets the choice of content and language. We will use the term *content generation* in referring to the generation of material intended for actual use in the text. The distinction cannot always be made confidently on the basis of thinking-aloud protocol statements. A statement of the type, 'The main point I want to make is . . .', may be a conceptual planning statement about the composition but it may also be a statement intended for actual inclusion in the text. In this section we examine a class of planning statements that are especially revealing as to the distinction between conceptual planning and content generation.

The general instructions, the videotaped modeling, and the cue cards were all designed with a view to encouraging conceptual planning. It is to be expected, of course, that some students would try to follow the model and the instructions even though they did not understand them. This could be observed in planning protocols when students used the vocabulary of planning that we had given them but used it in a way sharply at variance with its original intention. Examples of this occurred with each of the five types of planning highlighted by the experimental procedures.

With respect to thinking about goals, for instance, we get the following examples of students using the Goals card but with quite a different function from that of conceptual planning:

> The goal is that you have to be very good in school, and the thing that you're trying for is to get a good mark.

> Think about which subject would be helpful to you in the future, things like math or languages.

> I don't know if they mean it like that, but if they're picking their subject they should think about what they're going to be doing later in life.

Here we see that the idea of goal is used as a theme or cue for generating content to be used in the text, rather than as a cue for thinking about a goal of the text.

A similar phenomenon occurred with the Difficulties card, intended to elicit thinking about rhetorical difficulties or difficulties with the argument the writer was advancing. Instead some students used difficulties as a content theme:

> Like if you have a problem in math or something you should try to get a tutor.

> If you run into difficulties in a subject that you took as an option . . .

> You should pick like a subject that would help you deal with your difficulties.

One student was even ingenious enough to turn Organization into a content theme relevant to the essay topic:

> You should organize yourself so that you don't wind up in a trap like you take a course that you thought would be useful but it doesn't turn out that you really need it.

One of the cue cards, 'Remembering what you know about the topic', was a directive to generate content. Some students, however, took even this cue as a content theme rather than as a suggestion of a type of planning:

> If you forget about the topic later on when they come to mark it and you don't have that much information on it you won't get very good marks.

> Maybe you'd think back about what your teacher explained, and you'd remember it.

The extent to which students used planning cards for conceptual planning is shown in Table 3. Notice that 14-year-olds who saw the model videotape show a greater percentage of conceptual planning uses than others, which suggests that they, but not the younger students, were able to gain from the videotape some grasp of the implicit distinction between conceptual planning and content generation.

Table 3. Use of cards. Percentage of occasions on which cards were used for conceptual planning. (See text.)

	Group	
Age	Card	Card and film
10	8	0
12	12	27
14	14	60

The point we want to make from these data is not that many students misunderstood the directions. This may be true, but it is not enlightening. What is enlightening is that students who distorted the planning task did so in a highly systematic manner. It appears that for these students planning *is* content generation. When, as cooperative experimental subjects, they try to make use of the material and guidance given to them, the most they can do is try to incorporate it somehow into the process of content generation. As the examples show, they sometimes did this with considerable ingenuity.

The power of content generation as a planning mode is dramatized in the following instance of a 10-year-old student who seems to have come close to catching hold of conceptual planning but then had it slip out of his grasp. These are the student's notes:

NOTES

Getting basic subjects
Think about what you want to major in
Keep information remembered so you get smarter
Think of all the subjects to go together so you get a good education
Think how a reader would react to the story (kind of a story)
Remember how to figure out your problems

Notice that the last two notes reflect two of the types of planning encouraged by the experimental procedures—thinking about the reader, and thinking about problems or difficulties. The student did not actually get into planning in either of these areas but did record notes that might serve as reminders to himself to keep these matters in mind when composing the text. Here, however, is the text the student produced:

TEXT

I think students should be able to pick their own subjects if they had some guidance. One thing to start off with is for you to take your basic subjects like math, language, gym, music, and maybe history. In school start thinking what you want to be so you can take those subjects for a start. If you did want to be say a teacher (just math) keep remembering the things you've learned so you will be a better teacher (you will be smarter). So you do become a good teacher even if you just want to teach math you would still need other subjects so you would have to take ones that go together. To this story a reader's view may think it is kind of silly but maybe not. If you do run into problems you must learn how to cope with them and work them out.

It appears that when the student came to write his text, he used the conceptual notes as if they were content and worked them directly into the text.

Classification of Thinking-aloud Protocol Statements

In order to test further the conclusions suggested thus far, we classified statements in the thinking-aloud protocols so as to distinguish between episodes of content generation and episodes of conceptual planning. We tried to follow the same general approach to classifying protocol segments as used by Hayes and Flower (1980), with differences due to our interest in a finer-grained analysis of types of planning and to the fact that our protocols extend only up to the point where writing begins and thus do not contain episodes of transcribing and editing. Each transcript was first segmented into idea units and each unit was then coded as belonging to one of six categories: language considerations (spelling, grammar, vocabulary), content generation, organization, reader awareness, overcoming difficulties, and considering goals. The last four categories, when combined, make up the category of conceptual planning. The frequencies reported in Table 4 are the average of data from two independent coders.

Table 4. Analysis of thinking aloud protocols collected during planning in advance of writing. Length of protocol (in idea units) and percentage of total protocol devoted to each type of planning

Age	Length	Language	Content	Organization	Goals	Reader	Difficulties
10	18	1	91	1	5	1	1
12	42	0	89	4	3	1	3
14	37	2	90	3	3	1	1

As we have noted previously, it is often uncertain in judging individual protocol statements whether the statement is a statement *about* the composition, in which case it belongs in one or another category of conceptual planning, or whether it is a statement intended to be *part of* the composition, in which case it is an instance of content generation. In fact, one of the coders placed many fewer statements into the conceptual planning categories than did the other. The actual percentages indicated in Table 4 must accordingly be taken with discretion. They could move up or down depending on subjective criteria. We doubt, however, that by any reasonable criterion conceptual planning would be found to account for more than a small part of the planning done by students of the ages studied. Because the coders were blind to the ages and experimental conditions involved, greater confidence may be placed in the relative percentages associated with the different ages.

The number of idea units per protocol gives a rough index of the total amount of planning of any sort done at the different ages. There is a sharp increase from a mean of 18 units at age 10, to 42 and 37 units at ages 12 and 14, respectively. Thus the gross amount of planning activity revealed in the protocols more than doubles between the youngest and the older ages. This large age difference in the amount of planning is not accompanied by much of a change in the type of planning, however. Content generation remains at about 90% of the total at all ages, while conceptual planning remains at about 10%. The amount of planning in all sorts increases, but the amount of conceptual planning remains a constant, small percentage of the total.

Thoughts During Pauses

Earlier we noted a possible confound in the use of thinking-aloud protocol data for studying development. When children of different ages show a difference, it may be due not so much to what they think as to what they report of what they think. Similarly, when as in the present case children of different ages do *not* show a difference, this may be due to a failure of the older children to report fully what they think.

Although there is no fully adequate way to deal with such a suspicion, we did take the precaution of questioning students about what they were thinking whenever they lapsed into extended silence during a planning session. Replies were sorted into four categories:

Negative replies: 'I'm stuck', 'I can't think of anything', etc.

Direct content replies: These were replies comparable to those scored as content generation in the protocol analysis. That is, the subject responded with some item of content that seemed intended for inclusion in the text.

Indirect content replies: These replies took a form such as 'I was thinking that . . .' or 'It seems to me that . . .' Even though the idea that followed might be similar to the kinds scored as direct content, the presence of self-referencing phrases like those noted above suggested that the speaker was thinking *about* the idea or *about* its appropriateness for the essay rather than directly generating content of the essay.

Conceptual planning replies: These were replies such as 'I'm thinking about the reader' or 'I'm thinking how to write this', where the speaker indicated a concern about the structure, form, or style of the essay, or about some general issue of content, but was not proposing a specific item of content.

Briefly, negative replies and direct content replies were found at all ages. Indirect content replies and conceptual planning replies appeared rarely at age 10 but were common at ages 12 and 14, increasing from about 10% to over 50% of all replies. The age effect in conceptual planning is thus very clear here, in contrast to the regular thinking-aloud data discussed previously. Although these replies to 'What are you thinking?' are retrospective reports and thus have validity problems of their own (Ericsson and Simon, 1980), they suggest that the silent part of young students' thinking is not much different from the part verbalized in their thinking-aloud protocols, but that the older children are engaged in at least some conceptual planning that does not appear in the regular thinking-aloud data. At the same time, if the conceptual planning of the older children is still largely restricted to those brief periods when they are silent, it cannot constitute more than a small percentage of their total planning.

It is interesting that the older students do fall silent when they are engaged in conceptual planning, because it suggests that conceptual planning is competing with talking for their attentional resources. We have often noticed that subjects of all ages who are thinking aloud fall silent at exactly the point where the most demanding—and most interesting—thinking occurs. Their silence indicates that the 14-year-olds, in conceptual planning, are attempting something that is difficult for them to achieve.

Adult Replication

Six university undergraduates were tested in a replication of the Control condition of the main planning study (no cards, no videotape). There were two main reasons for this replication. The first was to get a more extended developmental picture. Although some striking changes were observed during the age range of 10 to 14 years, the incidence of conceptual planning in the thinking-aloud protocols appeared low at all ages. It appeared important to verify that there was in fact an age gradient in this planning behavior. The other reason was to ensure that there was not some experimental artifact serving to diminish planning even in proficient writers. We will not give a detailed account of the adult-level findings, but will give an overview that serves as well to pull together the findings on school-age writers.

With respect to the phenomena that we have noted thus far, the adult writers were very similar to one another and markedly different from the children and adolescents observed in the main study. The outstanding difference in planning between the adults and the children was that the adults explicitly planned out the organization of the entire essay during the planning period. Let us consider briefly the adult data in each of the areas of development that we examined in the main study, to see how this difference manifests itself.

The relation of the notes to the text in the adults is no longer traceable in the same terms that it was with the children. The notes have become much too complex and much too condensed. For most of the adults, the notes consist of multiple small lists of ideas here and there over the page, with arrows and lines connecting them. They have a diagrammatic, structural quality. They often are so abbreviated that they cannot be easily interpreted by a reader. Conceptual planning notes are everywhere. Marks that indicate the value of notes are frequent—asterisks, boxes, question marks, and exclamation points. Ideas are grouped and labeled according to content—'pros' and 'cons', 'early grades' and 'high school'—or structural position in the essay—'introduction' and 'conclusion'. There are sometimes notes that refer to the planner's current concerns—'this is no good', 'am I answering the question?', 'stay on topic', or 'relate paragraphs'. None of these features occurred in the notes of the children. They all come about because the adult is concerned with the structure of the essay during the planning phase, and most of the notes obviously play a supporting role for this type of conceptual planning.

The thinking-aloud protocols, too, show much more conceptual planning. We did not give cue cards to the adults, who no doubt would have used them correctly, but in any case they were not needed, as most of the areas of conceptual planning are represented (with the notable exception of audience considerations). The adults only infrequently had to be asked what they were thinking, so that there are few replies to compare to the children's, but the replies that did occur were of all types, with perhaps more indirect content replies.

About 33% of the protocol idea-units were explicitly concerned with the areas of conceptual planning that we defined. In fact, the adults' whole approach to content, which covered the other 67%, was also typically more goal-orientated, more orientated toward overcoming difficulties, and more orientated toward establishing structure ('putting your plan together' as the card said) than that of the children. There is a great deal of repetition of content in the adults' protocols, too, where they are reviewing and reconsidering aspects of the planned essay.

Finally, there are many cases of clear, explicit planning of the structure of the essay during the advance planning phase. The adults say things like 'I'll start with the idea that . . . then I'll talk about . . . and I'll finish with . . .', showing that they do consider the essay as a whole during the planning period. None of our school-age writers planned the organization of the essay in advance to this extent.

CONCLUSION

Let us briefly recapitulate our experimental findings on the development of planning abilities. At the level of metacognition — that is, the level of knowledge about the cognitive process of planning — 10-year-olds showed little accuracy in identifying the kinds of planning carried out by an adult model. By age 12 accuracy had risen to close to an adult level. In attempting to carry out suggested kinds of planning, however, students across the 10- to 14-year age range showed a tendency to distort all kinds of planning into content generation, although this tendency diminished significantly across the age range.

Between the ages of 10 and 12 there was also a major jump — a doubling — in the gross quantity of planning indicated in thinking-aloud protocols. Conceptual planning increased slightly across the 10- to 14-year age range, but was infrequent at all ages. Only 14-year-olds, however, showed evidence of a response to videotaped modeling of conceptual planning. Adults showed a higher incidence of conceptual planning, even without modeling or instruction.

At age 10 there was a close resemblance between notes taken during planning and the text written afterwards. This resemblance declined in the following years. With adults, planning notes were obviously a different kind of thing altogether from the text later produced from them, differing from it both in form and in types of content.

These findings are all congruent with the thesis that what happens in writing development is the increasing differentiation of planning from text production. Different aspects of the differentiation are observed at different levels. At the metacognitive level it is shown in an increasing ability to recognize a variety of planning activities involved in composition that are distinct from a direct 'thinking of what to write'. At the level of thought tapped by thinking-aloud protocols it is shown in the apparently slow emergence of what we call conceptual planning—planning that consists of thinking *about* the composition rather than planning that consists of mentally rehearsing or creating the composition. At the level of product it is shown in the emergence of the *plan* as a formally and substantively distinct entity that can be operated on apart from the composition itself.

Our experimental procedures, by forcing planning to precede text production, undoubtedly favored the creation of tangible plans. It is therefore noteworthy that, in spite of this bias, 10-year-old writers tended not to produce plans that were distinct from text. This strengthens, therefore, the conclusion that for children of this age planning is not differentiated from production. What the youngest writers seemed to do was discover a way to smuggle text production into the planning period by using note-taking as a way of producing a first draft of text.

We know that mature writers, left to their own devices, will often intermix planning with production (Hayes and Flower, 1980). In these cases there may not be a tangible plan that is elaborated to the extent that it warrants comparison with the text itself. Notes, if any, may be little elaborated and only local in their application. We believe, however, that in these cases it is still profitable to think of the plan as a distinct entity, even though it may exist only in the mind of the writer, with no physical embodiment, and even though it grows up along with the composition instead of antedating it. It remains in these cases that the plan for a text is conceptually different from a mental representation of the text itself. The plan exists on a different conceptual plane and has different content. It contains intentions, strategies, priorities, alternatives, evaluations, justifications. Much or all of this may be reflected in the text, but there it is implicit and deeply enmeshed, whereas in the plan it is more explicit and susceptible to direct operation. The plan may have strengths and weaknesses distinct from those of the text. Large changes in the plan may show up as small changes in the text or small changes in the plan may show up as large changes in the text. The plan, in short, represents a different sort of thing to work with, in which the writer can accomplish things that are not readily accomplished in working directly with the text. Conversely, as many a writer testifies, things happen in working directly with the text that could not have been prefigured in the plan. Expert writers keep switching back and forth between planning and production, we suspect, because each complements the other; it is not a one-way affair in which planning feeds production. This complementary function, however, is one that depends upon planning and production becoming sufficiently differentiated.

In our analysis the developmental scenario goes approximately like this: At first all the child's conscious attention is involved in the immediate written expression. Global intentions, world knowledge, discourse knowledge—these all have their influence on the child, as can easily be demonstrated, but it appears that their influence is tacit and unconscious, like the influence of our syntactic knowledge on our everyday speech. Over the course of childhood and early adolescence, thought becomes sufficiently detached from immediate expression that the young writer can generate text content in abbreviated forms and mentally manipulate it in advance of writing—delete, arrange, seek new content, etc. At this stage we may accordingly speak of the plan as distinct from the text and existing more or less as a mental table of contents for the text. Not until later adolescence do we typically see the plan taking on conceptual properties of its own, so that text organization, intentions, problems, strategies, and the like are clearly represented and capable of being operated upon, rather than remaining implicit and in the background.

In concluding, we need to say something about how firm and generalizable we take these findings to be. Let us first make it clear that we have no stake in assigning age norms to the developmental scenario we have sketched. Other student populations with different educational histories might be considerably advanced or retarded compared to the students we studied. Although age-norm questions are potentially interesting, our research cannot answer them, nor do such questions have a significant bearing on the conclusions we have drawn. We are interested in understanding the nature of planning in writing and how it develops. The developmental scenario that we have arrived at is supported by a sufficient variety of converging types of evidence that we have considerable confidence in it as a description of the student population we studied. The basic developmental process also seems to have such a strong internal consistency to it that we find it hard to imagine that it would not be found in other populations, even though the age norms might be considerably different.

One type of apparently contrary evidence may be anticipated, however. That is evidence from school situations that feature a great deal of social support for the composing process—peer discussions, cooperative writing, conferencing, etc. Anecdotal reports already suggest that instances can be found where rather sophisticated planning seems to be carried out by children of ages younger than the youngest in our population.

This raises an important issue. In one sense it can certainly be argued that young children already have competence in planning. They surely set goals in their daily lives, select strategies for reaching those goals, anticipate obstacles and think of ways to get around them, and so on. It is not surprising, therefore, that under the right sort of circumstances they can demonstrate these same kinds of planning abilities in writing. Doesn't this mean that the picture of a slow, difficult course of development in planning abilities is, if not a sham, at least a shambles?

It will be instructive to consider several different circumstances in which precocious composition planning may appear. First, it is no doubt possible to produce a demonstration such as Socrates did in the *Meno*, leading a child solely though questioning to carry out rather sophisticated planning. We have done something like this with individual students ourselves, and it is a key element in teacher-pupil conferencing. In Bereiter and Scardamalia (1982) there is a group planning protocol that shows planning far beyond the normal 12-year-old level, in this case stimulated by the group process. Because different children had different ideas about what to include in a story, the planning was forced to a more conceptual level where alternatives were explicitly weighed and analyzed. Another circumstance that might provoke higher-level planning would be one in which the child faced a significant communication problem—a strong need to convince a hard-to-convince reader, for instance. In such a case, problematic aspects of the communication task might be sufficiently salient that the child would be found giving conscious attention to questions of strategy, subgoal specification, anticipation of obstacles, and the like.

Educators, considering such instances, are sometimes inclined to declare that there is no developmental barrier to reckon with and that the problems of writing instruction are solved: simply engage students in the conferences, group efforts, and real-life problems that have been found to enhance planning and other aspects of composition. These may well be good instructional approaches, but one should be clear about what they are doing and how they relate to development.

Cognitive development, as Donaldson (1978) among others has argued, does not consist of the acquisition of new elementary logical operations. It consists, from one perspective at least, of the acquisition of knowledge structures and control structures that enable the child to bring these elementary logical operations to bear on increasingly complex tasks, in increasingly flexible and deliberate ways. This is, generally, how we see the development of planning in writing. Young writers may have the elementary logical operations of planning available to them, but it takes the guiding questions of an adult or a favorably structured situation for these operations to be brought effectively into use. With maturity, writers become less dependent on external conditions and events to organize and stimulate their thought. Instead of having to be led by questions, they ask their own questions. Instead of needing to argue alternatives with their peers they produce and analyze alternatives themselves. Instead of needing a real-life problem context to stimulate goal-directed planning, they can start cold with an unchallenging topic and begin to formulate goals and problems of their own. That is what the development of planning ability seems to be about. Our effort in this paper has been to look beneath the surface of this ability to learn something about the conceptual and procedural knowledge of which it is constituted.

REFERENCES

Bereiter, C., and Scardamalia, M. From conversation to composition: The role of instruction in a developmental process. In R. Glaser (Ed.), *Advances in instructional psychology* (Vol. 2). Hillsdale, NJ: Lawrence Erlbaum Associates, 1982.

Bereiter, C., and Scardamalia, M. Cognitive coping strategies and the problem of 'inert knowledge'. In S. S. Chipman, J. W. Segal and R. Glaser (Eds), *Thinking and learning skills: Current research and open questions* (Vol. 2). Hillsdale, NJ: Lawrence Erlbaum Associates, in press.

Britton, J., Burgess, T., Martin, N., McLeod, A., and Rosen, H. *The development of writing abilities (11–18)*. London: Macmillan Education, 1975.

Donaldson, M. *Children's minds*. London: Croom Helm, 1978.

Emig, J. *The composing processes of twelfth graders*. Champaign, IL: National Council of Teachers of English, 1971.

Ericsson, K. A., and Simon, H. A. Verbal reports as data. *Psychological Review*, 1980, **87**, 215–251.

Flavell, J. H. Metacognition and cognitive monitoring: A new area of cognitive-developmental inquiry. *American Psychologist*, 1979, **34**, 906–911.

Flower, L., and Hayes, J. A. The cognition of discovery: Defining a rhetorical problem. *College Composition and Communication*, 1980, **31**, 21–32.

Gould, J. D. Experiments on composing letters: Some facts, some myths, and some observations. In L. W. Gregg and E. R. Steinberg (Eds), *Cognitive processes in writing*. Hillsdale, NJ: Lawrence Erlbaum Associates, 1980.

Hayes, J. R., and Flower L. Identifying the organization of writing processes. In L. W. Gregg and E. R. Steinberg (Eds), *Cognitive processes in writing*. Hillsdale, NJ: Lawrence Erlbaum Associates, 1980.

Hayes-Roth, B., and Hayes-Roth, F. A cognitive model of planning. *Cognitive Science*, 1979, **3**, 275–310.

Jones, B. F., and Amiran, M. *Applying structure of text and learning strategies research to develop programs of instruction for low achieving students*. Paper presented at the NIE-LRDC Conference on Thinking and Learning Skills, Pittsburgh, Pennsylvania, October 1980.

Paris, P. L. *Discourse schemata as knowledge and as regulators of text production*. Unpublished Master's thesis, York University, 1980.

Robinson, F. G., Tickle, J., and Brison, D. W. *Inquiry training: Fusing theory and practice*. Toronto: Ontario Institute for Studies in Education, 1972.

Scardamalia, M., and Bereiter, C. *Audience-adaptedness in knowledge-telling and problem-solving strategy*. Paper presented the Conference on Models and Processes of Children's Writing, Albany, NY, 1980.

Scardamalia, M., Bereiter, C., and Goelman, H. The role of production factors in writing ability. In M. Nystrand (Ed.), *What writers know: The language, process, and structure of written discourse*. New York: Academic Press, 1982.

Simon, J. *La langue écrité de l'enfant*. Paris: Presses Universitaires de France, 1973.

Young, R. E., Becker, A. L., and Pike, K. E. *Rhetoric: Discovery and change*. New York: Harcourt, Brace and World, 1970.

PRACTICE

Explorations in the Development of Writing
Edited by Barry M. Kroll and Gordon Wells
© 1983 John Wiley & Sons Ltd.

8

Looking At What Children Can Do

Barbara Kamler and Gary Kilarr

When four-and-a-half year old Coline finishes writing her six-page story in a book of unlined paper assembled by her teacher, she moves to the teacher's desk to show her efforts (figure 1).

When nine-year-old Natalie and Bryan finish collaborating on their experience at the school athletics carnival, they make a more legible second copy on a single sheet of lined computer paper and place it in the conference folder on the teacher's desk (figure 2).

What can we say about either of these writing products? We can smile at Coline's cute little effort in writing, but other than three recognizable words, *I*, *can* and *no*, her piece is undecipherable. All other spellings are nonsensical; as well, she uses five misplaced full stops. Natalie and Bryan's writing lacks detail and interest for the reader. It is extremely untidy for a second copy. They misspell four words, misuse capital letters and quotation marks.

It is not difficult to see how these writers' efforts deviate from the conventions of our writing system. Such product evaluation, however, ignores the context of the writing process and the intentions of the writers. Without that information we have a very limited understanding of their capabilities. We can learn a great deal more about writing development if we look at what children can do rather than at what they can't. To do so we need to look beyond the products, to the individuals in the act of learning to write.

To learn what children can do when they write, we went to the classroom to watch the process of writing. We found a small school in a highly mobile rural community of New South Wales, where the principal was interested in improving writing. An initial presentation was made to the staff, using videotapes of real kids and real teachers from writing-process classrooms in the pioneering New Hampshire Study (Graves *et al.*, 1978/80). We wanted to give teachers a sense of what could happen when children were given responsibility for their own writing and allowed to experience writing as a process of rehearsing, drafting, and revising (Murray, 1980).

Page 2

Page 1

Figure 1

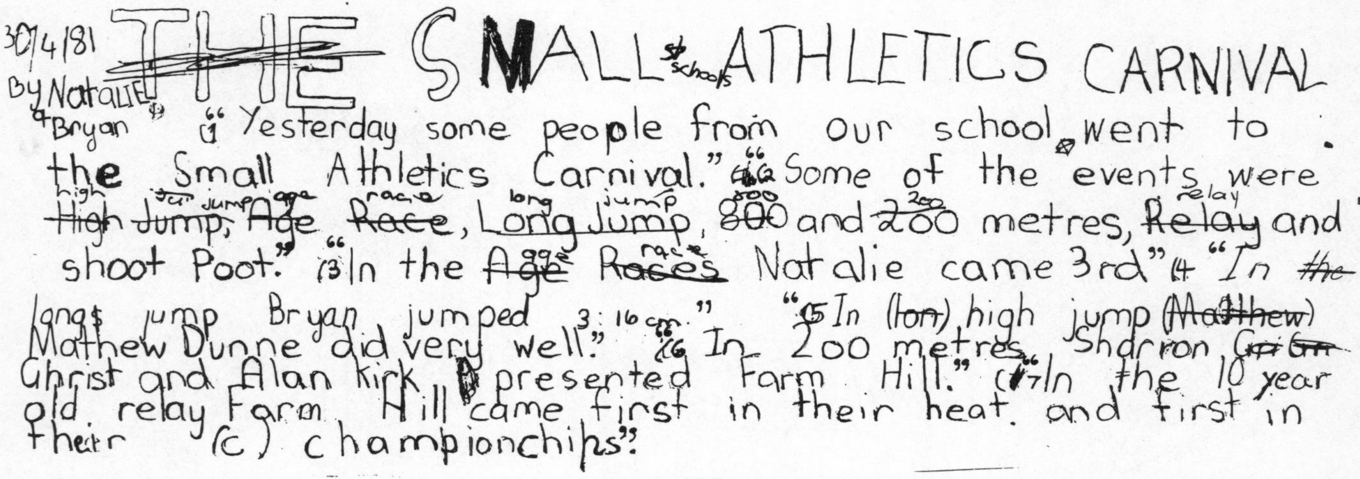

30/4/81
By Natalie

THE SMALL ATHLETICS CARNIVAL

¹ "Yesterday some people from our school went to the Small Athletics Carnival." ² "Some of the events were high jump, long jump, Age Race, 800 and 200 metres, Relay and shoot Poot." ³ "In the Age Races Natalie came 3rd." ⁴ "In the long jump Bryan jumped 3.16 cm." ⁵ "In (the) high jump (Matthew) jumped Sharron" ⁶ "In 200 metres" ⁷ "In the 10 year old relay Farm Hill came first in their heat and first in their (c) championchips."

Matthew Dunne did very well. Christ and Alan Kirk presented Farm Hill.

Figure 2

We were forthright about our intentions. We wanted to see writing-process classrooms develop in the local area; we wanted to collect data in such rooms to learn what kids could do as writers. A move in this direction would probably involve teachers in giving more time to writing and would encourage them to find ways of intervening during the process through the writing conference rather than at the end. We would be available to help by answering questions about their children and the writing process, but the teachers would be in control of the changes they made. The development of a writing classroom would take time and manifest itself differently for each teacher.

Our intentions were guided by Graves' (1981b) research challenge for the 80's: 'Slow down, look at the full context of writing, involve teachers, and get to know the full potential of children and teachers' (pp.496–497). The progress was indeed slow. Teachers struggled with what it meant to give young writers control and made changes at their own pace as they felt ready. Gradually we moved into the classrooms to work alongside teachers and collect writing-process data.

Two classrooms became our focus for finding out what children can do when they write: kindergarten and grade 4. To tap the intentions of writers in these rooms we relied on direct observation of the process during composing and writing conferences. When children were ready to write, we sat beside them to observe the full context of composing—to listen for the oral accompaniment to the text, the interruptions, the dialogue; to watch for aspects of the process writers struggled to control as the writing evolved. During writing conferences we observed teachers depending on children to create the context of composing after the fact; we watched them probing children's meanings, concerns and struggles by asking process questions, questions that provide information about learner's intentions.

Our earlier review of the products of Coline, a kindergarten writer, and Natalie and Bryan, grade 4 writers, gives a very limited explanation of what these children can do. Looking at their products in the context of process will tell us more. Accordingly, we will focus on Coline's composing process to see what she knows and on Natalie and Bryan's writing conference to learn about their control over the writing process.

COLINE'S COMPOSING PROCESS

Four-and-a-half-year-old Coline writes in a room that allows kindergarten children to experiment with writing from the beginning of the school year. The children control the writing; they determine what they want to write and figure out how to do it. There are no external demands for neat letter forms, proper spacing, writing on the line or conventional spelling. The only requirement is that children write, i.e. put pen, pencil or crayon to paper to express their meanings. What is eventually achieved varies greatly from child to child. Many children tell their story with pictures, some elaborated and coloured, others with only the barest detail. Many children add writing to their pictures; some use letter-like shapes or letter forms, while others combine letters into words to produce their messages.

Coline's use of letters is unconventional, but not random or disorganized. Her six-page book (see figure 1) makes perfect sense to Coline. She matches the print on each page with the story she reads aloud as follows:

Page 1:   The Front
Page 2:   There was
Page 3:   flowers in
Page 4:   the garden
Page 5:   someone came and watered them
Page 6:   The End

Coline has a coherent message to convey and does not need to rely on an adult to write it for her. She actively constructs written language using the knowledge she has. She relies on the letters of her name and other letters she knows, using both lower case and capital letter forms. The three standard spellings on page 3 (figure 1) result from copying 'I can write stories' from the front of her writing folder.

Coline knows a great deal about the conventions of print and books. She reads from the front of the book to the back, from the top of the page to the bottom. Consistently she reads the same story from her print and attempts to make a one-to-one correspondence between her spoken and printed word. Most fascinating, she deciphers her meaning from graphic symbols that bear no sound–symbol correspondence. We have labelled her use of graphic symbols, primary inventions (p.i.), letters combined into clusters that seem to function as words, and represent a stable verbal message. These inventions are prephonetic, i.e. lacking in sound-symbol relationship, and are different from spelling inventions. Unlike young children who invent their own spellings, Coline does not use letters to represent the sounds in words. Her primary inventions are not attempts to spell but rather to represent a general message.

Coline has a great deal to learn about writing in conventional alphabetic orthography. She needs to learn the relation between sound and symbol and how to put these symbols in a particular order. In the meantime, she *can* make symbols and understands what writing can do, so she begins to write using what she knows. To watch her growing control of the writing process and understand her use of primary inventions, we will examine five writing episodes at monthly intervals, from April to August. A writing episode will include not only the written product but process information as well; i.e. what the child does before, during and after a single writing.

April

Coline rehearses for writing by first drawing a two-storey house in pencil. She then fills her page with layers of crayon colour, red covered by blue covered by brown. Finally she scratches her message from the waxy surface (figure 3).

Figure 3

Coline's task seems to demand great concentration. She ignores the children around her and is silent as she composes. Graves (1981a) observes that 'most young writers who make the transition from oral to written discourse must produce language and sound when they write' (p.21). Coline, however, produces no sound as she writes. This may be because she is not attempting to attribute phoneme-grapheme correspondence to her primary inventions.

Many young writers who do not demonstrate the relationship between sound and symbol will not attempt to read their early attempts at writing. This does not stop Coline. She believes she can read her own messages and within the context of a writing episode, consistently reads back the same message, although the next day she cannot. When Coline finishes composing, she reads her message aloud, using her finger to match her p.i.'s to her spoken message as follows:

WWM	This is a
Ltol	double
Ltw	decker
ticoli	house

Although there are few cues in the print itself to help her read, she seems to create many boundaries to help her keep track of where she is in the text. In her earlier six-page story (figure 1), the individual pages create distinct boundaries. Her p.i.'s are further demarcated from one another by underlining and from the rest of the orthographic display on the page by a circle. In her April piece, however, she composes the entire message on one page. Having lost the page boundaries that earlier helped her consistently match p.i.'s with spoken message, she now relies on a vertical page arrangement. Her new boundaries include words following one another in column form down the page, an asterisk-like shape, and an occasional use of the full stop. Still she has difficulty. She reads her message aloud a number of times during this episode but has problems making her spoken words match the amount of print on the page as follows:

	Rereading 2	*Rereading 3*
WWM	This is a double	This is a
Ltol	decker	double
Ltw	house	decker
ticoli		house

On the second reading she matches different p.i.'s with her spoken message. Her voice stops with house and she still has one p.i. left over, *ticoli*. She scratches her head and sighs. She reads it aloud a third time to regain control; the message stays the same and she succeeds in making voice and print end at the same time, as in her first reading. This is the first indication that Coline will not be satisfied to leave a piece until she has manoeuvred a voice-print match.

May

While her peers put away their maths materials and gather slowly on the orange rug, Coline gathers her writing materials and moves to the back of the room, away from the commotion. She writes, oblivious to the noise at the front of the room. For the first time she produces her message orally as she composes. She makes her illustration to the right of her print (figure 4).

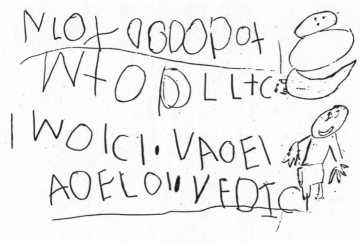

Figure 4

In this piece Coline does not list her p.i.'s vertically. Rather, she begins at the left of the page and moves right. At the end of each line of print she begins again at the left. This horizontal page arrangement seems to provide Coline with less distinct boundaries than before. Perhaps to regain some of this sense of boundary she again utilizes underlining and full stops. Visually the first two lines of print look like two words separated by underlining; the second two lines of print look like four words separated by full stops.

This conventional page arrangement is a step toward the left to right spatial arrangement of print. It is a step, however, that causes Coline a new difficulty in reading her message. As before, she knows what she wants to say and attempts to make her p.i.'s match the spoken message. She reads and rereads, clusters and reclusters her p.i.'s, attempting to match voice to print (table 1).

During the first three readings, Coline runs out of printed symbols before she can complete verbalizing her message. She seems confused and sighs, 'I forget'. She adds another p.i., *VFDICl*, to solve her problem, but she does not reread immediately afterward. Instead she draws a picture of a cat, a mat and a girl to the right of her p.i.'s. This drawing seems to be important as escape and breathing time rather than as illustration. The picture complete, she returns again to the task of rereading and makes a match on two consecutive attempts. To accomplish this, however, she abandons her earlier attempts to segment each line of print with her finger. Instead she treats each of the four lines of print as an entity. She briskly sweeps her finger across the print and divides her spoken message into four phrases which she matches to the four

Table 1

Writing	Statement of message during composing	Reading 1	Rereading 2	Rereading 3	Rereadings 4 and 5
NLOtOODOPOt WtoPLLtC wolcl	cat on the mat sat on	cat sat on the mat and the girl patted the cat on	cat sat on the mat and the girl	cat sat on the mat and the	cat sat on the mat and the girl ~~
VAOEl AOELOl VFDICl (not added until after rereading 3)	and the girl patted the cat on the mat		patted the cat	girl patted the cat	patted the cat ~~
					on the mat

lines of print. She is persistent and determined to make her message match the print. Unable to work out the match, she is still curious; she experiments. She is more bewildered than frustrated and concentrates for 15 minutes on reading alone.

June

Unlike the case in other writing episodes, Coline is not oblivious to the activity around her. She sits with a group of boys, rather than alone, and watches intently as Raymond draws rockets and creates the accompanying sound-effects. The entire writing episode seems to be surrounded by more language. For the first time Coline begins the composing by verbalizing her intentions. She lays two blank pieces of paper on the desk before her and announces: 'I'm going to do a picture on that one and write on this one.' This, in fact, is what she does. The numbers beside the p.i.'s indicate the order in which they are written by Coline (figure 5).

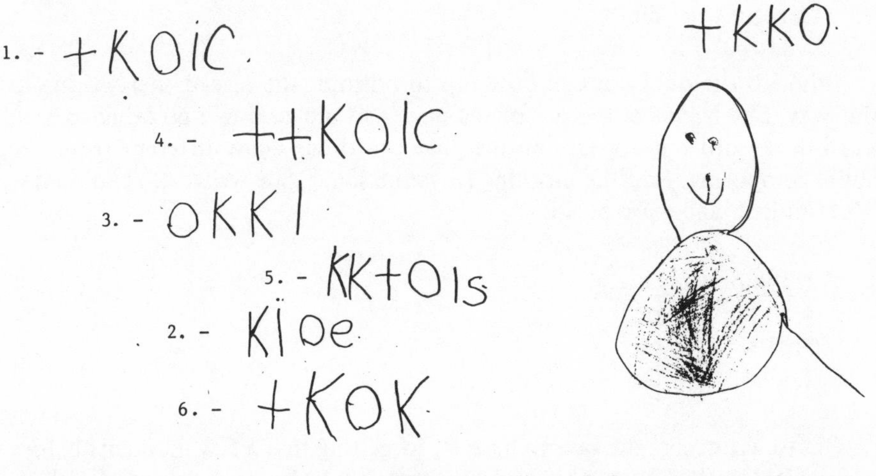

Figure 5

This product indicates more progress in Coline's writing. Her handwriting is more controlled, the size of her letters more uniform, her boundaries more defined than before. Her composing process shows how demanding this new step forward is. Coline spends 20 minutes just writing the first three p.i.'s and throughout the composing actively seeks interruptions. She chats with the boys and comments on their pictures. She writes two letters, then noisily taps her pencil on the table. She completes a p.i., then rocks her chair back and forth on its squeaky back legs. There is much physical turmoil in these pauses from the writing.

The length of time spent composing and the effort expended in making well-formed letters possibly affects Coline's page arrangement. Instead of composing horizontally as in the June piece, she returns to a vertical page arrangement. While composing, however, she does not proceed in a neat progression from the top of the page to the bottom. Instead, she begins by writing the first p.i. at the top of the page, the second at the bottom, the third in the middle as follows. The transcription to the right of the p.i. indicates Coline's reading:

1. tkoic	cat
2. kioe	sat
3. okki	mat

Coline pauses, then rereads what she's written as follows:

1. tkoic	cat
3. okki	sat
2. kioe	mat

Although she does not compose top to bottom, she rereads her writing in this way. She begins at the top of the page and moves down pointing to each word in the order it appears on the page, an order quite different from her initial composing. Still the meaning stays the same. She writes 4. *tkkoic* says, 'I'm finished' and reads again:

1. tkoic	cat
4. ttkoic	sat
3. okki	on
2. kioe	the

'Got to write mat' she says to herself, forgetting that a few moments before she not only called both *okki* and *kioe* 'mat' but also said she was finished. Each word addition demands a rereading by Coline. Each rereading in turn changes the correspondence between p.i.'s and her meaning for them. She writes 5. *kktols*, presumably to be 'mat'. But the positioning of the word on the page ensures that she calls it 'the' instead, as happens:

1. tkoic	cat
4. ttkoic	sat
3. okki	on
5. kktols	the
2. kioe	mat

Things seem to be going well for Coline. Her demand that voice and print match is being satisfied. She rereads again and maintains the same match. Then, composing at the point of her pencil, she says 'eating'. Realizing, of course, that there is no corresponding p.i. for 'eating' she adds one more, 6. *tkok*. The story complete, there are now six clearly defined p.i.'s on the page before her and six clearly defined words in the message in her head. The reading should be straightforward. This, however, is not the case. Seven oral rereadings follow until Coline finally makes the match as charted (table 2).

Table 2

Written text	Rereadings 1–3	Rereading 4	Rereadings 5–6	Rereading 7
1. tkoic	cat sat	cat sat	cat	cat sat
4. ttkoic	on	on	sat	on
3. okki	the	the	on	the
5. kktols	mat	mat	the	mat
2. kioe	eating	eating	mat	eating
6. tkok		oranges	eating	oranges

For some reason in the first three rereadings she pairs two spoken words, 'cat' and 'sat' with the one p.i. *tkoic*. Consequently she has one p.i. left over at the end, *tkok*, and no spoken word to go with it. On the fourth rereading she solves the problem by adding another spoken word, 'oranges'. All should go well now. On the fifth and sixth readings, however, she returns to her earlier behaviour of matching one spoken word to one p.i. As a result she now finds there is no written p.i. left to match the spoken 'oranges'. At last, on the seventh rereading she remanoeuvres and makes the match.

Such persistence! Coline will not stop until she reaches such closure. She adjusts and readjusts her division of the message until she succeeds. This self-imposed reading seems to be her way of gaining control of the writing.

Following her seventh rereading, she makes her illustration on the second piece of paper she put aside at the beginning of the composing. She seems pleased with herself as she draws a picture of a smiling cat and affixes a label *tkko* saying, 'See, I writed cat at the top'.

The message itself sounds like a rehash of a basal reader story line and is not interesting as a product. The process of getting there, however, is fascinating. Getting the message down in primary inventions is demanding. Coline pays most attention to the demands of making print and controlling the letters, less to her information. It is possible that while she writes she first makes her random clusters of letters and only later attributes meaning to them. Certainly children do this with their art. Perhaps there is a stage in the development of young writers where they write first, mean later.

July

In July Coline turned five, grew taller, and seemed more willing to assert herself. As a writer, she demonstrates a growing awareness of conventional orthography. Before school, she spends time in the classroom with Susan and Kathy cutting out butterfly shapes and colouring faces on them. She writes *To* on the inside of one and says: 'Look. It says To'. During writing time she sits beside Susan whose writing, like Coline's, is prephonetic. Unlike Coline, however, Susan does not worry about matching the print with her voice. Her message often changes from one rereading to the next. After composing this day, Susan reads her story aloud, as follows, while Coline watches closely:

Writing: PROOEO FOtO LOOtOtO TDZO XO IOTOT

Reading: This is a funny man and he is walking with me.

Coline looks at Susan's paper, then at Susan and announces knowingly: 'Susan, this is how you write "is" '. On the front of her own folder Coline then writes *is*. The surprises never end when we watch children in process. Coline's visual memory has been working hard. She writes in a classroom immersed in print, labels and story reading. Now she displays her awareness of conventional orthography by producing it.

Coline's own writing episode becomes almost more speech than writing. She is very talkative and chats with Susan and Kathy throughout the composing. She provides a running commentary on what she's doing:

> I'm drawing my picture. A spaceship. It's a mighty mouse space-
> ship. It's a big spaceship. Two windows. Colour it in. What colour
> is a spaceship? (*she takes a brown crayon*) Spaceship. Spaceship.
> Spaceship. There.

She interrupts the writing to draw the spaceship, but waits until the end of composing to make the picture of the girl. The drawing, as such, seems to serve as both illustration and context for the writing (figure 6).

In this piece Coline evidences the same persistent concern for matching printed symbols with her spoken message. This time, however, her task is even more complicated because during the composing she moves back and forth between the two pages while during the rereading she reads all the print on one page before she moves to the next. Full stops emerge again to define p.i. boundaries. As usual, she has difficulty matching voice with print. However, Coline works through numerous rereadings and reclusterings of p.i.'s and eventually ends up with this match:

Page 1

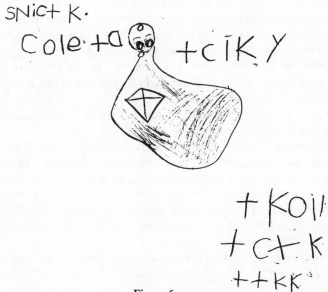

Figure 6

Page 1:		*Page 2:*	
IcNOile.	I	cole.td	my
YCOille.	was	SNiCtK.	dog
ICOle.	in	tciKy	was
ciot.	my	tKoil.	pulling
ttkaq.	space	tctk	my pants
ICtCi.	ship	ttkk	along

Three of Coline's p.i.'s begin with capital 'I'; but, in *IcNOile* she may be making her first one-to-one correspondence between sound and symbol! During a conference her teacher excitedly points out to Coline: 'I see that you've written *I* just the way adults do.' Coline nods in a matter-of-fact way. 'I know little *i* too,' she says, apparently meaning something quite different. She then proceeds to go through both pages pointing out the seven lower case *i*'s and three upper case *I*'s she has used in her message. This is a child gaining confidence and 'look what I can do' control.

August

Coline continues the slow move towards conventional orthography in her August piece. Her use of 'I' plays a crucial role in helping her read her writing. This may not, however, be evident from the product (figure 7).

She begins by composing *Molelttmclt*. She starts to read silently, pauses, then adds the *I* at the beginning of the line, reading aloud 'I wish'. She pauses again, muttering 'Oh boy', then adds a second *I* between the letters *t* and *m* and reads aloud 'I was'. She is revising the first line of print and consciously making a sound–symbol correspondence between the spoken and written 'I'. A major step forward. She does not sound the 'I' beforehand, but does read it aloud in context after the addition has been made.

She continues composing this line of print, saying the next word aloud before she writes it, 'a' for *a*, another correspondence. She draws a window shape explaining, 'See that's just a little picture of my jewel box. I got a piano jewel box. It's not a real piano. It's a painted on piano'. She concludes the line by saying 'queen' before she writes *kEl*.

This may be the first time Coline invents a spelling. When children begin to spell inventively, they hear and write the initial consonants of words. Here Coline uses *k* for the initial consonant of queen followed by *E*, the letter name of the vowel sound in queen. This may be accidental; this may still be a p.i. As Coline does not sound the individual letters, it is difficult to support one way or another. It does, however, seem to mark her first step away from primary invention and toward spelling invention.

Coline reads this first line of print four times, meticulously and consistently segmenting the print with her finger as follows:

> *Print:* I moleltt I mclt a kEl
> *Voice:* I wish   I was a queen

Coline maintains the same voice–print match on every rereading without confusion. She has created signals within the print itself to cue her reading. The three standard sound–symbol correspondences seem to function in her piece as clear boundary markers:

Figure 7

I ——————— I ——————— a ——————— .

Coline hums while she draws a girl's figure, then a series of blocks, which she colours in and embellishes with 8's, a carry-over from her work with the number 8 in the lesson preceding writing. After ten minutes of drawing, which seems to act as rehearsal for what follows, she begins to write again. She says each word aloud as she composes, places them vertically down the page and rereads as she goes.

This story addition demonstrates no sound–symbol correspondence, but Coline has no difficulty consistently matching p.i.'s to the voiced message through several rereadings:

ttktolc	My
lotoL	baby
tole	was
tole	playing
tol	with
tkol	her
told	blocks

This second sentence has nothing to do with the first. The relationship between them, however, is not important to Coline in terms of a final product; instead she seems to use her messages as a vehicle for working through her understanding of how reading and writing work. A review of her messages from March through August seems to confirm this:

> *There was flowers in the garden. Someone came and watered them.*
> *This is a double decker house.*
> *Cat sat on the mat and the girl patted the cat on the mat.*
> *Cat sat on the mat eating oranges.*
> *I was in my spaceship. My dog was pulling my pants along.*
> *I wish I was a queen. My baby was playing with her blocks.*

We can say many things about these messages. They are not very interesting. They are not personal. They do not seem overtly related to Coline's current interests, daily life, or school experiences. This, however, is analysing the product out of context. Graves (1981a) helps us look again taking context into account:

> There is much for children to learn to control in writing that is very different than speech. They must supply the context, write in a certain direction, learn to control the space–time dimensions of writing on a flat surface, understand what the medium of writing can do, know the relation between sound and symbols, know how to make the symbols, learn to put symbols in a particular order, and while composing one operation understand its relation to the entire order of what has been and will be in the message and compose in a medium where the audience is not usually present (p.19).

When learning to write, children need to solve a complex array of problems. Because Coline is given control of the writing process from the beginning, she is allowed to solve these problems in the context of creating her intended messages. Coline's messages are well-informed and meaningful. She does not write nonsense. Her focus is on meaning to the extent that, once conceived, she consistently reads the same message back from the page. The demands of making print, however, require enormous concentration. It is not surprising that beginning writers, like Coline, may need to pay less attention to their information, and more attention to controlling the conventions.

This does not mean that Coline's story-making ability is limited. Compare her six messages with this dictated story composed by her in April, but scribed by her teacher:

> Two fairies flew up into the sky and they saw a big tree. The tree was nice and leafy and they got a branch off the tree and they used it for a fly swat. They killed three flies. The flies didn't like it so they got a dog to bark at the fairies. The fairies scared the dog with their fly swat and flew away somewhere else, where they couldn't get the flies on them.

The story is more complex and elaborated than her other messages; it shows a strong sense of story convention and structure. Well then, shouldn't Coline be dictating all the time and not waste her time eking out little meagre, uninteresting messages? Her teacher thinks not. She allows children to dictate stories from time to time, in order to see the complexity they are capable of emerge on the page in visual form. More often, however, she expects and encourages children to write their own stories; she knows they are not going to be like dictated ones because the children are struggling to control reading and writing in an holistic manner.

Aware of the discrepancy between her young writers' intentions and what they get down on the page, she encourages children in conference to explore these intentions further. She asks for more information, for the story behind the approximations on the page, for the context. With this information out, the children can begin to hear their writing voices and the teacher can understand and encourage them in the process. She does not worry about product; she knows the process will show her how her young writers are developing.

Coline likes writing and believes she can do it. She works very hard and concentrates deeply on the task. Her teacher has described her as the most stable writer in the class in terms of positive attitude and ability to apply herself to writing for extended periods of time. On most occasions, the minimum time spent is 20 minutes, the maximum 50 minutes.

Coline has gained impressive knowledge as she learns to solve the problems of writing. She uses 19 letters of the alphabet, 11 in lower case and 18 in capital letter form. Her growing mastery of letter formation indicates control of shape, uniformity of size and appropriate placement orientation. She is aware of the left-to-right, top-to-bottom spatial and sequential arrangement of print, and most importantly to her development as a reader and writer, she knows that print must make sense. She knows that letters can be combined into words, that there is a one-to-one correspondence between the spoken and written word, and that writing conveys a meaningful message. Coline knows a lot about writing. It would be so easy to underestimate her knowledge, however, if we had prevented her from experimenting and controlling the writing, by doing it for her or not asking her to write at all.

NATALIE AND BRYAN'S WRITING CONFERENCE

Although Natalie and Bryan are older writers (in grade 4) and their efforts are closer than Coline's to the conventions of our writing system, it is easy to underestimate their knowledge of writing too. In our earlier focus on their product (figure 2) we looked at what they didn't know. To learn about what they do know, we need to look more closely at them in the act of writing.

Although Natalie and Bryan were not observed during the composing process itself, they were observed in a writing conference discussing their piece with their teacher. In this conference the teacher tries to get back to the composing context and gain knowledge of Natalie and Bryan's intentions by asking process questions: 'What is this for?', 'Tell me why you did this?'. She wants to know why the children have made certain decisions in order to respond fully to their intentions and learn what they can do. Questions of this nature put the teacher at great risk because the answers children give are often not expected. She knows, however, that each conference will be different and the unexpected is her expectation.

When the teacher looks at Natalie and Bryan's piece in conference, she is not unaware of the errors they have made. She expects errors, because she encourages children to experiment with written language, but treats the errors as a source of information for instruction. The piece is not there to be evaluated and marked—it is there to be 'conferenced', listened to, developed. Her process of teaching is positive; she tries to establish a primary focus on what her writers can do.

To this end, she develops a list of *Things I Can Remember to Do* with individual children in conference. The teacher uses this list to help her focus on what children can do and it is recorded on the back cover of their writing folders. When children show in drafts that they are able or desire to use a particular convention, an addition is made to the list, worded by the child and scribed by the teacher. A comparison of Natalie and Bryan's lists indicate how each child is developing control over written language (figure 8).

Natalie and Bryan are encouraged to experiment with ways of controlling their writing, rather than to strive for adult-like products. They write in a room where children choose their own topics, initiate and guide their writing

Bryan	Natalie	
*	*	Title
*	*	Author's name
*	*	Date
*	*	Capital for a person's name
*	*	Comma for word lists
*	*	Full-stop at end of sentences
	*	Revision
	*	The end
	*	Circle misspellings
	*	Guessing
*		Capital at beginning of sentence
*		Illustration
*		Question mark
*		Quotation mark

Figure 8

through rehearsing, drafting and revision. When four or five stories are completed, they select the one they wish to publish. They discuss the piece with the teacher in conference and when it is ready for publication, the piece is typed by a volunteer parent, illustrated, bound, and finally shared with classmates and others.

Bryan and Natalie's piece on the athletics carnival is one they have decided to publish. Their initial conference on this piece was reduced to confusion as they attempted to sort out their collaborative effort from their very rough first draft. The teacher responded to their content as a reader, asking questions to clarify their intentions. The conference ended when Natalie and Bryan decided revisions were necessary to make better sense of the piece for themselves, and their readers. In the ensuing week they prepared a second draft and submitted it for conferencing.

The teacher is aware of the difficulties these young writers experienced in their first conference. She begins this second conference with process questions that will help her understand the changes the children have made in the second draft. We will examine sections of this second conference and examine how the teacher clarifies the children's intentions by looking at process.

T:	*You've written the story now, twice?*
N:	*Yes.*
B:	*Yes.*
N:	*We had to do it neater because we couldn't understand it. It got a bit messy.*
T:	*Yes that's OK* (Teacher acknowledges child's concern about messiness, but also suggests that mess is acceptable when drafting.)
N:	*We cut some parts out of it because some didn't make sense and some sentences were a bit long for a picture.*
T:	*I see.*
B:	*And some were shorter than some.*
T:	*Have you got the first draft that you did?*

The teacher establishes both drafts as a context within which the conference will develop. She is interested in the changes the children have made and in the reasoning behind their decisions.

T:	*Right, now this is the second draft?*
B:	*Yes.*
T:	*Okay. Will you read what you've done so far, Natalie.*
N:	*Yesterday, some people from our school went to the School Athletics Carnival. Some of the events were high*

jump, age race, long jump, 800 and 200 metres, relay and shot put. In the age races Natalie came third. In the long jump Bryan jumped 3 and 16 centimeters. In high jump, Mathew done very well. In 200 meters, Sharon, Chris and Alan Kirk presented Farm Vale. In the ten year old's relay, Farm Vale came first in the heat and first in the championships.

T: What changes have you made in the second draft?

B: We left out this sentence: In the eight hundred metres, Scott Connelly came third, because this other boy cut across all the lanes. It was a bit too long for a picture.

N: Yes.

T: What do you mean too long for a picture?

The teacher asks for clarification not of the content but of the children's decision to leave out the sentence. This is a direct focus on the process. Why did the writer make the change?

N: Well, if it is typed out, it might be a bit too long when we illustrate it.

T: Hmm . . . (Teacher nods and waits for elaboration.)

B: Well for our picture there'd be this boy cutting across the lane cutting Scott coming third and getting the ribbon and it would be a bit hard.

T: It would be a bit hard for drawing?

B: Yes.

It is clear that Bryan and Natalie have made a decision based on their understanding of the publishing process. The teacher then tries to clarify their original intention by moving to the specific content that was rejected.

T: Was it Scott who was disqualified or was it the boy?

N & B: No, it was the other boy.

B: Because Scott finally came fourth and the boy who came third was disqualified for cutting across lanes all the time.

T: In this first draft you've talked about Scott Connelly but when you've written it again, you've told me that you've left it out altogether.

B: We were going to draw a picture of him running in the relay.

N: We crossed that out and kind of mentioned him in the relay.

T: *If it was too long for that one page for your picture what*
        you can do if you like . . .

The teacher begins to suggest an alternative for the children
to consider. She is sure that the children are being hindered
by consideration of form. She wants to expand their
notion of the publishing parameters in the classroom. But
before she can complete her suggestion, Bryan jumps in
with a possible solution. It is at this point that the teacher
demonstrates a significant strategy that appears to be the
key to letting children control their writing. She lets Bryan
talk. She does not try to take over by making the children
listen to her suggestion. She gives the children control over
their work. The teacher waits.

B: *We could just split it up.*
T: *Yes, keep that whole sentence in and split it up, because if*
        you are thinking of the pictures, we can work it somehow
        so that we can get the picture . . .
B: *Yes, I've seen a book that's illustrated on one side with the*
        sentence and on the next page it's got a picture with the
        writing on it.
N: *It's got a little picture up the top.*

Again Bryan interrupts. The teacher waits. Natalie picks
up the thread. She has been pondering the concept also.
Both children discuss what they intend among themselves.
The teacher is ignored. She waits and nods or restates the
children's intent. In this way the teacher shows the children
they control the writing. The teacher follows, does not
lead.

T: *Hmmmm.*
B: *And on the next page after that, it's got a great big picture*
        of the next part that happens and it's got a little bit of
        writing down at the bottom.
N: *Yes. That's what we wanted to do! Wasn't it?*
B: *Yes, I think it was.*
N: *Yes, that was what we wanted to kind of do.*
T: *Have a picture?*
B: *Yes. Have a whole picture on just one page.*
T: *With just a tiny bit of writing?*
N & B: *Yes.*

T: *And what about on the next page? Have all the writing? . . .*
N & B: *Yes, have all the writing and a little picture.*
T: *So, you've got a big picture . . .*
N & B: *And a little writing and a little picture and big writing.*
T: *Got it. Well, in that case you shouldn't cross out sentences
you like just because they won't fit in with the picture. It
can be typed specially so that it will fit in and you can do
the pictures that you'd like to do. Did you like that sentence or did you only leave it out because of the picture?*

The teacher's role has been that of catalyst. She has
removed form as a hindrance and the children have found
a different solution. As a conclusion she restates her
understanding of Natalie's and Bryan's intention and ends
with a question, offering them the possibility of returning
to their original notion. The teacher has clearly expanded
the children's notion of things they can do. They now have
greater freedom to make changes.

N & B: *We only left it out because of the picture.*
B: *The sentence was real good.*
T: *Okay.* (Bryan begins to write the sentence on the draft.)

In a conference there is always the possibility that writers
will want to make changes. These revisions can take any
form from the addition of a full stop or sentence to a
rearrangement of the entire piece; they may be the result of
discoveries made while rereading the piece or discussing it
in conference. While Bryan is busy adding the sentence
they have agreed on Natalie reads the piece silently and
states in an embarrassed tone:

N: *You see this. It doesn't make sense because we've got
championchips instead of ships.*
T: *Alright, change it then.*

In this fourth class the children are expected to write words
correctly if they know them, but also expected to 'have a
go' at any words they want to use while composing. In this
way the teacher promotes getting the meaning down during
the writing process — a matter of fluency. This is not to say
the teacher ignores spelling. Quite the contrary. The
teacher looks for opportunities to refine the spelling skills

of the children during conferences. Natalie discovers her misspelling while rereading and makes the change. The teacher has decided this spelling is not a problem; her response is quick, supportive and non-judgmental. She wants her children to learn to be self-reliant spellers; she encourages them to discover their own misspellings and gives no penalty for making them. During this conference, spelling is incidental to the main purpose of clarifying their meaning. At a subsequent point in the conference, however, the teacher spends more time dealing with a misspelling, setting aside temporarily the purpose of the conference.

B: *So I'll finish it off. Where is it?* (Bryan continues to add the sentence reading from the first draft as he writes on the second.) *Scott Connelly came third because the other boy cut across the lane and the other boy got dis . . .* (He begins to sound out the word.) *How do you spell disqualified?*

N: *It's on there, Bryan.* (Natalie points to the first draft.)

T: *Who guessed this spelling for disqualified?*

B: *Me . . . dis . . . qual . . . i . . . fied.* (Syllabifies his spelling.) *Is that right?*

T: *You did it all right except for the ending, that's all. That's really a good guess. Did you guess that, Bryan?*

B: *Yes.*

T: *Good on you, that's a really good guess.*

B: *So what's on the end?*

T: *You've got disqualified ending in f.i.d.e. You've got all the letters right except . . .*

B: *Oh . . . f.i.d. is it?*

T: *No.*

B: *F.i.e.d. . . . uhh . . . fied, that's it.*

The word disqualified is a crucial part of their athletics carnival experience, but one that is new to them. The teacher can see that Natalie and Bryan have used their knowledge of other words they are familiar with, i.e. side, outside, seaside, to spell disqualified. She continues to support the practices she has instituted in the classroom: *'That's a really good guess'*, and responds with the only No in the entire conference. This No is direct feedback to Bryan which causes him to make another guess; he then decides the proper spelling without further clarification.

It is interesting to note the children make these changes

during the conference rather than later back at their desks.
This allows the teacher to help Natalie and Bryan with
their intentions and also provides an essential opportunity
to observe the children in process. When Bryan adds the
sentence to their piece, the teacher observes him adding
quotation marks at the end. Curious about his intention,
she opens the discussion with a question. Quotation marks
are referred to as sixty-sixes and ninety-nines in this
discussion.

T: *The ninety-nines you just added here, what are they for*
     Bryan?
B: *Umm . . . because we're really saying the whole story.*
     It's kind of like Natalie and I are telling it to someone else.
T: *So you . . .*
N: *Yes, I don't think we need them with each sentence,*
     because they know that we are talking so they should just
     be at the beginning and ending of our story.
T: *You put those in . . .*
B: *Do we need it for events?*

It is obvious the children are not entirely clear about the use
of quotation marks. They have over-generalized the use of
the punctuation to include when they as authors are
'telling' the story. The teacher does not tell them they are
wrong. Instead, she attempts to build on what she believes
Natalie can do. Natalie has used quotation marks successfully in a previous story and this process knowledge has
been recorded on her writing folder. The teacher tries to
provide an opportunity for Natalie to control the conference
and solve the problem.

T: *Well, I know from Natalie's writing folder she's used sixty-*
     six and ninety-nine to show someone is talking in her Junee
     Museum story. You used them to show people were
     talking, didn't you, Natalie?
N: *Yes, I added them in when I had my conference with you.*
B: *Why don't we just forget about the sixty-sixes and ninety-*
     nines when we talk about the heats, and just use them here:
     'Some events were' and all that?

Before the teacher continues, Bryan speaks directly to
Natalie. He has some idea the punctuation is not necessary

in every instance. He has unintentionally taken control away from Natalie. The teacher leads the children back to the purpose of the discussion with a question.

T: *Are there people talking in this story? Are there people saying things in this story?*
B: *No it's kind of like we're just saying it.*
T: *You're telling the story?*
N: *Yes, we're telling the story.*
T: *Well?*
N: *Do we still need those sixty-sixes and ninety-nines every . . .*
B: *That's what I was going to say, because if we are saying it and we are writing the story, do we have to do the sixty-sixes and ninety-nines?*
N: *Yes?*
B: *Because we are saying it?*
T: *Do you know when to use sixty-sixes and ninety-nines?*

It would appear easier to answer directly, and tell the children how to use quotations. It would take less time. This teacher's response tells us two things. She is not going to take control away from Natalie and Bryan; she suspects the children's concept of using quotations may be more confused and complex than anticipated. She takes this opportunity to explore more fully the children's knowledge of quotation marks.

N & B: *Yes, when someone is talking.*
T: *Is there someone actually talking in your story, like Natalie or Bryan said, something like that?*
B: *No.*

It appears Bryan is beginning to get the idea, but we can see in the dialogue following that confusion still exists. The teacher has made a wise choice in exploring the extent of their knowledge.

N: *Well, in the age race, it said I came third, so that was Bryan talking.*
B: *And some of the events were 800 meters and all, that was Natalie talking.*
T: *So it's you talking?*
N: *Yes, just here, 'In the age race, Natalie came third', well Bryan is talking there.*

B: *And you're talking when it say, 'Bryan jumped . . . .'*
N: *'Three meters and sixteen centimeters.'*
B: *Yes.*
T: *When an author is writing a book, it's their words that they use when they write it. They're doing the talking when they are writing the book.*

The teacher decides it is pointless to continue unless the children can view the problem differently. She tries a new tack.

N & B: *Uhuh* (nodding yes).
B: *But they are talking to say it.*
T: *Yes, they are talking to say it, right, but in the story on the page . . .*
B: *Who's going to know who you are?*
T: *Yes, that's right, so you only need sixty-six and ninty-nine in the story . . .*

The teacher believes she has made progress and attempts to make a clarifying statement. Bryan interrupts and seems to be on the right track.

B: *The only way they can find out is by looking at who the author's name is.*
T: *They can find out by looking at the author's name on the cover of the book. But is there anyone in your story, any person who is actually talking, not you talking, telling the story.*
N: *Bryan there* (pointing to a sentence he authored on the draft).
B: *And where Natalie is saying . . .*
N: *Yes, when I'm talking here.*
T: *Well, what about your Junee Museum Book? Did you use sixty-six and ninety-nine there in the whole book?*

Again a dead-end. The teacher tries to return to her original strategy of using what Natalie knows.

N: *No.*
T: *You were telling the whole story.*
N: *Yes, but the only time I had sixty-six and ninety-nine was when Dad was talking.*
T: *Right.*

N & B: *Ohhhhhhhhhh.*
T: *Are you right now?*
N: *Yes.*

It would appear the children have finally got it. Using what Natalie can do has paid off. The teacher continues the discussion comparing Natalie's use of quotations in her previous story with this piece of writing.

T: *So you told the whole story . . .*
N: *And when my Dad was talking, I did sixty-sixes and ninety-nines because I wasn't talking, Dad was talking.*
T: *Dad was talking, right. So do you need any sixty-sixes or ninety-nines in this story?*
N: *No.*
T: *Is there anyone speaking other than the authors?*
B: *Us two.* (Bryan refers to Natalie and himself.)
T: *Other than the authors?*
N: *No.*
B: *No.*
T: *Well, the authors are speaking in every story.*
B: *Yes, they are too. So we just cross out all the sixty-sixes and ninety-nines in this story.*
T: *Unless someone is speaking.*

The children now seem to have a clearer understanding of using quotations.

B: *Let's get going.* (Bryan begins to cross out the quotation marks as Natalie watches.)
N: *Well, don't cross out that part there Bryan, because you're talking there, and I'm . . .*

Evidently, it isn't all that clear to Natalie. Bryan takes over to straighten her out.

B: *Yeh, but I'm the author.*
N: *Uhh . . . (giggle).*

Realization at last. The children are in greater control over written language. The teacher asks one more question to check the results of this discussion. Bryan has the final word.

B: *Back to the start!*
T: *You are going to cross them all out now?*
N & B: *Yes.*
B: *After I went through and spent half of my lunch time the
            other day doing some sixty-sixes and ninety-nines and now
            we don't need them.*

It is obvious a lot of time is spent in this conference on understanding quotation marks. It may have been a more economical use of time to tell the children outright how to use them. There were several opportunities when the teacher could have done this. Instead, she spends time teaching by asking questions to find out the information the children know. The teacher provides *no* new information. She guides the children to draw new conclusions by examining what they know. By involving the children in the process she is learning what they can do. By participating in the process the children are learning what they can do.

CONCLUSION

Our process observations of Coline, Natalie and Bryan suggest that these learners are acquiring knowledge of written language by inventing it for themselves. As Bissex (1980) observes in her five-year study of Paul's reading and writing: 'Language and art are not only culturally transmitted; they are also re-invented by children who increasingly shape their inventions to cultural forms', (p.203). She notes that 'just as writing was not originally a way of encoding speech but a separate system, so Paul's first writings were not attempts to spell but to print letters with a communicative intent', (p.6). This is exactly what Coline seems to be doing in her creation of primary inventions. Like Paul, she reinvents the historical evolution of the writing system in her own development as a writer.

Bryan and Natalie also invent as they solve the problem of how to represent their meaning in conventional form. This is most obvious in their use of quotations. As a result of their collaboration they invent an unorthodox use for the punctuation which fits their intention. We might even suggest that they have over-generalized a convention. Particularly significant is the recognition by the teacher that the children have invented. As an adult she does not impose the correct conventional form. Instead, she uses the strengths of the children to help them examine their unorthodox invention and to allow them to determine further refinement.

Graves (1979) observes that 'Children have a natural urge to express, to make marks, to "play" with writing, to experiment boldly with new ways to put messages on paper' (p.2). From an early age children want to make sense out of written language; they build models of how writing works from their natural, ongoing encounters with print; they display their growing awareness of our writing system by producing it.

Children at school will remain active participants in control of their writing acquisition; they will write in order to solve the problems of writing. To encourage, rather than obstruct such experimentation we need to pay more attention to the process of writing. Our observations of Coline, Natalie and Bryan seem to confirm Piaget's view that 'Children have real understanding only of that which they invent themselves, and each time we try to teach them something too quickly, we keep them from re-inventing it for themselves' (in Chomsky, 1974, pp.13–14).

Young learners do not see the world as adults do. What makes sense to children does not necessarily make sense to adults. All the more reason why we need knowledge of learners' intentions as they solve the problem of learning to write. We can best gain such knowledge by looking at learners in process, while they are composing or recreating the composing context in conference.

Process knowledge will give us the fuller context of meaning. Process knowledge will allow us to see how children learn. Without such information we have only a limited view of children as learners; we underestimate their ability and impose our knowledge on them. With such information we can look at what learners can do; we can allow them to invent and support their natural inclination to learn.

REFERENCES

Bissex, G. L. *GNYS AT WRK: A child learns to read and write.* Cambridge, MA: Harvard University Press, 1980.

Chomsky, C. *Invented spelling in first grade.* Unpublished paper, Harvard Graduate School of Education, 1974.

Graves, D. H. *The growth and development of first grade writers.* Paper presented at the meeting of the Canadian Council of Teachers of English, Ottawa, Canada, May 1979.

Graves, D. H. Patterns of child control of the writing process. In R. D. Walshe (Ed.), *Donald Graves in Australia.* Sydney: Primary English Teaching Association, 1981. (a)

Graves, D. H. Where have all the teachers gone? *Language Arts*, 1981, **58**, 492–497. (b)

Graves, D. H., Calkins, L. M., and Sowers, S. *A two-year case study observing the development of primary children's composing, spelling and motor behaviors during the writing process.* Report for National Institute of Education, 1978–1980.

Murray, D. M. How writing finds its own meaning. In T. R. Donovan and B. W. McClelland (Eds), *Eight approaches to teaching composition.* Urbana, IL: National Council of Teachers of English, 1980.

Explorations in the Development of Writing
Edited by Barry M. Kroll and Gordon Wells
© 1983 John Wiley & Sons Ltd.

9

Growth, Community and Control in Secondary School Writers [1]

John Hardcastle, Alex McLeod, Bronwyn Mellor,
John Richmond and Helen Savva

In this chapter we want to discuss the ways that different pupils in secondary schools (aged 11–16) respond to the demands of the writing process. We report a number of studies in which we have observed pupil writers at work, both alone and in collaboration with each other. Analysis of the pupils' completed writing provided some insights. Direct observation and the use of video cameras provided many more. On the basis of these studies we shall offer some recommendations for classroom practice.

Writing remains, and seems likely to remain, the dominant language mode in secondary education. A range of recent work has highlighted the crucial significance of talk in classrooms, and pointed to the fact that, given that the written language is dependent on the spoken language in the first place, this dependence should be recognized in the many secondary classrooms where it is still largely ignored. However, the eventual goal of most lessons in the secondary academic curriculum is a piece of writing. The public examination system relies almost entirely on writing to make its judgements about children's futures. Whatever the rise of telecommunication and plastic tape in the world's efforts to communicate with itself, compete with itself and entertain itself, there is no evidence that the output of print is abating. Writing is, actually, an enjoyable and fulfilling activity—for some. And here we are writing this.

Many people who would like educational issues to be simpler than they are, believe that the quality and correctness of children's writing would improve

---

1 Sections of this chapter originally appeared as 'Craft and Art' and 'Designing the Workshop' in numbers 6 and 9 of *The English Magazine*, published by the English Centre, Inner London Education Authority.

dramatically if teachers, and particularly English teachers, got back to teaching 'grammar' or 'the basics' in the first years of secondary school, if not before that. Such people often point to a mysterious dereliction of duty some time in the 1960's, when some teachers somehow stopped bothering, which has led to the malaise of doubt and despond we are supposed to be in now. Neither the fact that before the Beloe Report (1960) and the introduction of the Certificate of Secondary Education, eight out of ten British children left school without any paper qualification whatever, nor the steady rise in Ordinary and Advanced Level passes per 16- and 18-year-old during that guilty decade, nor the fact that the number of students in higher education in Britain more than doubled between 1960 and 1970, tarnishes the image of a golden age shining through the fogs of contemporary uncertainty, an age when teachers somehow 'got it right'.

It is a mark of the uneven distribution of knowledge in education that the myth persists as an uneasy groundswell in spite of the certainty of almost all linguistic and educational researchers on this question, that there is no connection between the preliminary teaching of 'formal grammar' of a pre-Chomsky variety, and proficiency or correctness in children's writing. See, for instance, Chapter 1, section 5, of Wilkinson (1971).

Nevertheless, the written English language is a profoundly structural affair. It is foolish to see 'structure' and 'creativity' as unfriendly opposites, glowering at each other from red and blue corners. They are essential to each other, and anyway, the distinction between them is in reality bogus. It's the old form and content debate. That is, if we make the distinction at all, we make it for ease of analysis, and not because the whole reality on the page is better represented in distinct parts. A metaphor that might serve is that we take a machine apart in order that, when we put it back together again, it will work better. It is not more of a machine when it's in parts on the garage floor than when its humming under the bonnet.

Any attempt to say something useful about children's writing in school must start beyond old, false dichotomies, beyond squabbles over spelling and punctuation versus personal expression. We must come out of our camps, abandon our sects, and grow up to a position which recognizes the deep level of organization *and* the rolling, unpredictable creativity of the written language.

Writing is a craft as well as an art. The difference between a craft and an art is that good craftsmen always know what they are doing, good artists frequently do not. In reality, most constructive activities have craft and art about them: working confidently, pleasurably within yourself, using skills you know you have; also daring, pushing open doors to as yet unexplored rooms, frightening the first time, less frightening the next. In writing, craft and art are tangled together in the process, and writers make both sorts of decisions—the calculation and the gamble—all the time. Just as it is important not to see calculation and gamble, craft and art, as opposites, so it is important not to see them hierarchically related either, with craft cast as Cinderella and art as Muse. At the most accomplished level, the poet takes no less pleasure in the formal qualities of a poem than in its meaning, or mood, or intensity of emotion. At the level with which this chapter is mainly concerned, pupils who see that they have learned to punctuate, or to handle sentences with more than six words and more than one clause, or simply to write a page which looks nice, may gain as much from knowing that as from the pleasure of having expressed a strong personal feeling accurately on paper.

The distinction we have been operating in the last paragraph could be expanded into two complementary views of children writing in school, two constellations of ideas. (Except that constellations in the heavens appear to be close together and in fact are not, whereas our constellations appear to be separate and in fact are entwined.)

Emphasis on the craft of writing leads to a focus on: pre-writing (what pupils do or think before the pen hits the page); scanning back and revising during writing; proof-reading after writing; discussing the writing with an adult or, less usually, a friend; second (and subsequent) drafts. This approach tends to concentrate attention on: errors, miscues and confusions in writing; stylistic or grammatical complexity; conformity to the norms of the writing code.

Emphasis on the art of writing leads to a focus on: the topic of the writing; the writer's sense of purpose, intention, direction, involvement; the writer's sense of audience — the reader — and therefore of message; writing as a means of expressing and/or redefining oneself, a catharsis, a therapy. This approach tends to concentrate attention on: the writer's confidence; the writer's view of writing as a medium and of self as a writer; motivation, stimulus to write; originality, individuality.

These two emphases, held together and allowed to nourish each other, will serve us better than banners and battle-cries.

OBSERVATIONS IN CLASSROOMS: THE STARTING POINT

The present authors have been meeting as a group since 1977. The direction of our interest has shifted somewhat during this time. When we started, we were concerned with the writing done by the substantial numbers of pupils of West Indian origin in the schools where we worked. The West Indian-ness of the writing was central to our interest then, and we were looking at conscious dialect writing, at pupils who could move efficiently from dialect to standard in their writing, and at the intervention of non-standard grammar and vocabulary in pupils' mainstream school writing. By now, the West Indian-ness of the writing has moved off-centre, and we seem to be trying to swallow the bigger question of how any children's writing develops, and how to help it to develop more effectively.

Our first detailed study was of Pat, a pupil in a south London girls' comprehensive school, and of the development of her writing between the end of her third year (14-year-old) and the first term of her fifth year at the school. That study has been written up as 'Progress in Pat's Writing' (in Richmond, 1982). It takes eight examples of Pat's writing, the first four written during the last term of her third year, the second four written at intervals during her fourth year. The study was intended to be longitudinal and to show progress, so it seems perverse to pull bits out of it, but perhaps a flavour and the outline of a way of working will be better than nothing. Here is Example One of Pat's writing:

Mohammed

Muhammed was born on Monday the 20th of April 571. Muhammed was brought up in a famous tribe called Quraysch tribe before both of his parents died. before[1] Muhammed was born.[2] Muhammed[a] Mother[3] had a very strange insight saying that Muhammed was going to be the lord of the people. Few days when[b] Muhammed was born is[4] farther[5] died. Couple years later[c] is[4] mother died, so his grandfather had too[6] look after him[7] 2 years later he died so his uncle looked after him. Muhammed was a good boy[8] he didn't cause is[4] uncle any trouble. While Muhammed was with his uncle he looked after his uncle he looked after his uncle[9d] sheep[7] in[10] this way he was able to earn a small amount towards his keep. Muhammed[a] uncle,[d11] business took him off to far off places. Muhammed,[12] accasionly[13] Muhammed goes[14] with him. Muhammed[a] uncle was going to Syria and Muhammed asked him if he could go and his uncle said yes. as[15] they were going to Syria they passed some few places until they Came[16] across some christain[17] monks,[18] Bahira[19] told the christian[20] monks that Muhammed would become the greatest prophet of Allah[7] ~~and he~~ When Muhammed learnt a great deal from the christian[20] monks, he became a very good buisness[21] men,[22] he[23] came to be known as 'Sadiq' the truthful one. Then later on Muhammed fell in love with a women[24] twice is[4] age. He was twenty five when he married his wife Khadijah. Khadijah had some children but they died very young. Kadijahs[25] and Muhammed gave most of their property to the poor. most[26] of his life time[27] was with his wife and his people[7]

Pat wrote this piece in a Religious Education lesson, in response to the teacher's request to write about the life of Mohammed. The class had had some lessons on Islam, and the teacher had talked about the subject; additionally, Pat had access to a book on comparative religion, and could use encyclopaedias and other books in the school library. However, there is no direct copying in Pat's piece. She used the resources available to make a statement of her own. Here is that statement in an 'error-free' version:

Mohammed

Mohammed was born on Monday 20th April 571. Mohammed was brought up in a famous tribe called Quraysch tribe before both of his parents died. Before Mohammed was born, Mohammed's mother had a very strange insight saying that Mohammed was going to be the lord of the people. A few days after Mohammed was born his father died. A couple of years later his mother died, so his grandfather had to look after him. Two years later he died so his uncle looked after him. Mohammed was a good boy; he didn't cause his uncle any trouble. While Mohammed was with his uncle he looked after his uncle's sheep. In this way he was able to earn a small amount towards his keep. Mohammed's uncle's business took him off to far off places. Occasionally Mohammed went with him. Mohammed's uncle was going to Syria and Mohammed asked him if he could go and his uncle said yes. As they were going to Syria they passed some few places until they came across some Christian monks. Bahira, Mohammed's uncle, told the Christian monks that Mohammed would become the greatest prophet of Allah. When Mohammed learnt a great deal from the Christian monks, he became a very good business man. He came to be known as 'Sadiq' the truthful one. Then later Mohammed fell in love with a woman twice his age. He was twenty five when he married his wife Khadijah. Khadijah had some children but they died very young. Khadijah and Mohammed gave most of their property to the poor. Most of his life time Mohammed was with his wife and his people.

This is the substance of what Pat wrote. The 'error-free' version has made no stylistic changes, merely skimmed off the features which hit and offend the eye of the normal adult reader at first reading. Let us look at the substance.

The most general of overall reactions to the substance is one of pleasure and admiration, particularly if we remember that the writer is 14. A considerable amount of information is conveyed—and clearly. The writer's style is confident, relaxed and varied. The only stylistic strains or infelicities are 'Two years later he died so his uncle looked after him,'—where we have a surfeit of masculine pronouns—'took him off to far off places'—where the repetition of 'off' is awkward—and possibly 'some few places', which is an odd phrase in the context. Readers might find one or two more, or decide that we have been too harsh in mentioning these; that is the nature of stylistics. The justification of our generally positive feeling may lie in the anatomy of Pat's sentences. We find a wide variety of sentence lengths, from five to 23 words, with a mean sentence length of just under 13 words, indicating that Pat is at home with fairly long strings of words. The number of clauses per sentence varies similarly, with seven single-clause sentences, two three-clause and two four-clause sentences. One of the four-clause sentences is worth looking at more closely:

> Before Mohammed was born, Mohammed's mother had a very strange insight saying that Mohammed was going to be the lord of the people.

This complex sentence contains an initial temporal clause modifying the main verb, as well as a double subordination whereby 'saying that', subordinate to 'had a very strange insight', itself subordinates the clause which follows it. The word 'insight' is elegant and appropriate.

The interest in Pat's piece is further sustained by the variety of sentence introductions she uses; sometimes the straight main clause, 'Mohammed was born . . .'; sometimes a subordinate time clause, 'While Mohammed was with his uncle . . .'; sometimes a phrase, 'In this way . . .'; or an adverb, 'Occasionally . . .'. These flexible details of style make the difference between an interesting and a tedious piece of writing, though of course they lie below the threshold of conscious appreciation of the reader who reads once only. And lest we appear to have gone overboard about form, let us repeat that the piece does its job as well; it carries considerable information in its 21 sentences.

By this time readers should be muttering, 'This is all very well, but the girl didn't actually write the "error-free" version. She wrote the first version.' Let us come to that now, pausing, at the risk of stating the obvious, to explain the reason for the process we've just been through. Most teachers, confronted with an equivalent of the handwritten original of 'Mohammed' (Pat's handwriting is quite clear and bold, incidentally), will see at first glance a mass of errors. They may decide, especially if they are not English teachers, that the errors are not their business, and look merely to see whether the pupil has done the job set. (All tribute, however, to teachers of all subjects who do see the form as well as the content of their pupils' writing as their responsibility.) At the other extreme, they may decide that the only way the pupil is going to reduce errors is by having errors pointed out, and correct everything. Between one reaction and the other, it is quite unlikely that Pat or Pat's equivalent will be offered adequate praise and encouragement for quite considerable achievements in grammatical control, style, and informational content, as well as strategic help with error, miscue and confusion.

This is not teacher-bashing. It is recognizing the true difficulty of the task.

If readers look back to the first version of Pat's piece, they may like to check the notation of numbers and letters against the list which follows. In the list, Pat's errors, miscues and confusions are followed by a slash, and then the notional correct equivalent. Her use of non-standard forms, in this case two time phrases and five examples of the signalling of possession by juxtaposition rather than by *'s*, are followed by a stroke, and then the notional standard form. This difference in notation is intended to be significant. We're not going to say any more about the very important question of the intervention of non-standard forms in mainstream school writing. This is discussed in detail in 'Progress in Pat's Writing' and elsewhere in Richmond (1982).

1. *'before'*/'Before'
2. Unnecessary full stop after *'born'*—comma may have been intended
3. *'Mother'*/'mother'
4. *'is'*/'his' (but probably affected by dialect pronunciation) (×4)
5. *'farther'*/'father'
6. *'too'*/'to'
7. Omission of full stop (×4)
8. Omission of some medium strength punctuation mark, or full stop, in the latter case leading to non-use of capital in following word
9. Duplication of *'he looked after his uncle'*
10. *'in'*/'In'
11. Unnecessary comma, probably induced by *'d'*
12. Duplication of *'Muhammed'* in advance, together with unnecessary comma, leading to non-use of capital on following word
13. *'accasionly'*/'Occasionally'
14. Change of prevailing tense
15. *'as'*/'As'
16. *'Came'*/'came'
17. *'christain'*/'Christian'
18. ,/.
19. *'Bahira'* not explained; presumably name of uncle
20. *'christian'*/'Christian' (×2)
21. *'buisness'*/'business'
22. *'men'*/'man'
23. Non-use of capital as a result of *,/.* after *'men'*
24. *'women'*/'woman'
25. *'Kadijahs'*/'Khadijah'
26. *'most'*/'Most'
27. Omission of 'Muhammed'

34 errors, miscues and confusions

a. *'Muhammed'*—'Muhammed's' (×3)
b. *'Few days when'*—'A few days after'
c. *'Couple of years later'*—'A couple of years later'
d. *'uncle'*—'uncle's' (×2)

7 non-standard features

In 'Mohammed' there are 34 separate errors, miscues and confusions (EMCs). That long-winded phrase, or its slicker abbreviation, seems to us a necessary safeguard against the easy assumption that all mistakes are evidence of ignorance or carelessness. Some mistakes are literally mis-takes in the sense that correct knowledge in the head didn't get translated into correct marks on the page—slips of the pen which all writers commit from time to time, particularly when the brain tries to compose too far ahead of the hand. Some errors are evidence that a developing writer hasn't yet grasped a convention of the code (e.g. the marking of sentences) which mature writers agree is useful and correct. Yet other errors are actually evidence of learning. The long march of becoming a writer involves crossing rivers without bridges. If you're going to try to handle a written form which you've never handled before, it's highly unlikely that you'll handle it perfectly first time. You may still be having trouble with it the tenth or the twentieth time. Your trouble may be overkill, or overenthusiasm for your new tool. Here's a nice example from the eighth of Pat's pieces, written over a year after 'Mohammed', when her writing had moved on considerably:

> They were in Italy; she was 30 years old; her first child John was
> five years old; *(end of sentence).*

The semicolon is a delightful tool when you first try it out confidently; it's like learning to ride a surfboard; gives such steadiness in midsentence; but as Shaughnessy (1977) remarks, 'The semi-colon usually becomes epidemic when it is first learned'; (sorry).

Another kind of trouble a developing writer might have with a new form is the difficulty of incorporating it into an existing set of structures and making the necessary adjustments to them. Here is Anthony, a 13-year-old, writing the first sentence of the second draft of a story called 'Death under the Tree':

> 'There were these three men in this pub called the Swan having a
> few pints when they heard a Ambulance van came outside the pub.'

This is a long sentence—25 words. The main verb is right at the beginning. The clause which starts with 'when they heard' is complicated because it is governed by a distant main verb, and 'they heard' is separated from what should be the infinitive 'come' by the three-word phrase 'a Ambulance van' (more of an obstacle than, say, 'him' in 'they heard him come'). For any or all of these reasons Anthony has played safe and incorrectly tried to start a new main clause with 'a Ambulance van came'. An error, certainly. But an error which has come about because he is tangling with a long and, for him at that point, grammatically complex sentence. Should the teacher advise him to 'avoid long sentences' because he might run into difficulties? Do we advise babies to stick to crawling if, after lurching across the carpet, they fall on their nose?

Of the 34 EMCs in 'Mohammed', numbers 4, 7 and 20 occur more than once, as shown by the extra number in brackets. We can categorize the types of EMC as follows:

Misspellings	12
Absent or redundant capital	9
Absent or redundant full stop	7
Absent or redundant comma	2
Duplication of word or phrase	2
Change of prevailing tense	1
Obscurity of meaning	1
	34

Let us look merely at the first three categories, accounting for 28 of the 34 EMCs. But before doing that, let us consider the significance of the fact that 28 of the 34 EMCs *are* accounted for by only three categories. What looked like a disorderly mess of errors begins to have some organization to it. If, instead of conscientiously correcting everything in the hope of doing some good, or ignoring errors as being someone else's business, we began to look at the system behind the errors, perhaps we could then begin to devise more effective strategies for helping with the errors.

Of the misspellings, four are the same word, 'is'/'his'. So in reality we have nine separate misspelt words. A further two of these, 'men'/'man' and 'women'/woman', are almost certainly not spelling problems, but confusion over singular and plural forms. In other words, Pat probably knows how to spell 'men', 'man', 'women' and 'woman', but is not sure which to use in a singular or a plural context. The misspelling 'Kadijahs' after two correct spellings of a name she had got from print, is an odd mis-take which we can leave aside. 'accasionly' is a good stab at a word Pat has possibly never written down before.

The teacher, on the evidence of Pat's spelling in this one piece, would be best advised to do two things. First, say something about homophones (words that sound the same but are spelt differently) like 'is'/'his' (normally homophones in Pat's casual speech), 'farther'/'father' and 'too'/'to'. Secondly, say something about reversal of letters within words as in 'christain' and 'buisness'.

The majority of the EMCs which make up categories two and three (11 out of the 16) actually combine to form one compound category, which is the marking of sentences. It becomes clear that if the teacher only has time to say one thing to Pat about the technicalities of her piece, the priority should go to some advice about sentence-marking. That sounds rather glib, because it really is very difficult to do that job helpfully. An important confusion to avoid is the one which decides that since Pat is having problems with sentence-marking, she must be unsure of what a sentence is. All normal children know what a sentence is, or they wouldn't be able to speak. Having a conscious, abstract definition of what a sentence is, is another matter, one which linguists find deeply challenging and perplexing. Marking sentences correctly is yet another matter. It would be nice (and probably newsworthy) to report that we know *how* Pat learned to mark sentences correctly during the time we worked with her. She did learn; a year after 'Mohammed', sentence-marking was a minor and receding hiccup in Pat's confidence, rather than a major difficulty. The method used was to point out to her frequently the places where the sentence-marking was going wrong, and to do so in a tone of voice which suggested that we'd got a problem rather than that she'd had a moral lapse; to appeal to her sense of Sentence, the sense which, as a native speaker of English, she carries in her head ('Can you see that this string of words makes a sentence?'); to set her detective tasks ('Right, in that last paragraph you've missed out four capital letters, three full stops, and you've got two commas where you should have full stops. Can you find them?' She usually could.); finally, to encourage her to write and read and write and read so that the stock of sentences in her experience grew always larger and more varied. She did learn, but what the crucial moments of meaning were, when brain, language, code, hand and pen began, regularly, to SEE, is still a mystery to us.

Eighteen months after writing 'Mohammed', Pat was working over a story, with one of us (J.R.) helping her. A video camera was watching them. At one point she made the statement of statements, 'Sir, I don't really understand what a sentence is,' and the videotape recorded the teacher pausing, breathing in deeply, before attempting the traditional definition involving subject and predicate. 'Does that make sense?' he asks. 'No,' she replies honestly, and he then proceeds to more liberal definitions about a sentence expressing a complete idea, a finished thought, and so on. Hopefully, he concludes, 'Is that any help?' and she, to reassure him, says, 'I think so sir.' Teacher and learner sigh reverently at the complexity of the problem, and go on to the next sentence. At the time of asking the question, Pat had very nearly beaten the problem of marking sentences.

We'll leave Pat there. One disclaimer: the lessons learned from working with her emerged from the luxury of one-to-one collaboration between teacher and learner. Both gave up their own time, and also bent the school timetable to make space to work together. Clearly, the harassed manager of 30 will not be able to devote such care, attention and time to each learner. But nor should that manager dismiss the insights Pat offers us for that reason. The insight that the same piece of writing may simultaneously show evidence of considerable achievement and considerable confusion, is a crucial one for all teachers. And the development of a strategy for identifying where pupils need help, so that it can be offered economically rather than haphazardly, could make our lives more successful, not more onerous.

To go with the disclaimer, three articles of faith—but faith got from experience:

(1) When making any judgement about a pupil's language activity, whether talking or writing, it is important to see that activity as a process of development and change. The activity has come from somewhere, and is moving towards somewhere else. Therefore, cross-sectional leaps into a pupil's work are of very limited value.

(2) It is exciting to see a writer developing. It is essential to look at a pupil's writing through the primary perspective of progress and development, and not of defect and deficit. Only once this primary perspective has been established is it possible to get close enough to the pupil to offer real help with error, miscue or confusion.

(3) We learned at least as much as Pat did, as a result of our collaboration. We did not always learn the same thing; who ever does? One-to-one communication is a rare privilege within the confines of the secondary curriculum. Nevertheless, the only living educational interchanges are those where, as time passes, the teacher learns as much as the learner; where 'teacher' and 'learner' are interchangeable titles.

The principles of looking longitudinally at a learning writer, of taking time over it, and of establishing the perspective of progress, are the central ones. The limitations of the Pat study are three-fold. Pat is a solitary writer; all her writing is considered as finished product; and the main effort of analysis (though not the main effort of teaching) is directed towards technicalities. The second stage of our work is attempting to address and overcome those limitations.

OBSERVING THE WRITING PROCESS

Three of us (J.H., A.McL., and J.R.) chose to look at the writing being done in a whole class. We picked a group of boys who were second year (12- to 13-year-olds) when we began our study of (and with) them, and who are currently (summer 1982) coming to the end of their fourth year. We shall stay with them as a group for one more year. The class numbered about 25 when we started;

there are now around 15 regular attenders, mainly because at the beginning of the fourth year the school splits the six lower-school classes into eight, but also because one or two boys have stopped coming to school. We started off by focusing on five boys in the class who represented a wide range of achievement as writers; during the course of the three years virtually all the boys in the class have aroused our interest at different times and for different reasons.

We began to observe writers actually while they were writing, by using videotape. The first time we tried this we had a camera on a high tripod looking over a boy's shoulder as he wrote. We looked at three of the five boys in this way on the first occasion, and two months later refined the process with the other two boys by having an extra camera which looked straight at the writer from across the table, picking up eye movements, references to book, blackboard or worksheet. Using a hand-controlled mixer means that the screen can be split half and half between the two cameras, or either picture can be diminished so that it is an inset in the corner of the other.

What can we learn about writing from videotape? What particular virtues does it have? One virtue is its impersonality. If a human being, an adult, stares at a pupil writing, the writer is likely to become disturbed and embarrassed. The camera doesn't provoke that effect if the pupils have seen video before, have seen themselves on the screen, and the machinery has been at least partly demystified. The camera is quite likely to encourage the writer to work with more sustained attention than otherwise, but that's actually a good thing, for the writer in any case, and also because it drives performance closer to competence. There's a better chance that what appears on the page will reflect what the writer really can do, as well as what he or she can't. A second virtue of videotape lies in the range of supportive activities, essential or at least helpful to the arrival of words on the page, which the camera can notice. These will include the prewriting activities of thought, consultation of available texts, collaboration or discussion with friends at the same table. During writing these activities may be continued and supplemented by checking back, crossing out, starting a new draft, putting in extra words or details of punctuation after checking back, pausing, changing speed of composition. After writing, how much full-scale revision and alteration happens? Can this be related to the level of commitment to the writing, or to the proficiency of the writer?

Let us look at three of the pieces written during the first videotaped lesson. The lesson had begun with a dramatic telling of Chaucer's 'Pardoner's Tale', retitled 'Death Under the Tree'. The class's work at that time in the integrated Humanities programme they were following was on life in medieval England. The story took about 40 minutes to tell, and then the boys were given a sheet of paper on which the main points of the story were outlined in ten short sentences. They were asked to write the 'Death Under the Tree' story in their own words, using the sheet for guidance, but changing the story if they wished, by giving the characters names, or setting the action in modern times, or altering details of the plot. The boys wrote for the remainder of the lesson — another 45 minutes — and some of them finished the story later on.

Audley, the boy out of our five who is certainly having the most difficulty with writing, wrote an unfinished story of 262 words which was made up of 26 sentences. While the camera was on him, he wrote the following, in a small, scrimped-up, barely legible hand:

> They carared on
> warking they wen a mile oit of the vilig
> they saw a odl man   wrking and they sied hey
> do you now were death is   they sarted to kechim
> and ponc him   the odlhim by is solders
> and the men sied   I been har 85 years
> and pard that I   leve this vild
> thay said no thats not it
> and they srted kechim on to the floor
> and they pitkend him ip of the floor
> and he sied you find daeth on the Hill
> *(turns page)*
> and they sitof to the Hill they war sagling
> ip to the Hill when they arid up thay
> thay did see nofing
> thay sied les ga and find the odl men
> and dohim over
> one of vine fept somting and he looked and it was
> a gold pes   they serted to look   foir   more

Clearly, Audley has a long way to go. (He *has* come a long way in the 2½ years since he wrote this, but whether he will get anywhere near independent confidence and autonomy as a writer before the end of his schooling is still a distinctly uncertain question.) He wrote fast while the camera was on him, and he had been writing fast before the camera got to him. He actually wrote more in 45 minutes than the other two boys we looked at closely that morning (262 words as against 133 words by Kevin S. and 159 words by Anthony — 38 of these 159 being an abandoned first draft).

Here is the writing which Anthony and Kevin S. did in the 45 minutes (i.e. not just the bits they wrote while the camera was on them).

Anthony DEATH UNDER THE TREE

First draft

There were these three men in this pub called the Swan having

a few pints when they heard a Ambulance van came outside
the the pub, I said what was that noise I said to the pub boy

Second draft

There were these three men in this pub called the Swan having
a few pints when they heard a Ambulance van came *(later
corrected to 'come')* outside the pub, I said what was that
noise, I said to the pub boy that to go and see what the noise
was, the boy huried outside to see what it was I came back is
slowly telling them the bad news that that one of their best
friened had died. The men in the pub were very unhappy
because they thought that Death had killed there best friened,
they went outside the pub and said that we are going to get
death or I am going to kill anyone in the way on the way
looking for

Kevin S. SLEEP

This is the story of three wariors from the Kabala tribe named
Ejo, Oju, and Fola. They went out looking for the thing they
called mind snatcher we know as sleep.
'How far do we have to go?' said Oju tiredly.
'About another seven suns and seven moons.' Ejo said
'Can we go to the Grendel river to pray to our monster god
Grenda.' said Fola
'alright, but we have a long journey ahead of us.' Oju said
'I'll be back when the sun sets on the mountain side. Is that
okay?'
'Yes it's fine, but make sure you don't get up to mischief.'
'Obala (goodbye)' said Fola
'let go and hunt some lion for supper' said Ejo
'Alright with the bones I can make my mum new earings and
necklace.' said Oju

Here is an 'error-free' version of what Audley wrote while the camera was
on him:

They carried on walking. They went a mile out of the village.
They saw an old man working, and they said: 'Hey! Do you
know where Death is?'
The old man said: 'No, I don't know where Death is.'
They started to kick him. They held him by his shoulders,
and the man said: 'I've been here eighty-five years, and prayed
that I could leave this world.'

They said: 'No, that's not it.' And they started to kick him
on to the floor, and they picked him up off the floor, and he
said: 'You'll find Death on the hill.'
And they set off to the hill. They went staggering up to the
hill. When they arrived up there they did see nothing. They
said: 'Let's go and find the old man and do him over.'
One of them felt something and he looked, and it was a gold
piece. They started to look for more.

So, we're not looking at a boy who has no written language structures. He
writes in sentences, though he has no idea how to mark them. We're not
looking at a boy who has no memory. He has a good aural memory, at least.
We are not looking at someone who is scared of the blank page. He covered
one and a half of them. But we may be looking at someone who has very little
sense of himself as a writer. While the camera was on Audley, he didn't check
back over what he was doing, at all. There are only four crossings-out in the
262 words he wrote that morning. It came out in a flow. Kevin S. and
Anthony, writers with some degree of competence and control, and with the
potential (which they have since realized) to become successful writers, were
constantly revising, checking back, collaborating (they sat next to one
another), occasionally actually correcting something on the other's script.
Between a half and two-thirds of the time spent observing them was taken up
with these para-writing activities; the actual making of marks on the page
depended enormously on them. These two boys had achieved the beginnings of
an objectivity which was ready to mature into a sense of the craft, into an
autonomy. Audley had got nowhere near that, at this point.

It is an interesting phenomenon of watching children at work, that those
who have the most to learn are those who teach you most. Audley and his
difficulties acted as a kind of archetype for us at this early stage. We knew
that, for him and for others, we needed to find ways of making writing a less
lonely, isolated, chancy business. We needed to take writing from being the
constant, perfunctory duty which it mainly is in secondary schools, towards
becoming a process where community, growth and control actually mean
something.

COLLABORATION IN WRITING AND REDRAFTING

In the two and a half years since that videotape was made, we have kept a close
watch on the writing development of Audley and Kevin S. Kevin is fluent,
confident and discriminating. He can cope with most writing assignments
without much hesitation, and often with flair and a strong sense of purpose.
Audley's progress has been more hesitant but he has shown, again and again,
the ability to hold a complicated narrative in his head, and in spite of his

continuing struggle with and against the conventions of spelling and punctuation, any sympathetic reader is immediately impressed by the stark presentation of urban living in his writing. His best achievement has been in the imaginative use of dialogue.

Some of the later writing of Kevin S. and Audley has been reported extensively elsewhere (Richmond, 1982) and will be mentioned in the rest of this chapter only in relation to collaboration with others.

Close study of the first videotape convinced us that these writers know much more than they know that they know. There is no doubt that our pupils have a highly developed tacit understanding of how the writing system works. Our concern is not to provide them with prepackaged linguistic definitions of what they know, but to help them explicate *for themselves* the tacit understandings that they already have. We thought that for most writing activities our pupils could make these self-explications, but very often they appeared not to have much confidence in their own knowledge and ability. Their comments on their writing were mostly remarks about what they thought they couldn't do: 'I'm no good at writing stories.', 'I can tell you about it but I can't write it.', 'I don't know how to punctuate speech.', 'My spelling is terrible.' Our view was almost the opposite. Every piece of writing we discussed at meetings of our working party showed emerging abilities that we hadn't noticed at the first quick reading. Almost every kind of writerly competence was shown by someone in the class, and they were learning from each other. Kevin J. and Simon C. could handle with ease almost any kind of writing function that would be looked for in writers of their age. Michael S. had become a humorous story writer whose satires caused a lot of laughter and one fight. David L. wrote at great length on religion and evolution, drawing skilfully on the rhetoric he heard regularly at church.

There were others who still found writing a struggle. For some it was a struggle they thought they could win. A few were still very hard to persuade that their efforts could ever succeed.

Their feelings about their writing—those completed or half-completed sheets of paper that piled up in their folders—covered a range from pleasure, or at least silent satisfaction, to total disregard; from those who never left anything incomplete, kept it carefully and in the right order, liked others to read it, and might be prepared to make revised drafts, through those who did some of these things, to those whose written efforts were quite likely to be found on the floor, only partly completed, when the class went off at the end of the lesson.

We decided to pay particular attention to three aspects of their writing: collaboration, redrafting, and the provision of real purposes for writing at all. Fortunately, these three could be combined, because collaboration, especially in redrafting and revision, could be related to interesting them in thinking about readers other than teachers, people who would read their writing because they wanted to. The Humanities programme continued to provide plenty of starting points for autobiography, imaginative narrative and discursive writing, but we knew we would have to help them choose topics, and ways of approaching those topics, which would be likely to make them feel committed, so that the writers' voices, their individuality and conviction, would be in their minds as they wrote, and would be felt by the reader.

Few pupils in the middle years of secondary schools are enthusiastic about making a second version, or subsequent versions, unless there is some good reason. Most examinations at 16+ encourage—actually require—writing that should be 'right first time' and teachers with examinations in mind may in practice discourage redrafting because they know that in the exam room it can't be done.

Almost all the work we read in the first year of the Hackney Downs study was written only once. To encourage redrafting, we would have to extend the boys' view of the process, because their reluctance was based on their belief that redrafting was just a matter of correcting mistakes and neater handwriting. Thorough redrafting, which would take into account the response of their readers, could best be achieved by encouraging something they had already begun to do. They often read each other's work, especially narrative, and talked about it, but the comments were always made when the writing had been completed. The authors took note of these remarks, of course, but hadn't yet thought of using them, incorporating their friends' suggestions and observations in the making of another draft.

An experienced writer, rereading his or her own text, attempts to do so with a certain amount of critical detachment, almost as he or she would read the work of another person. Young writers often need help if they are to decentre in this direction successfully. It is hard to think of someone else reading something you have just struggled to express, so when you reread you are more likely to re-enter the struggle rather than distance yourself from it. We have seen competent writers aged 14 or 15 who just do not notice serious blunders— omissions, contradictions and redundancies as well as formal mistakes—in their own writing which they would instantly jump on in the writing of another.

So it seemed that if we tried to promote close reading of each other's work, they might be helped to shift from the stance of the writer to the stance of the reader, first in making helpful comments, but later, we hoped, in thinking about redrafting. This approach in any case reinforced our belief in collaboration in the classroom. In Humanities they work together most of the time, so working together on writing wasn't anything strange for them.

The first videotape had shown us one writer (Kevin S.) who regarded revision *while writing* as a very important activity, but who resisted the idea of thorough redrafting, and another (Audley) who never revised and hardly even checked what he wrote. A second videotape, made in March 1980, showed a writer (Kevin J.) who was already so confident that he hardly ever needed to check his attention to the conventions. Self-monitoring in fluent writers tends to occur at the extreme of competence: you pay most attention to the thing you feel you haven't quite mastered. Kevin J. had moved forward to the point where he was mainly monitoring subtle details of informational accuracy.

For our third videotape, in December 1980, we decided on a writing operation which, without taking the boys away from the kind of thing that would normally be doing in Humanities, would put revision and redrafting fairly and squarely into their thinking. It was a turning point in our study, and it became a turning point for many of the boys too, because they have changed their view of redrafting, and the change began when we made that videotape. Instead of thinking of revision as a chore and a bore, they now regard redrafting as something well worthwhile, and they are doing more and more of it.

They were at the end of the first term of their third year in school. The subject matter of the Humanities course at this time was migration; why people have moved or have been moved, to and from Britain, or as a result of British actions, in the last 350 years. The class had a choice of writing either a factual piece explaining what they had learned about migration during the previous weeks, or a story about an important journey. On this occasion, there was an additional dimension built into the activity. The class was working in pairs. During the first lesson they did the writing individually, consulting with each other if they wanted to, but not being obliged to. At the end of the lesson, we collected what they had written and photocopied it. A week later they got their own writing back, unmarked, plus a photocopy of their partner's writing. They were then asked to do an editing, correcting and improving job on the photocopy, in consultation with their partner. At some point in the lesson, when they had done that job, the photocopies were swapped back, and the original writer could incorporate such suggestions, corrections and improvements as he agreed with into a second draft. As well as our spoken guidance about this process, the boys had some advice written on a sheet:

> *Talking about your writing*
> We've made photocopies of what you wrote last Thurday about *Why People Moved*. Here are some suggestions. You don't have to follow them exactly, but we would like you to discuss your writing with each other.
> (1) Read it right through, to find out what it was all about.
> (2) Are there any questions you want to ask, like:
>   (i)   Is there any part of it where you would like to know *more* about what happened?
>   (ii)   Is there anything in it you don't quite understand? Ask for a more detailed explanation.

(iii) Is there anything you don't agree with?

(iv) Can you suggest anything that *should* have been mentioned?

(3) Do you think there are any mistakes:

(i)   in spelling

(ii)   in full stops

(iii) in Capital Letters

(iv)   in commas, question marks, etc.

(v)   in speech marks.

You could try reading it, sentence by sentence, one at a time, and talk about anything that seems important.

When you have read it together, and talked about it, you can make changes and alterations on the photocopy.

THEN DECIDE WHAT TO DO NEXT:

I.   Add your comments at the end of *your own* writing.

II.   Add your comments at the end of *your partner's* writing.

III.   Change or add anything you think is needed.

IV.   Make a *revised version* of what you wrote, if you think you can do it better.

If you like, you could help each other.

If you prefer, just make *your own revision*.

V.   Ask the teachers to help with anything you are not sure about.

If we were right in our hypothesis that they know more about writing than they know that they know, this collaborative redrafting might help them to use their knowledge.

Let us look now at how this was tackled by Sunny. On the first day, this is what he wrote:

The earliet people to go to America in the 1600 were the British
some were Quakers or Roman Catholices there thought that in
America they would be free to practise their religion.
Other people hoped to become rich in America. There was plenty
5 of space and the calnate was good for growing sugar, cotton
and tabacca. in America were Irish, Dutch, French protestants
and Swedish.
in the 1700's Scoltish and Irish people were driven off their
land sometimes the British took the land I mean the goverment.
10 Between 1610 and 1810, there was a steady stream of Africans
coming to America by force as slaves working on the plantations.
The plantations were owend by absentee English landlords who
were making an enormos profit. Some plantation owers

wont to work they slaves to death.
15 Why did people move because of better prospects and Job opport.
and good money. The Jews move because the Germans took them out
so they had to new plaece some of then went to America and
brought weath to the county

At some time during writing Sunny changed *america* to *America* (line 1), *Afroicans* to Africans (line 10)—he may have written *Afro* with some other word in mind—and there are five other minor changes relating to what are probably slips of the pen.

Sunny's partner was Kevin S. (see Richmond, 1982). They worked together on the first draft, but that conversation was not recorded, so we don't know much about who contributed what. We do know that they were enthusiastic and committed to the topic. Sunny's family came to Britain from Nigeria, and Kevin's from Montserrat. They had by now overcome the bantering rivalry, the custom of making sharp insults about each other's country and people, which is fairly common between West African and West Indian boys and girls. The Humanities programme had shown them a little of their common heritage, and everyday life in London was teaching them that people from African and Caribbean countries living in London have a great deal in common as well as their history.

Kevin wrote the following changes and additions on Sunny's first draft:

Line	Improvement suggested
1	earliet/earliest
1	1600/1600's
1/2	British some/British, some
2	there/they
5	calnate/climate
8	Scoltish/Scottish
9	land sometimes/land, sometimes
9	the British took the land/the Lord chucked them of the land
9	I mean the goverment (*deleted*)
12	owend/owned
13	enormos/enormous
13	owers/owners
14	wont to (*deleted*)
14	work they slaves/worked their slaves
14	because it was cheaper to buy new slaves (*added after 'death'*)
15	move because/move? Because
15	opport./opportunity
16	took/cruely chucked
17	to new/to find a new
17	plaece/country

18   weath/wealth
18   county/country

Kevin's amendments are mainly in the conventions; these are helpful and necessary, but they make no impact on the writers' involvement with the subject. However, Kevin made two changes which strengthen Sunny's statements, in just the same way as Sunny's changes in Kevin's first draft added extra force to it (see Richmond, 1982).

'Sometimes the Lord chucked them of the land' is a fairly terse way of summing up the expropriation of Scots and Irish farmers; it is a reminder that there were class issues involved as well as national ones. 'Sometimes the plantation owners worked their slaves to death because it was cheaper to buy new slaves' makes explicit the meaning that Sunny probably intended. It is closely parallel to a sentence in Kevin's final version. They are, in fact, joint authors of this powerful statement of something that excited and angered them.

The video camera was on Sunny and Kevin when they were completing their second drafts. Both had already written more than half. At the end of the 80-minute period, several other pairs had been videotaped, but not these two. They demanded to be included, staying on into lunch time to do so. Although they had already written most of their second drafts, and had been working together for over an hour, they were still asking each other questions, mainly to check or confirm changes that had been suggested. The transcript which follows mainly concerns the major amendment of Sunny's draft suggested by Kevin, in lines 14 and 15.

> Sunny: S_____! (Kevin's surname) What did you put here?
> Kevin: Pardon?
> Sunny: Didn't you think it . . .?
> Kevin: (Takes Sunny's paper) What? (reading) . . . *plantation owners worked . . . worked their . . .* cross off . . . *slaves to . . . to death . . . because it was cheaper to work them . . .* You know? (returns to own writing, saying *twenty-four million,* as he writes it).
> Sunny: Now listen to this then . . . Look, S_____. Let's return to facts. I can hear. That's copyright.
> Kevin: (writing his own draft) Oh, my God!
> Sunny: You done it again, S_____!
> (They work silently for a time)
> Sunny: (whispering) S_____! What you think about my writing, right? It was . . . . Took that out of the book.
> Kevin: Mm.
> Sunny: You did.

Kevin: Uh?

Sunny: You did.

Kevin: (Takes up Sunny's paper) I read it to you again, OK?
        . . . *plantation owners worked their slaves to death.*

Sunny: How'm I spell that, all right?

Kevin: . . . *because it was cheaper* (following the words on the
        page with his pen) *to work to . . . to work them to a . . . to
        work to do.*

Sunny: Help me with that later.

Kevin: . . . *to work them to . . .* (sighs, pauses, crosses out *work
        them to death*, which he had earlier written in on Sunny's
        photocopy, and writes in *buy new slaves*).

Sunny: Finish it off . . . . I just gonna have a little nap.

Kevin: It won't be a very long one.

Sunny: What man? You finished that off quick!
        (Kevin returns to his own writing.)

Sunny: (saying the words as he writes) *It was cheaper to . . . it was
        cheaper to buy more slaves . . .* umm . . . *new slaves.*
        (Sunny interrupts himself to look at what Kevin is writing.
        He follows it closely, with visible satisfaction.) Kevin is
        writing: *Some slaves, newly imported to Jamaica, immedi-
        ately escaped to the Blue Mountains and set up their own
        culture. They called themselves the Maroons. Maroons
        comes from a French . . . .* How do you spell patois?

Sunny: Don't know. Sir! Sir! Sir!

JH: How do you spell what?

Sunny: Patois.

JH: P-A-T-O-I-S.
        (Kevin writes . . . *patios word.*)

It is in the nature of the early stages of learning to redraft that the conversation produces more of interest than the revised draft itself. Sunny's second
version is a distinct improvement, but his contribution to the joint effort, and
his commitment to it, hardly show in it. One longs to know what is intended by
his claim: 'That's copyright'. More than a year later, in a conversation about
Nigeria, he said, 'I particularly liked those slave trade books.'

This is his revised version:

   The earlist people to move to America in the 1600's were the
British, some were Quakers or Roman Catholices. They thought
that in America they would be free to practise their religion.
   Other people hoped to become rich in America. There was plenty
of space and the climate was good for growing sugar, cotton, and

tabacca. In America were Irish, Dutch, French protestants and Swedish.

In the 1700's Scottish and Irish people were driven of their land, sometimes the Lord chucked them off the land. Beteen 1610 and 1810, there was a steady stream of Africans coming to America by force as slaves working on the plantations.

The plantations were owned by absentee English landlords who were making a enormos profit. Some plantation owners worked their slaves to death because it was cheaper to buy new slaves.

Why did people moved? because of better (*unfinished*)

As redrafting, it's a rather meagre beginning. It wasn't finished, and Sunny didn't take on all the improvements offered by Kevin. There are even two new accidents with spelling, *beteen* and *driven of*. But he was learning the process, and the second draft is a fairly crisp, succinct account of the topic that they had been asked to write about. Sunny covered a lot of ground; Kevin wrote only about the slave trade. Sunny here was following more closely the intention of this writing assignment—to see migration, whatever the reason for it, as part of British history. It was, for him, a success, though a modest one.

Simply urging Sunny to redraft would not, on its own, have persuaded him to pay this much attention to the crafting of his writing. It was collaboration with a friend that led to his willingness to redraft constructively. Collaboration has now become an accepted procedure in this classroom. Stories and discursive writing are now read by others at first-draft stage, and at all later stages, as a matter of course. Notes like: 'Editor, Simon Y.' or 'Title supplied by Ahmed.' appear at the end. It's worth pausing here to mention the other means we have employed to encourage the collaborative redrafting processes.

When a piece of work is finally completed, we often type it. There are two ring binders in which the collected writings are kept; it may take a boy about an hour to read through one of them, and they are in continuous use. Some writing by young people in other schools has been put in the binders as well, and a few pieces of published work by young writers on themes of particular interest to our pupils.

They also see us writing. Whenever we can, we write alongside them. They can see us struggling with the words and ideas in much the same way that they do. Some may be rather bemused by our eccentricity, but they are always curious to see what we've written. With some, it is becoming a written dialogue.

REDRAFTING AS A LONG-TERM PROCESS

A number of the stories written in the first half of 1982 took several weeks to complete. They were much longer than anything their authors had attempted before, and were all substantially redrafted. Redrafting often begins before the first draft is completed.

Sunny is now working on a long story. He began it at the end of March, and it still isn't finished. He now regards redrafting as an essential part of writing. He has gone far beyond the minor changes (and the major matter of the elimination of errors) of the first pairing occasion. He starts with a draft he clearly intends to work on later. It is written at high speed, in handwriting very different from the boldly elegant script he uses for final drafts. He makes changes as he writes, crossing out and altering, sometimes words, sometimes whole sections. He usually makes the first draft in ball pen, and adds or changes in pencil.

Sunny's story is called 'The Fattest Mother in the World'. He chose to write this story. No one gave him the topic. A week or two earlier he had written a story called 'A Test of Skill'. It is his version of a Nigerian story, probably a very old one, as it concerns a chief and his three sons, and a contest in which they try to outdo one another. One of us (A. McL.) asked Sunny if he knew any more Nigerian stories, and whether his parents ever told him stories from Nigeria at home. Next week he came in with the first four pages of 'The Fattest Mother in the World'. He told us that he talked about the story with his father as he wrote it. 'My father reads a lot of books', he said. This of course is something we have always wanted to encourage. Most children hear stories from their parents; some, frequently those whose families have come to live in Britain, have amazed and delighted us with stories told by their parents and grandparents.

The following is the final draft of the first page. It is presented here in the form in which it appeared in the ring-binder collection. Two minor slips in spelling have been corrected, and one missing apostrophe added, in the typing.

The Fattest Mother in the World.

Winston's mother was the fattest mother in the world.

Around the vast breasts, like hundredweight bags of McDougall's Self Raising. We were in the war at this time, and the wool she used to clothe herself could provide socks for half of our Air Force.

When Winston's mother opened her mouth every dog and chicken and hollyback braced itself for shock waves. She used her capacity for noise as her special expression of behaviour, as if by drowning her house, furniture, garden, husband, son with her voice she was drinking them down into that great bosom to be trapped in a blubbery fastness.

'Winston . . . . I'll cut y'arse off.'

This happened because Winston was late for doing some vital duty like fetching the bread.

It was never known to the rest of us whether Winston's mother put these awful threats into physical effect.

Some of the phrases are probably taken down directly from Sunny's father. This seems to us to be in every way a good thing to do.

The story itself makes excellent reading. Some will complain that it's sexist. It is, but perhaps we may forgive it for that; the mother is certainly not a submissive female. The collaboration of father and son, in the telling and to some extent in the redrafting, is something we would be happy to see everyone do. It adds another dimension to the collaborative learning we do our best to promote in school. The story is much longer and more ambitious than any story or other writing that Sunny has done before, and he is very proud of it.

We have three separate drafts of most of the story. Sunny says he has written some of it four times. The following is a representative sample. The first draft is on two separate pieces of paper, apparently written at different times.

First draft: fragment one. This is mostly in pencil. Some changes have already been made in ball pen. Winston's mother has joined in a boys' boxing contest, demolished all the competitors and collapsed on the ground.

> . . . . it was all that boxing Winston said it seand that he loved his mother even after the things his mother did to him in past years. Winstons father was sitting dranking a cup of tea he even had the guts to ask for some cookies and at that time it seem to him it was funny

Fragment two. This is all in ball pen, with many words crossed out and others added, including a sentence written in the margin.

> Winston was laying on his mothers breasts like a baby who his socking his mothers breasts for milk then the amublnce came in they came with doctour ners etc. it seem the whole hopital becaues horn and then on and off, (the men came in whith a stump carryer. When they saw who the victim was they have to bring a crnae if you saw Winston mother she woud of made a great actor even getting an award.

Altered version, written over. From *the amublnce came in*, down to *on and off* has been crossed out, and the following written in:

> with our help we got an amublnce They came in with the doctour ners etc because this had happen before. it seem the whole hopital staff was they becaues this happen on and off

Addition, in margin.

When they is the (indecipherable) as big daddy and giant haystack then they new what they nebe to bing her to the hoptail

Second draft. Written in ball pen. Some later changes made using another pen, and some in ball pen.

'It was all that boxing' Winston said, the expression on Winston was not the same expression as if his mother had betten him and for that would like to kill her, but not half all the years he was with his mother he never showed the love and passion for her.

He was crying they on his mothers breast like a young child wanting his daily milk with help from us we got an amublnce When they hread this call they knew who they enemy was

Doctour's and Nurses came in to see Winstons mother, there were a lot of people. It seemed it was the hole hoptsial had moved in two men with a stser came in to take Winstons mother to the hospital when they saw who it was one of them said bleime she is has big has big daddy and giant haystack put together we will have to get a bigger one, and two more helpers, to me I thougt Wintons mother would have made a great acter if she really wented to do it.

Even a academy award.

Third draft. Written in ball pen, very neatly. Three corrections, also in ball pen.

'It was all that boxing,' Winston said, the expression on Winston's face was not the same expression like his mother wanted to kill him, but not for the years he had lived with her he would had killed her but this was different Winston did not showed his love passion for her like this before.

He was crying there on his mothers breast like a young child wanting his daily milk. We mange to call for a amublnce it took about 10 minutes to get to our house.

In they come, one, two, three, four, five six. It same that they had brought the whole hopstial in to Winstons mother because these had happen before and happen to be a false alrm. Two amublnce men came in to carry Winstons mother to hostial but when they saw how the victim was they said 'blame she's a big one you have to get big daddy and giant haystack put together to make her size We'l have to get a bigger and larger carryer.' If you had see the agny on Winston mothers face I thought for minute that she would make a great acter or even getting an academy award.

This extensive redrafting has not diminished as the story has grown longer and longer. Watching Sunny at work is interesting, because he writes the first draft at high speed, and pays very little attention to whatever may be going on round him. When he is redrafting he works quite slowly, writing in some but not all of the changes on the first draft. He is willing to show the first draft to only two or three other boys, but he is happy to discuss it with us and with his father.

Here is part of a taped conversation. At this time the redrafting was about half done.

Alex McLeod: I wondered how you came to choose this topic, for this story.

Sunny: Well I dunno, because I haven't wrote a long story before. I just wanted to get a long story out, and see how it come out, see how many pages I could do. I just tried this out for the first time, you know . . . If this story comes out good this long, I'll do a second time round, do another story. It'd be longer.

A. McL: Did anyone else read it in the rough?

Sunny: No. I mean, mm, well. My Dad did. Well of course when sometimes if I was going to do a story, I'd just write it rough first, right, all the ideas come out, right, cause you want to take your time. Your ideas won't come, you know, so I just write it rough, and then I know what I'm writing so I just do it easily, redraft it four times, so it would come out. Four times.

A. McL: Terrific. Did you talk to him much about it?

Sunny: Yeh.

A. McL: I think that's great. When you were redrafting, I noticed that you made a lot of changes. Do you read it out loud, to yourself, or do you just look at it and think?

Sunny: If I read it by my . . . If I read it out loud then I know the mistakes; if I read it by myself, in my head, I think I've done it all right.

A. McL: Good. I think that's true.

Sunny, and the other boys, are now used to the idea of both short consultations, and long conversations, with us about their writing. We think it's essential to respond first to the story, or the ideas, or the argument, before we even begin to mention redrafting. Generally, we prefer to refrain from any comments on spelling and punctuation until they are nearly at final-draft stage, though sometimes they insist on help with spelling much earlier. A large proportion of the mishaps of spelling and punctuation they put right themselves, frequently with the help of other boys. Most of these pairings are now stable.

When a final draft is typed we try to make it error-free, and then we ask them to read through the typed version and tell us whether we have made any mistakes or altered their meaning. Then we make photocopies, giving the writer one to keep, and putting one in a ring binder. Parts of this chapter have been read in typescript by Kevin S. and Sunny, and they pointed out two errors of fact.

This method of working is now fairly well established. The school enters its pupils at the end of the fifth year for examinations in English, whether Ordinary Level or Certificate of Secondary Education, in which substantial amounts of course work are included, redrafting is encouraged, and early drafts can be retained in the pupils' folders.

We hope, after another year, to report more fully on the development of writing in this class over four years. We are particularly interested in the composing processes of young writers and how teachers can help those processes become easier, and in how writers become committed to the various enterprises of writing.

A SYSTEMATIC APPROACH TO COMPOSING AND REDRAFTING

Let us move now to a second-year class in a mixed comprehensive school. Two of us (B.M. and H.S.) used the evidence from our work with the boys' class to develop ways of systematically encouraging composing, revising and redrafting. What had been learned piecemeal, in the heat of the moment, sometimes in front of the video camera, was now used to devise ways of helping younger writers. Questions we had been discussing in the group were reformulated. In particular, we asked ourselves:

— do we 'teach' pupils to write in the secondary school, or do we simply dictate the terms and leave the writers to produce the goods?
— to what extent do we work with the writer, share the experience or interact in the process?
— will children, many of whom consider writing a painful experience to be avoided at all cost, develop both the art and craft involved in writing if they are isolated and left alone with the task?

It had become increasingly clear to us that it was not enough to provide children with the opportunity to write in a variety of modes. The act of writing, in or by itself, does not secure the development of children as writers; on the contrary it can confirm in them a perception of themselves as people who are constantly failing to write effectively.

Our shared starting point was a belief in the need to work collaboratively with our pupils in order to assist their development as writers. We had known for a long time about the importance of talk to writing; we were convinced of the need for drafting and for real audiences for writing; we were committed to the idea of the learner's active role. But there hasn't been a great deal of help on writing offered to teachers on an informational and practical level—as there has been on reading and talk—so we were unsure of many aspects of the nature of the collaboration we proposed. We needed to look at the writing process over a sustained period of time; to look closely at what and how children write, and also to listen to what they had to say about writing. So we decided to set up a 'writing project' with this second-year mixed-ability class. There are 29 girls and boys in 2E; one third of them had been selected in their first year for 'extra help' with reading and writing, which is given by a remedial teacher in three out of four of the hour-long English lessons—thus providing opportunity for team teaching. The focus of the project was to be on writing itself: a process-based curriculum unit in which we raised issues about writing explicitly with the pupils.

The writing project with 2E began with a short talk given by one of the teachers about writing, and writing in school. She explained the project and made it clear to the pupils that she wanted them to regard writing as a creative and developing process over which they exercised control. It was emphasized that collaboration, revision and redrafting, critical comment on their own and other people's writing (including the teachers') would be important features. Notes made by one of us observing the pupils' reactions during this talk include the following comments: 'the kids are clearly responding, if in a slightly shocked manner to the mention of "meaningless writing tasks", and several nodded when the teacher said, "You do a hell of a lot of writing"', and 'The kids seem interested, some a little embarrassed by the different atmosphere, but there's total silence and most eyes are looking directly at the teacher as she speaks. This is something different, serious and the teachers are not absolutely sure of what is going to happen either. I think the kids feel it, at least a little . . .'

The class discussion which followed sustained this feeling of involvement and seriousness. All of the pupils said they thought writing was important: all of them wanted to improve their writing. There was no need to sell them the idea of the writing project. It reminded us of James Britton's remark: 'Motivation is the word we've invented to fill the void we've created.'

In the next phase of the project we invited pupils to reflect on their ideas about and attitudes to writing. Needing to listen to what they had to say about writing, we designed various activities around writing which involved them in group talk. We hoped that these activities would help the pupils not only to air their thoughts but also perhaps to begin to disencumber themselves of mystifying and confusing ideas about writing.

In the first activity the pupils, in pairs or threes, were given four pieces of writing to read which were stylistically very different (a pupil's story, a Caribbean folk-tale, an extract from the novel 'Ruby' by Rosa Guy, and the account of the unfortunate bricklayer that Hoffnung made famous), but which all contained the theme of pain, accident or misfortune.

Each group, having read the pieces, had to put them in order of preference, and to be prepared to justify that order. 'Preference' simply meant 'the one you like most through to the one you liked least'. In the whole-class discussion which followed the groups and the teachers (who did it too) compared their choices.

In the second talk activity the class were given a list of 20 statements about writing (from which there are examples below). Again they worked in pairs or threes. They were asked to cut out the statements and put them in three columns, 'agree', 'disagree' and 'don't know' (which became 'maybe' by common consensus) — again being prepared to justify their decisions.

— Handwriting matters a lot.
— A story with lots of spelling mistakes can't be good.
— Poor punctuation and spelling spoil a good story.
— It's important to write about things that matter to you.
— Either you can write or you can't, that's all there is to it.
— Writing is the most important thing you can learn in school.
— Teachers don't teach you to write; they just tell you to do it.
— Girls tend to be better writers than boys.
— It's important to know what you are going to write before you begin.
— You can't write the way you talk.

At this stage one of the teachers read out a piece she had written about her own writing: how she does it, what she finds difficult about it, how this compares with writing methods of friends, what she'd like to be able to do, and so on.

The class then, individually, wrote their own pieces called 'My Writing'. They found this quite difficult, but were helped by the talk that had gone before. Afterwards several pupils read out their pieces to the whole class, and again the discussion was serious and interested. Things like wanting to have control over what to write about, having sufficient time to write, and teachers' responses to writing came up both in what they said and wrote:

My writing is not bad. But when I start writing I like writing.
When I stop writeing I don't like to start again. I only like writing
storys.

I don't like people telling me what to write. I'll would rather like to
get my ideas because I think I would rather write by myself.

I think my writing is a bit untidy sometimes. I can't spell very well.
I write good poems but my stories are boring. I write long stories
and when I read them I feel they don't make any sense.

Sometimes I don't care what I write and the teacher just writes
good. Its not good its rubbish . . . .

I think my writting is pretty good now and again. I could set out a
good piece of work when I have the time But usually I haven't the
time.

My writing is bad when I do not feel like writing or when I do not
like the kind of writing I am doing. But my writing is a bit better
when we are writing something I am interested in.

My writing is not bad. One lesson in school is not enough time to
write a story.

Sometimes I like my writing because people can read it, sometimes
I hate my writing because people can't read it.

I get mixed up when I have to keep putting ' + ' everytime some-one
says something.

We wanted to look then more specifically at the issues raised in the two talk
activities and in the pupils' writing by focussing on a single piece of writing
and what other people said about it. In pairs or threes the class read a story,
'Do You Believe in Ghosts?' written by a pupil in another class. The groups
were given a photocopy of the handwritten piece together with the following
'teacherly comments' on the story. They were asked to put the comments in
order of fairness and helpfulness:

(1) Your story is spoilt by careless mistakes. You are not putting
    '-ed' on the ends of words to show the past tense, and you have
    left out fullstops and question marks. Use a dictionary to check
    spelling.

(2) You have some good ideas and your story is quite exciting. But your story is difficult to follow because of the incorrect way you have set out the speech. Try to do better next time.

(3) You are a good story-teller. I really enjoyed reading this because you built up the suspense very well indeed. Also there are some clever unexpected twists in the story. Perhaps some of the description is overdone.

I don't think you need the last line of the story, what do you think?

Any idea why I say this?

You handle conversation well.

(4) Good.

(5) 6½/10.

Not all the responses were quite as we would have wished ('Number 5 is rubbish—it should be at least 7½'), but at least reactions got an airing. In the whole-class discussion which followed the groups explained their decisions: why and how they thought a particular comment was fair and helpful. The groups were then given a typed and corrected version of the story, and asked to compare it with the original. This was in response to the vociferous opposition of some pupils to the apparent finality of most of the teacherly comments on what was only the first draft of the story. Many pupils found confirmation of their earlier objections in this final draft:

> Janice: See! She's changed lots of bits, and she says 'he stabbed . . .' and left out that other lot . . .
>
> Teacher: Isn't that because the teacher has told her to?
>
> Janice: No (emphatic) . . . it was only a first draft. She . . . what does the teacher say to (do)? . . . They don't say . . . nothing . . .

2E enjoyed these activities very much. Important questions had been asked and basic assumptions queried, and we had learnt a lot about what struck each individual as important or pertinent. We felt that we had begun to create a real dialogue, and we were not disappointed at the perceptiveness of the pupils' comments. But we also found that they were often obsessed by the mechanics of writing, so much so in some cases that they found it difficult to focus on anything else. The habit of separating out the craft from the art, the form from the content, and treating them as 'unfriendly opposites' is deeply embedded in some children's minds. It was also becoming increasingly apparent to us that writing and its development is, in an essential way, an individual, even idiosyncratic, business, and that the secondary school is frequently an unsympathetic place in which to create room for pupils to find their way as writers.

Therefore, we attempted to set up ways of working that offered pupils an opportunity to search out their own ways of developing as writers. We began the first writing session by reading and talking about the short story 'Time, Thelma and Carnival' (in Searle, 1973) which is written by a girl in Tobago about going to carnival and being late home. The pupils could then choose from six or so writing suggestions we made to them, or ignore them and choose their own subject.

Uppermost in our minds was the need to move away from the idea of writing as something which begins and ends as it hits the page—first go. During our discussions we had emphasized the importance of talk for writing and the need to write drafts incorporating significant revisions before writing a final version. So we offered the following framework for writing sessions, which was presented to the class in the form of guideline sheets.

STAGE 1
(1) Talk about ideas for writing with your partner if you want to.
(2) Begin writing. At any time that you want to, read bits with your partner.
(3) When you have finished writing the first draft, read it with your partner and talk about it. Make any changes you want to.
(4) Give this draft to your teacher for photocopying.

The pupils' writing was then photocopied, and the teacher wrote a comment on a separate piece of paper. A week or more later the following things happened, as outlined in stage 2 of the guidelines.

STAGE 2
You will get back from your teacher:
(a) your writing
(b) a photocopy of your writing
(c) your teacher's comment on your writing.

(1) Give a copy of your writing to your partner.
(2) Read your story with your partner and talk about it.
(3) Read your teacher's comment on your writing and talk about it with your partner.
(4) Ask your partner to write a comment on your writing.
(5) Talk to your teacher about her comment on your writing.
(6) Read your partner's comment and talk about it.
(7) Now go through your writing with your partner and make any changes you want to.
(8) Do the same things with your partner and her/his writing.
(9) When you are satisfied with your writing, write a final copy.

During these writing sessions most of the pairs or threes talked at some length and in some depth about each other's writing. We tried to make our comments positive and encouraging, but also suggested ways in which the first draft might be extended or developed. We feared that the pupils' comments on each other's writing might be too negative and aggressive but we were surprised not only by their helpfulness but also by the perceptiveness of their suggestions. The class worked together with a high degree of concentration and enthusiasm. Here is an extract from an animated discussion between Neil and Steven on the content of their stories.

N: I don't get the bit about your mum nearly trying to kill you.

S: Well. Well I really mean that the conversation of the story is like it ain't really actually killing, right it's another way of beating us . . . getting angry, beating. It ain't exactly killing it's just a hiding, hot temper, attacking, it's just attacking.

N: But in the story you said you said your mum would be worried but when you get home she beats you.

S: I know. She thought we was, I was lost but I think I mentioned . . . that um er oh (looking at his story) well I never mentioned where I was right . . . She may have thought I . . . like I done something, um ran away . . . In another way, um another way, I mean that she was worried about me, thought I was lost but when I came in one o'clock in the morning she was very angry because I was alright . . . nothing happened to me and I should have come home at nine instead of one o'clock the next morning.

N: Oh I didn't know you had one o'clock.

S: So in other words right I get in trouble for coming in later . . . that's why it's called 'Late Home'. . . .

When it is Steven's turn to talk about Neil's story he initially praises but then mounts a severe and systematic attack on the credibility of several aspects of the story. Neil stands his ground though and, with some difficulty, argues back. It seems to us unlikely that he would have done so if he'd been talking with a teacher.

S: Now Neil your comment (reading) . . . *Neil your story is very good and funny but the part about the football match is not very good* . . .

N: What do you mean?

S: Well I mean like, hold it . . . because it says they wanted you to play for them and you said 'Yeah' and then you asked them that and you said, 'Can I play for you?' and they said

'Yes' and then you said 'What time?' and then you asked
them what time it was. Then you asked them what time the
game was and they said 'Any minute' but you can't have a
game just any minute. You will find the player before um
the game starts. You will find it on the day before but . . .

S + N: But, but, but . . . (fighting for space)

S: In other words right, in a minute like . . . you should have
said the game . . . they should have said the game started er
um like the game should have started in half an hour's time
instead of any minute.

N: No but it would be late . . . it would be too dark to play
football.

S: Anyway you never mentioned what time it was. All they
know it says here *if they wanted me*, right, *I saw a notice on
a venture wall* . . . look it says . . . one day . . . that's in the
morning . . . in the morning, evening or what?

N: It was after school (indignant).

S: Oh after school . . . but . . . and plus if it was like you know
half an hour you could have prepared . . . like um get
prepared.

N: But they hadn't . . . but they had players . . . they had
players but the one thing . . . but all the players who they
named and put them on a list they were sick and all that lot.

S: Oh.

N: And they need one more extra.

S: Oh.

N: To play the game.

S: Oh.

In a rough and ready way Neil and Steven are perhaps getting near to
considering what the writing must make explicit for the reader. They go on
then to grapple with the complicated issue of direct and reported speech in
Neil's story:

S: Speech . . . speech mark . . . *and I asked them* . . . speech
mark.

N: Where?

S: And . . . where it says . . . *after play* . . . *and I asked them if
they wanted me to play*.

N: No that ain't a . . . you stupid idiot, *and they asked me*
(teacher arrives and looks on without intervening). You only
put speech on those if I'm talking but I ain't talking.

S: *They said and I asked them if they wanted* . . .

N: But I weren't talking! Miss but I weren't talking.

S: Miss. Here um here it says that um it's like he's speaking and *I asked them if they wanted me to play for them.*

T: Let me see . . . *One day* . . . Well Neil as you wrote it you weren't actually speaking there were you? You were kind of reporting (Neil agrees) what happened but it's not terribly clear because um . . . *and then they said alright, then I asked them* . . . you see you started off there as though you were reporting something that had already happened and then you slipped into writing as though there was a conversation actually taking place. Do you really see what I'm saying there? So you've got to clear that up. If you want to write it as though you were reporting back on something that has taken place you are going to have to change . . . change it slightly. Do you see what I mean? Talk about that for a few minutes and see what you decide. O.K.?

S + N: Yeah.

The teacher is clearly struggling to explain an important distinction at this point, and it seems that Neil and Steven's 'Yeah' is largely out of politeness. But later the same problem comes up again.

N: Where does it say that bit . . . *I better be going* . . .? Oh yeah.

S: *I better be going I said but . . . they told me to score my hat trick. Then the whistle went . . . then at the end of the match they said I had . . .*

N: *Played well.*

S: Wait . . . *at the end of the match they said* . . . speech mark.

N: Where?

S: New line . . . speech marks . . . new line.

N: Don't need speech marks.

S: *I had played well.*

N: But they ain't saying it!

S: So how are they gonna say I played well?

N: At the end I said that they said I played well . . . I'm talking . . . I ain't . . .

S: Oh . . . oh . . . oh . . .

N: It should be . . .

S: You're right, you're right, you're right.

Here it seems that Steven is beginning to understand what Neil and his teacher have been trying to put across to him, but from his concentration on the writing in front of him at this point, it is clear that he is not just being told the difference between direct and indirect speech; he is sorting it out for himself.

We were pleased to see that, within the opportunities given to pupils to work in an extended way on a piece of writing, attention was paid to content and style as well as to spelling and punctuation. But clearly the problem of surface features as opposed to content wasn't altogether solved. Even when teachers are convinced of the value of drafting incorporating significant revision, it is hard to persuade pupils to go beyond seeing drafting as merely 'rough copy' and 'neat copy'. We hoped the structure outlined in the guidelines would extend the notion of drafting beyond this, but we also devised two more group talk activities which we hoped would confirm tendencies towards useful revising. The activities were not seen as exercises for teaching pupils to 'do drafting' but were designed to raise just what might be involved in drafting — apart from surface corrections.

In their pairs or threes the class read a story, 'The Mepher' (methylated spirits drinker), written by a pupil in another class. It had been typed up with spelling and punctuation corrected. The groups were given the following instructions (which were adaptations of comments made by the pupils in previous discussions):

(1) Read and talk about this story.
(2) Then on the story
    (a) mark the bits of the story that you think are most effective
    (b) underline any parts of the story that don't make sense to you
    (c) ring any words you would change
    (d) put a ' + ' by any parts where you think the writer needs add something to the story
    (e) put a '-' by any parts where you think the writer would be better leaving out something
    (f) put a squiggly line near any bits that you think don't sound right.
(3) What would you tell the writer to do now to help her/him to improve the story?

Afterwards, in a whole class discussion, the groups explained their decisions and commented on ways in which the story might be developed.

In the second activity of this stage the pupils were given first, second and third versions of the same story written by a pupil in another class. The drafts had been typed out with spelling and punctuation corrected, so that the visible revisions between the drafts were matters of content, structure and style. Each group was asked to put the drafts in 'chronological' order, and to be prepared to justify their choice.

It's early days yet with this class; what we have seen sustains our confidence, but as yet we have no substantial evidence that it makes any ultimate difference to the pupils' writing. But nor did we expect it to in the short term; the time scale is necessarily a long one. What we do have so far is pupils talking about writing and reflecting on the process—having an opportunity, in particular, to think about writing as something that can be altered and as something within their control.

The activities and discussions have been most useful in that they have allowed us access to what the pupils think and feel about their writing. This is not only a manifestation of an enthusiasm on our part for pupils' talk; it is inescapably where the information is. It is unfiltered and disconnected information but it is still the main source. For this reason we find taping and interviewing essential. This has been one of the most valuable results of having more than one teacher in the room. Most schools can manage to organize two teachers in a class for two hours a week. But while it may need the initiative of colleagues working together within a department to achieve this, from such an initial experiment we believe that individual teachers working alone could operate a similar writing project.

The next stage of our project with 2E will take us more fully into the following areas: the tricky question of audience, and the distribution of 2E's own writing; a closer study of the nature of possible teacher intervention and collaboration with pupil writers; writing ourselves on a regular basis with our pupils.

RECOMMENDATIONS FOR CLASSROOM PRACTICE

The work described in this chapter, though unfinished, gives us enough confidence to offer the following assertions and recommendations in conclusion.

We began by suggesting that a sense of the craft of writing, and a sense of the self as a writer, were essentials in the development of writing abilities. We believe that our classroom studies demonstrate how it is possible to encourage young writers to think about themselves as writers.

If there is any validity in our claim that they provide a way of explaining the difference between success and failure in the business of writing in school:

    (1) We must stop being the only assessors of pupils' writing. Pupils must begin to assess their own writing, and to assess each other's. How can you become a craftsman or artist if you don't get a chance to judge what you do?

    (2) We must reduce the practice of single-draft, once-for-all efforts. Experience comes from working on something until it's near-enough right, not having single stabs at temporary targets.

(3) We must widen the range of real purposes, real audiences, and real modes of distribution, if more pupils are to see writing as a real activity.

(4) We must become less interested in what offends our 'teacherly' eye at first glance, and more interested in why it's there.

(5) Collaboration — apprentices working together, commenting on each other's artefacts — might become not just desirable but essential in writing workshops.

ACKNOWLEDGEMENTS

Acknowledgements to Lesley Hensman, 2E's class teacher, to Pat, and to the boys in 4BH, and the boys and girls in 2E, including those whose work is not quoted here.

REFERENCES

Beloe, R. (Chairman). *Secondary school examinations other than GCE.* Report of a committee appointed by the Secondary School Examination Council. London: HMSO, 1960.

Richmond, J. *The resources of classroom language.* London: Edward Arnold, 1982.

Searle, C. *The forsaken lover.* Harmondsworth: Penguin, 1973.

Shaughnessy, M. *Errors and expectations.* New York: Oxford University Press, 1977.

Wilkinson, A. *The foundations of language.* Oxford: Oxford University Press, 1971.

Explorations in the Development of Writing
Edited by Barry M. Kroll and Gordon Wells
© 1983 John Wiley & Sons Ltd.

10

A Child's Power to Share: The Development of A Personal Experience Model of the Writing Process

Robert E. Shafer

During the spring of 1980, I had the occasion to spend a considerable amount of time in an English primary school located in Waterbeach, a village between Cambridge and Ely, just off the Ely road.[1] Each year hundreds of thousands of tourists from all over the world go up and down that road, savoring the splendor of Cambridge and the magnificence of Ely without visiting the 'island' villages which lie in what was once Hereward's treacherous fen—a unique part of English history. When I arrived at the Waterbeach County Primary School, I found an infant's class teacher who was willing to work with me on some naturalistic observations of children's writing, a project which I proposed to pursue during the spring months. I've recorded elsewhere some details of my experiences as a participant-observer in that classroom (Shafer, 1980). My aim here is to pursue some broader questions which became quite poignant as a result of my experiences at Waterbeach school, especially questions concerning the origins and development of a 'personal experience' model of writing.

Both the headmaster and class teacher at Waterbeach school informed me that 'progressive' and 'informal' methods were used there. I had read accounts of these methods by such writers as Featherstone (1971), Marsh (1970), and Silberman (1970). But, despite my reading—as well as a series of visits to primary schools in England in 1973—I was surprised by the openness of this school. I noticed that much of the classwork was related to the exploration of a particular theme, such as 'water'—the topic underway when I arrived. The

---

1 The author wishes to thank Roger Kilsby, Headmaster, Waterbeach County Primary School, Cambridgeshire, and Janet Ardavan, teacher, as well as all members of the school staff for their fullest cooperation.

children pursued their work on various aspects of the theme for varying parts of the school day. In addition, each child worked independently at a painting, sketching, or writing task, usually also related to the theme.

As I watched the children at Waterbeach read and write fluently and joyfully over the course of several months, I recalled one of King's (1974) observations about informal learning: 'Learning comes about as children find their own questions in real first-hand experience and have the opportunity to pursue their investigations in a school setting' (p.7). The statement seemed to characterize well the school setting I was observing.

During my third week in the school, I began to focus my attention on the ways in which the children began and sustained their writing. I observed immediately that writing—as well as reading, drawing, and painting—was the daily expectation not only of the teacher but also of the children. It seemed as natural for them to write, draw, or paint about things they had read or experienced as it was for them to breathe. For these children, writing was a way of interpreting experience—a way of synthesizing new experiences with previous ones. What I was observing, in action, was the 'personal experience' model of writing. As Judy (1980) points out, what is central to this approach is the conviction that personal experience 'can serve as the starting point for writing: hopes and fears, wishes and ambitions, past events in their lives, even fantasies. What seems most important is that students recognize that whatever they write . . . should grow from fully synthesized experience' (p.39). The personal experience approach seemed to work very successfully at Waterbeach school. I watched six- and seven-year-old children write page after page, story after story, without the direct and systematic teaching of specific skills of reading and writing—and before reading and writing are typically expected to begin. My observations led me to formulate many questions: What were the assumptions underlying the personal experience model and from whence did they stem? How was it that the personal experience approach had developed in England? What was the relationship of 'informal methods' to the personal experience model of writing? To explore such questions I began to spend time in the library of the Department of Education at Cambridge and to discuss these questions with primary teachers and teacher educators at Cambridge and elsewhere. My goal was to find the backdrop of ideas which had fostered the personal experience model of writing. My explorations led me to focus on the period between 1920 and 1940, a time during which the personal experience model of writing became a firmly established part of educational practice in many British primary schools.

In the period between the world wars, a distinctive view of education was beginning to develop in England. This view of educational theory and practice was shaped, in part, by a new science of psychology, resulting, for example, in new views of cognitive growth and new ways of studying and dealing with the period of adolescence. Another result was a concern for individual growth. In educational terms, this meant that the teacher's task was to help each individual grow 'to full stature', a favourite phrase of the time, using the individual's personal experience as a source for learning. As Percy Nunn (1920) proposed, the primary objective of education was to reassert 'individuality'. Norwood (1929) emphasized that 'we must stress individuality in education . . . individuality of the pupil, of the teacher, of the schools . . . If this principle is lost, all is lost' (p.309). Such ideas brought about changes in the organization of classrooms. The old idea of children sitting in rows, heads bent over copy books, was becoming unfashionable in many quarters. As Shayer (1972) has pointed out, many teachers began calling for a more 'creative, self-expressive approach to English' (p.93). Many parents— particularly working-class parents-supported proposals for educational change, demanding a better education for their children and the right to a secondary education for all.

The result was a slow but inevitable growth in the direction of child-centered, informal education for the primary school. Not that all teachers were, by any means, convinced that the new theories were workable. Mr Aldous Huxley (1927) pointed to the fact that many teachers still believed in 'knocking it into their heads' — in pumping 'information into this mental receptacle':

> Ram it in, ram it in!
> Children's heads are hollow.
> Ram it in, ram it in!
> Still there's more to follow. (p.4)

Nevertheless, a revolution was clearly taking place during the 1920's and 1930's. The British educational historian, W. O. Lester Smith (1957), has commented on this transformation.

> Charles Lamb, in a famous essay tells of the wide gulf between the old and the new schoolmasters of his time (circa 1800). But in the 1920's and '30's the gulf between the veteran teacher and the younger teacher was much wider . . . at least as wide as that which in the sixteenth century separated the disciples of Colette and Erasmus from teachers during the medieval pedagogics. (p.35)

Progressive education, as it came to be known, had its origins in the work of such psychologists as Pestalozzi, Herbart, Froebel, the MacMillans, Montessori, Caldwell, Cook, Dewey, and Dalton. The educational thought of these individuals and many others forms a backdrop for the development of British primary schools and the concept of open and informal education as exemplified in these schools as we know them today. We must look back to the eighteenth century, however, to Jean Jacques Rousseau, to find the major prophet of the progressive educational revolution and the major influence on those thinkers mentioned above. Although Rousseau's work began to influence education in the nineteenth century, it did not become a dominant force in Britain until the progressive movements of the 1920's and 1930's. Rousseau stressed the undesirability of a rigid curriculum and proposed the value of activity and experience in learning. Today 'learning by doing' has become a cliche, but it was a revolutionary idea when Rousseau suggested it by saying, 'Teach by doing whenever you can, and fall back upon words when doing is out of the question' (*Emile*, p.144). The outstanding aspect of *Emile* was the complete abandonment of a predetermined curriculum. Emile was to be educated entirely through activities and by first-hand experience. In his emphasis on the use of first-hand experience as the basis for all types of learning, it is clear that Rousseau can be considered the first major proponent of the personal experience model for writing.

Another major influence on the progressive movement in England was the American philosopher John Dewey. As Smith (1957) points out, 'from the 1920's onward, the educational creed of John Dewey also became dominant in British education' (p.56). One of Dewey's major concerns was to individualize education, and the Dalton plan—the first example of a way of achieving this goal—also influenced education in England. It was enthusiastically received in England in the 1920's and was later modified to include group work as well as individual teaching (Parkhurst, 1923). The purpose of this plan was to provide a method of teaching children as individuals instead of as a class. The pupils entered into a monthly contract with their teacher to carry out a syllabus or course of study, but were free to distribute their time within the month as each thought fit. The classrooms ceased to be classrooms and instead were called subject-laboratories; the pupils had free access to them and in each was a teacher to offer guidance on a particular subject; and the pupil would also find there suitable books and illustrative materials.

It is clear that John Dewey's position in the 1920's and 1930's as the chief exponent of progressive education in the United States influenced the development of education and the personal experience model of writing. Dewey regarded education as growth and its purpose, therefore, was to encourage growth—mental, moral, and physical. Dewey stressed the nature of personal experience and the ways that it could be used in the classroom to promote thinking (Dewey, 1916). It is possible to see many of Dewey's theories still in evidence in British schools today. Wherever children are busily active in working at various crafts and carrying on elaborate projects such as building a castle or a harbor, as I had observed in the Waterbeach Primary School, the children are being educated as Dewey and other progressive educators intended (Galton *et al.*, 1980).

Moreover, progressive educators encouraged such practices as having children write about personal experiences, often in response to an activity, such as a field trip. What might be called today a 'prewriting activity' became a fundamental tenet of progressive education as it became applied to teaching writing in the 1920's and 1930's in England. Shayer (1972) cites the recommendations of Finch and Crimmins in their 1932 book, *The Teaching of English and Handwriting*, wherein they list a variety of creative activities to stimulate writing, among them 'writing to express feeling and to communicate experience in a free situation', and 'writing dreams as composition exercises' (Shayer, p.119).

A significant testimony to the influence of the personal experience model as an organizing principle in school life is a now famous comment in the Board of Education's *Report on the Primary School* (the second Hadow Report published in 1931): 'The curriculum is to be thought of in terms of activity and experience rather than of knowledge to be acquired and facts to be stored' (p.10). This emphasis on creativity, imaginative work, and experience could well be related to the work of Susan Isaacs, whose book, *Intellectual Growth in Young Children* (1930), described her work with children between the ages of two and ten at the Malting House School. Isaacs based her work on the importance of fantasy, imaginative play, and personal expression for children, stressing that these activities enable children to come to terms with the realities of their world. The emphasis on creativity foreshadowed much of what was to come in the development of writing based upon the child's experience and imagination.

There were, of course, objections from the more conservative educators, who were particularly concerned with the neglect of grammar. There were constant calls from English associations and the writers of English methods texts for more 'old fashioned parsing and analysis' and for the teaching of formal grammar from the very 'lowest forms upward', as well as proposals for a return from the 'modern tendencies' to 'stimulate the imagination and develop free composition'. Despite the fears of conservatives, the personal experience model of writing was assimilated into English primary schools — and without shedding some of the best traditional elements in the British educational tradition. It seems clear that many contemporary British primary schools embody a synthesis of the old and new, incorporating the concepts of experience and activity into day-to-day educational practices without turning the school over to the child and without losing sight of the traditional aims of education in Britain (a point supported by Tibble, in Washburne, 1953, p.10).

There were, of course, excesses in the implementation of progressive ideas. For example, in 1931 the Hadow Committee made a strong recommendation for the adoption of methods better calculated to develop individuality and foster mental growth. But many teachers, anxious to be in the forefront of the new educational theory and not having fully comprehended the tenor of this well-balanced report, interpreted its advice in ways that were clearly not intended. In some schools, therefore, 'activity' was given very little guidance and there was a tendency for some activities to have little purpose. On the other hand, most educators interpreted the report as recommending the adaptation of an experience model to various aspects of the school program, without suggesting an abandonment of the many excellent practices which had come to characterize British primary education in the 1920's. The experience model, therefore, continued to evolve against the backdrop of a developing progressivism in educational thinking.

During the 1940's and 1950's the British primary school became widely recognized as a model of excellence in education. The Education Act of 1944 extended the influence of the progressive education movement into the post-World War II period in England. Although terms like 'informal education' developed during this period, the emphasis for many primary school teachers remained the same. The focus continued on personal experience and activity as the basis for classroom organization, teaching, and learning, giving shape to an integrated primary curriculum in which reading and writing were used as means of learning and were not taught exclusively as ends in themselves. Visitors came from a variety of countries to see these primary schools in action, although the more conservative elements of British society continued to stress that the schools organized on the 'informal or progressive model' were not serving the best interests of many children (Bantock, in Cox and Dyson, 1971, p.115).

In August of 1963, the Minister of Education, Mr Edward Boyle, asked the Central Advisory Council for Education in England to review primary education in England in all its aspects and also to consider the transition to secondary education. The report of this review, *Children and Their Primary Schools* (more widely known as the Plowden report), was released on October 28, 1966. The recommendations of this report for children's writing were entirely consistent with the personal experience model and proposed that the primary schools continue in the progressive tradition:

> What is most remarkable now in many infant schools is the variety of writing: writing rising out of dramatic play, writing associated with and explaining the models that are made, writing which reflects the sharpening of the senses . . . Much of the writing derives from the experience of individual children. (p.218)

It seems clear that the Plowden Report cemented many of the practices of primary education which had developed during the child-centered decades from 1920 onward and which had become known as 'open education' or 'informal education' or the 'unified curriculum' (Galton *et al.*, 1980, p.40). Such educational practices also came to be called the 'integrated day' or simply the 'informal approach' to education. Using personal experience in writing and reading was a substantial part of educational theory and practice arising from this position, placing value on using children's interests and experiences in all areas of schooling. What I had observed in the Waterbeach County Primary School in the spring of 1980 was a particular version of these theories and practices worked out in a particular village school.

The concept of personal experience and informal education were tested again in the 1970's, when the then Secretary of State for Education, Mrs Margaret Thatcher, set up a committee under the chairmanship of the noted Oxford historian, Sir Alan Bullock, to inquire into the teaching of reading and other uses of English. The Committee report, *A Language for Life*, proved to be another endorsement of the personal experience model. In the recommendations devoted to writing, the Bullock Report came out strongly in favor of writing as an activity integrated with other language experiences and not as a separate subject. The Report commented on the fact that writing in the secondary schools had traditionally been used to assess the students' knowledge of subject matter, but noted that there had been an increase in the amount of personal writing in recent years. In acknowledging the necessity to encourage personal, spontaneous writing, but also noting the teacher's desire to foster growth of technique in writing, the Report recommended attention to 'the fact that the writer's intention is prior to his need for technique . . . the teacher who aims to extend the pupil's power as a writer must therefore work first upon his intentions and *then* upon the techniques appropriate to them' (p.164). Such statements served not only as a confirmation of the personal experience model of reading and writing within the British educational tradition, but also as a validation of the efficacy of the model in educational practice in primary and secondary schools.

In 1966, when English, Canadian, and American educators gathered at Dartmouth College to discuss the future of English teaching, the 'personal growth model of English' was one of the most significant aspects of discussion brought across the Atlantic by British educators. John Dixon's account of the conference and the implications of the 'personal growth model' — as outlined in his book, *Growth Through English* (1967) — has shaped subsequent discussions and debates concerning that conference. It is now clear that, at the Dartmouth Conference, John Dixon and other British educators who espoused the 'personal growth' model of English brought the personal experience model of writing and other aspects of progressive education back to an America which had rejected them in the 1950's as 'life adjustment' education.

Kantor (1975) has studied the development of creative expression in the language arts curriculum against the backdrop of the ebb and flow of the progressive education in American schooling. Kantor discovered that an interest in 'creative expression' was present in English teaching, particularly in the teaching of writing, in all the decades of the twentieth century, but that the flowering of the progressive movement in the 1920's and 1930's led to specific proposals for a personal experience model of writing—for example, in W. Wilbur Hatfield's *An Experience Curriculum in English* (1935) and in the six volumes produced by the Commission on the Curriculum of the National Council of Teachers of English and known as the *English Language Arts* series (1952). The work of others, such as Lou LaBrant (1936) and Lawrence Conrad (1937), praised the value of personal experience in writing as helping the student examine his or her inner life. In addition, the endeavors of such teachers as Hughes Mearns of the Lincoln School at Teachers College, Columbia University, stand out as symbols of the best uses of the personal experience model in teaching writing. Mearns book, *Creative Power* (1929), tells of the unlocking of children's creative powers in writing, drama and the arts. Mearns had much in common with the British teacher and writer David Holbrook, who, a generation later, used the term 'secret places' both as fuel for the creative process of writing and as a title for a book about the personal experience model of writing. Holbrook's (1965) work, with that of John Dixon's 'personal growth model', were clear indices of the continuing viability of the personal experience model of writing for many primary and secondary teachers in England. The impact of these models was clearly in evidence at the Dartmouth Conference. The recommendations of that conference were in many ways an endorsement of the continuation of the progressive tradition in Britain with strong recommendations for a rebirth within the United States.

Yet another Dartmouth participant, James Britton, has become in the past decade the chief spokesman for a personal experience approach to writing, influencing educators in Australia, Canada, New Zealand, and the United States, as well as in Great Britain. The work of Britton (1970), with his colleagues (1975), must be given credit for keeping the personal experience model of writing alive and well in the English-speaking world, despite the assaults of cutbacks in funding for education and a large-scale 'back to basics' movement.

As I watched the life of the school unfold during the days I spent at Waterbeach, I thought often of the comments of Connie and Harold Rosen (1973): 'Language is for living with. Children's language emerges from the lives they lead and we cannot hope to make sense of it without understanding their lives. A considerable portion of their day is lived in school and this life too becomes woven into their language' (p.21). The central meaning of life at Waterbeach school was to be found in the interpretation and reinterpretation of experience through the free interplay of symbols in various media— painting, sketching, talking, and writing. I was particularly impressed by the children's zest for writing. They took on each writing task with a spirit of exploration, or, as I would prefer to call it, 'creative inquiry'. They talked about the writing activity as a problem, read about it together, and then began to write. What I noted day after day was a method of inquiry that consisted partly of a sharing of personal experience and partly of group interaction—

first an exploration of personal experience through talk, then an investigation of whatever resources were available, and ultimately a continued exploration of the topic individually, through writing. Such an approach has its roots in the progressives' emphasis on informal learning and on the centrality of personal experience. It is an approach to writing that has been refined and reinterpreted in the last 50 years, as the English primary school curriculum has evolved—an approach validated in the lives of individual children and confirmed by national studies. What I found at Waterbeach school leads me to believe that the personal experience model of writing will continue to prosper in the British Isles.

REFERENCES

Britton, J. *Language and learning*. Harmondsworth: Penguin Books, 1970.

Britton, J., Burgess, T., Martin, N., McLeod, A., and Rosen, H. *The development of writing abilities (11–18)*. London: Macmillan Education, 1975.

Bullock, Sir A. *A language for life* (The Bullock Report). London: HMSO, 1975.

Conrad, L. *Teaching creative writing*. New York: Appleton, 1937.

Cox, C. B., and Dyson, A. B. (Eds). *The black papers on education*. London: Davis-Poynter, 1971.

Dewey, J. *Democracy and education*. New York: Macmillan, 1916.

Dixon, J. *Growth through English: A report based on the Dartmouth seminar*. Reading: National Association for the Teaching of English, 1967.

Featherstone, J. *Schools where children learn*. New York: Liveright, 1971.

Galton, M., Simon, P., and Croll, P. *Inside the primary classroom*. London: Routledge and Kegan Paul, 1980.

Hadow, Sir W. H. *Report on the primary school*. London: HMSO, 1931.

Hatfield, W. W. *An experience curriculum in English*. Report of the curriculum commission. National Council of Teachers of English. New York: Appleton-Century-Crofts, 1935.

Holbrook, D. *The secret places*. Tuscaloosa: University of Alabama Press, 1965.

Huxley, A. *Proper studies*. London: Chatto and Windus, 1927.

Isaacs, A. *Intellectual growth in young children*. London: Routledge, 1930.

Judy, S. The experiential approach: Inner worlds to outer worlds. In T. R. Donovan and B. W. McClelland (Eds), *Eight approaches to teaching composition*. Urbana, IL: National Council of Teachers of English, 1980.

Kantor, K. J. Creative expression in the English curriculum: An historical perspective. *Research in the Teaching of English*, 1975, **9**, 5–27.

King, M. L. *Informal learning*. Bloomington, IN: The Phi Delta Kappa Educational Foundation, 1974.

LaBrant, L. The psychological basis for creative writing. *English Journal*, 1936, **25**, 292–301.

Marsh, L. *Alongside the child in the primary school*. London: A. & C. Black, 1970.

Mearns, H. *Creative power: The education of young in the creative arts*. New York: Dover, 1929.

National Council of Teachers of English. *English language arts*. Commission on the English curriculum, New York: Appleton-Century-Crofts, 1952.

Norwood, C. *The English tradition of education*. London: Murray, 1929.

Nunn, P. *Education: Its data and first principles*. London: Edward Arnold, 1920.

Parkhurst, H. *Education on the Dalton Plan.* New York: Bell, 1923.

Plowden, Lady B. *Children and their primary schools.* London: HMSO, 1967.

Rosen, C., and Rosen, H. *The language of primary school children.* Harmondsworth: Penguin Books, 1973.

Rousseau, J. J. *Emile.* London: Dent, 1911.

Shafer, R. E. *Children's interactions in sustaining writing: Studies in an English primary school.* Unpublished manuscript, Arizona State University, 1980.

Shayer, D. *The teacher of English in schools: 1900–1970.* London: Routledge and Kegan Paul, 1972.

Silberman, C. E. *Crisis in the classroom.* New York: Random House, 1970.

Smith, W. O. L. *Education: An introductory survey.* Harmondsworth: Penguin Books, 1957.

Washburne, C. *Schools aren't what they were.* London: Heinemann, 1953.

Explorations in the Development of Writing
Edited by Barry M. Kroll and Gordon Wells
© 1983 John Wiley & Sons Ltd.

11

Getting a Theory of Writing

Marie M. Clay

In the last decade there have been many observational studies describing children's writing. The young child, who in the past was assumed to be incompetent, has emerged as an active participant in the process of becoming a writer. In these studies one sees the influence of three other movements of the same period—an emphasis on behaviour as the basic data to be gathered and explained, the ethnographic study of contexts where learning takes place, and recent theorizing about language acquisition. These have been important influences for, to understand how young children learn to write, we must go beyond the analysis of their writing samples (Clay, 1975). There is a need to observe them in the process of writing.

However, it is essential to remember that most of the child's opportunities to write occur in school and schools are institutions which reflect in some ways the expectations held within society. If a society values correctness, or originality, or personal responses expressed in writing, then school programmes will reward these and children will produce more of what is valued. This was demonstrated in the cross-national IEA studies in which adolescents in USA, New Zealand and Great Britain responded to literature (in written reports) in ways that differed but which were consistent with the emphases in the instruction programmes of those three countries. Differences in expectations will thus influence the research results that emerge from different countries; what researchers describe in each country may seem to tell a different tale. Can we, however, despite cultural differences, reach some conclusions about the changes that occur in writing as children move through their schooling? Observational studies of children learning to write may point to some common ground underlying the cultural and institutional differences which create outcomes or which lead to different interpretations of these outcomes. In the following section I shall review a number of such studies of the earliest stages in learning to write.

OBSERVATIONAL STUDIES OF CHILDREN AS WRITERS

Preschool Play and Exploration

Goodnow (1977) studied the ways in which preschool children's drawings change with experience. She considered any piece of graphic work — scribble, pictures, letters, maps — and she noticed that children:

- were thrifty in their use of units.
- were conservative when they made a change, usually varying only one unit at a time.
- were consistent in the ways that they related one part to another in their drawings; they did not work from sheer whimsy nor from the rules of adults.
- related parts one to another in sequences, which changed as they attempted more drawing.

Goodnow's children copied simple shapes, they developed conventional equivalent forms, and they moved from old to new equivalents. She found that the need to communicate did not emerge strongly in the early graphic activities of children.

In several studies of Mexican and Swiss children, Ferreiro (1978a,b) described the early writing of children from literate and illiterate families. Her three- to five-year-olds seemed to work on simple hypotheses about writing, which changed slowly with experience. One sequence of changes which one little girl made over a year was

- writing has shape (circles).
- shapes can be separated (several circles).
- shapes go in lines (several circles in linear arrangement).

Children seemed to shift to new hypotheses when their current theory conflicted with their new experience. Ferreiro described a series of such shifts occurring before the children began to use the alphabetic principle of letter-sound relationships, which we commonly think of as the beginning of early writing.

In these early hypotheses about writing conceptual identity usually predominated. A big house needed more letters than a small house, and three girls needed more letters than one girl. Identical texts represented the names of different objects, so that *hens* and *chickens* might be written in the same way, and very different texts could be used for identical objects. There were three limitations on the texts produced by the children: a tendency to use the minimum quantity of letters (often three), a restriction in the stock of letters known to the child, and an avoidance of repeating the same letter more than twice.

Children discovered that the same elements could be varied in linear order to produce different statements. This is the beginning of an understanding of permutations and combinations in the middle of Piaget's preoperational period and before letters have acquired a relationship to sound. When the children first began to use sound as a guide, a series of letters as a whole corresponded to a stated name. Then the children came to a new question. What was the value of each letter? A decisive step was then taken. To one part of the writing the children matched one part of the name and usually each letter corresponded to a syllable. This represented a clear linking of writing with the formal aspects of speech. However, the speech did not guide the writing; rather the text that was read about was adjusted in reading to what had already been written. If the child sensed that there were too many letters, some could now be erased. From there, it was a short step to using speech to anticipate how many letters would be needed.

Ferreiro observed that children clung to their hypotheses rather than shifting at the first instance of conflict. However, when they had encountered sufficient evidence that did not square with their present assumptions they formed new hypotheses. New conflicts emerged as more was attempted, and resolutions were found. These preschool children were making discoveries; they constructed the writing system, making it their own. The writing that preceded the alphabetic period was far from unstructured and it provided evidence of children's efforts to search for an understanding of the laws of the system. It seems probable that a great deal depends upon the opportunities available to the children to make discoveries about print. However, the illiterate and literate families both produced children who explored print.

Invented Spelling

Children who invented systematic ways of spelling their messages before they had received any instruction were reported by Read (1975). Independently of adult help, they conducted an analysis of their own speech and their knowledge of the forms and names of letters and, negotiating these two sources of knowledge, they found ways of constructing a written language. Some of their discoveries are easy for the adult writer to decode: BAT (bait), KAM (came), FEL (feel). But what does such a child do if he or she wants the first sound in 'chick'? Saying ABCDEFGH reveals a letter with CH in it and the child writes HEK (chick), WHT (watched). Read's children noticed that we lose much of the vowel quality when we speak and so they produced KLR (colour), BRD (bird), LTL (little). Children's analyses followed their own pronunciation: I NO MI ABC WOT (won't) U PLA WF (with) ME. The invented spellings differed from standard spellings in many ways but children

applied common principles in creating these spellings, based on the phono-
logical perceptions of the four- or five-year-old. The child was having fun,
being creative, searching for system and carrying out an analysis of the sound
system of his language. On the basis of letter names and attending to the
phoneme sequences in their own speech, children were able to negotiate one
area of knowledge with another to explore a third.

Carol Chomsky (1979) encouraged nursery school, kindergarten and Grade
1 children to try to write using invented spelling. She found that, providing the
children knew their letter names, they could teach themselves

    — that letters have some relation to sounds.
    — that one-to-one correspondence does not exist in English.
    — that a system exists and rules do operate.
    — that this process can generate products beyond the remembered.
    — that there are more abstract regularities (orthographic rules).

She wrote

> This hypothesis construction was an active process taking the child
> far beyond the rules that can be offered him by the best patterned,
> programmed or linguistic approaches. The more the child is
> prepared to do for himself, the better off he is. (Chomsky, 1975,
> p.513)

Research has also shown that, early in schooling, children begin to discover
groupings of letters that they can work with in going from words they speak to
words they can write (Gibson and Levin, 1975). According to Francis (1975)
we would do well to leave them to discover these higher level units themselves
and not give them inaccurate and over-simplified information about spelling
patterns. This implies that what the competent readers and writers discover for
themselves about the orthography is more efficient for reading and writing
than what we, the adults, have chosen for drilling the less competent children.
Increasing exposure to written language in reading and writing in programmes
which allow children to be constructive learners should produce readers and
writers who maximize the usefulness of higher-order units in sound-to-print
relations and build an internalized model of the orthography. As Francis
(1975) points out, 'Perhaps, as in speech, it is better that they grope for
meaning and search for regularities in interesting material than they have them
thrust upon them in a form which runs the risk of being essentially boring'
(p.168), and, more to the point in the light of recent linguistic knowledge, in
programmes which misrepresent the nature of language and how we operate
on it.

According to Chomsky (1979), Ehri (1980) and Henderson and Beers (1980), children who begin with invented spelling shift to more conventional spelling:

> As the inventor became more familiar with standard spellings his choices of letters to map sounds became more conventional and morphemic patterns rather than single letter–sound mappings were adopted (i.e. past tense sound /t/ spelled first as WALKT shifted to the letter *d* and became WALKD). (Ehri, 1980, p.337)

What is not clear from the reports to hand is whether the shift to conventional spelling occurs simply as a result of teachers fostering large quantities of writing without their giving specific attention to the factors which encourage these shifts, or whether such additional factors as the reading programme, the questions teachers ask, who reads the child's stories and how they react to these stories, among others, are necessary to bring about the conventialization of spelling.

I suspect the shifts occur because of active comparisons that the child engages in. The teacher, in interaction with the young writer, has something to do with some of the shifts that occur. I am always wary of statements which imply the naturalness or inevitability of learning something as complex as the spelling of English. Undoubtedly children can invent for themselves something like written English, but not all children will invent it. Knowing what helps the successful ones to make the necessary shifts for themselves will help teachers to assist the unresponsive or confused children.

Creative Writing

Not all research has been concerned with children's mastery of letters and spelling. The five-year-old children I observed in New Zealand schools every week in their first year at school were expected to negotiate a knowledge of the world with an urge to express ideas and so produce 'a scrap of personal news' (Marshall, 1974). This is called 'creative writing' to emphasize that the starting point is the child's ideas and discoveries. The term captures the generative nature of the activity. Unlike American school entrants, these young children knew few letter names. In this programme the children showed many of the behaviours described by Ferreiro (Clay, 1975):

— Children drew pictures and dictated captions.
— They traced over the teacher's script or copied underneath it.
— They constructed messages using words and captions around the room.
— They remembered some word forms and wrote them independently.

— They invented word forms, writing independently.
— They asked the teacher for words.

The negotiation was between the child's drawing skills and his control of language, with the teacher acting as mediator-scribe. The statement of meaning in the form of a drawing seemed to hold the ideas while the child worked on the messages. Some of the early behaviours like tracing or copying were dependent on the teacher, but slowly children took over the task. The child produced messages, broke them down into units to be written, coded them into letter sequences, arranged them on a page, reread and checked the message, detected some things to be changed, and sometimes sought outside help. Editing was part of this early writing, and these checking processes sharpened the child's discrimination of what he knew and did not know. Such procedures build personal stores of written language knowledge that are very different from one child to another because of the personal nature of the expressive writing experiences and of the individual choices made (Clay, 1975).

Describing ways of teaching to foster different drafting and redrafting purposes for secondary pupils, Binns (1980) touched on a critical issue to be borne in mind. The teaching points for individuals, for classes and for the curriculum depend on the pedagogic procedures used previously. If earlier teaching has stressed the improvement of written language to make it consistent with correct English, then it may well be necessary for the present teacher to use strategies to develop a greater concern with meaning. On the other hand, if pupils had been encouraged to write from a spontaneous use of their own language, then they will probably need to learn how to recover a more formal expression of meaning from their original wording. Or, the rule-conscious, audience-aware child may need to rediscover his playful roots (Calkins, 1980). Present procedures must help students to integrate the approaches they currently control with further development towards fluent writing. No matter how 'whole' our approach to language learning, emphases will have emerged in the programmes of other teachers which will lead to a diversity of needs in any one class. Children can only grow from where they are. Working from such assumptions, Binns used several teaching ploys to bring particular features to the attention of students.

— He reread the student's writing aloud making the meaning clear, unhampered by the spelling, punctuation and handwriting.
— He read phonetically exactly what was written, creating a contrastive analysis from which the desired form and meaning could be extracted.
— He applied vocal emphasis with intonation and stress to those parts he particularly wanted to draw to the student's attention.

As well as using the oral mode, Binns used an overhead projector to display the passage to the student, covering a word, part-word, sentence or phrase to make a teaching point. In these examples the editing process has been translated into an interaction — teaching.

Longitudinal Study of Change Over Time

A study, described as outstanding and seminal by Burrows (1977), recorded a case study of Michael as he wrote in his classroom over a four-month period (Graves, 1973). Four second-grade classrooms in Buffalo, New York, were visited in two public schools in a community where the adult males were largely blue-collar workers. Seven pupils of the average age of 7.7 years were studied with equal care but Michael was the focus of the report. He showed a great amount of behavioural change from December to April, 1972/73. Graves recorded his writing progress in the context of classroom activities and the work of other children. He emphasized the need to study the writing episode, the life of the child who writes, and the socioethnographic context of the episode. The research techniques revealed the uniqueness and complexity of the composing process and showed that even early writing is a many-faceted operation and that the natural setting in which it occurs has its own contributing characteristics. In a review of writing research, Burrows called for a replication of this research with older children and further applications to other young children to add to our knowledge about the nature of, and relationships among, the many variables involved in composing.

THE CHILD AS AN ACTIVE CONSTRUCTOR OF THEORY

An important theme that emerges from these observational studies is that young children are motivated to explore writing because the task invites exploration and can be rewarding in itself. Durrell suggested to Graves (1978) that the child's first urge may be to write rather than to read, and that we have not taken full advantage of that. The power of making one's own statement and getting better at it is self-reinforcing for the child, whether it is the preschooler's efforts to say something in print or the school entrant meeting new expectations. This child's comments reflect the pride he felt in controlling this important task:

> I made my own words and I didn't copy people. The more I learned
> to write good letters the better they got. (Florio, 1978, p.9)

It helps the child if the expectations concerning what he does are commensurate with his stage of writing development and if the product is understood and valued in that perspective, be it scribble, invented word, garbled story, polished essay or first steps into poetic forms. Where the child is the originator of the task in hand, he is likely to have a much greater commitment to it and to take much greater responsibility for formulating his ideas in a manner which is clear and explicit enough for others to understand.

If we take the observations of Goodnow and Ferreiro as evidence that the child acts on his own theories of how things work and changes those theories in the face of conflicting evidence, then Duckworth (1979) has provided us with a powerful Piagetian statement of explanation that can be applied to the forward movements that occur in children's writing. If the child already has a theory, says Duckworth, no matter how primitive, that child will pay attention to instances which confirm or contradict his theory. Noticing a novel feature in print or in his own inventions may activate a search. A contradiction may lead the child to figure out some other theory that would take the new feature into account. In this way a few examples can raise the child's understanding to another level. Even a single instance can contribute to the development of understanding in this process. This is a cognitive theory of developmental change which can be applied to oral language learning. It is also close to what Frank Smith (1971) has said about learning to read, and seems to be applicable to early writing. The work of Read (1975), Goodnow (1977), Ferreiro (1978a,b) and Chomsky (1979) is consistent with this position.

One of the problems with school curricula which work against pupils wanting to read and write is a failure to understand a basic point in Duckworth's idea of getting a theory. The child needs to come to an understanding of the consistencies of the system: what works in what ways. A few instances are enough; probably too many cloud the issue. To come to the awareness at five years that four letters in a fixed linear order make up a particular word is a big step forward. It will take the child many years to master all the fixed linear orders of letters in words. The overarching concept is exciting and testing it out is fun, whereas having to discriminate ten four-letter words or build a seemingly nonsensical word family of ten similar words will probably dampen down the natural curiosity.

Within this description of the child as constructor of theory we must also emphasize the central role of meaning, indicated both by Harste (1980) and by Halliday (1975) in 'Learning how to mean'. In cognition, in oral language and also in early writing the young child is motivated to make the world make sense in terms of his present theory of that world. Correctness is an additional yardstick used by the adult, who has the benefit of having accumulated years of appropriate learning.

As active processors of information about their world, preschool children have many strategies for relating what is understood to the language forms that can be used to talk about what happens. Children learning to talk, and Ferreiro's children learning to write, have developed what might be called a self-improving system. They carry out an intentional search to resolve uncertainties; they relate what is observed to what is known; they search for a new theory which will guide behaviour. Further experience will call for further reorganizations. In early reading when the child suspects from the picture what the text will say, moves a finger left to right across the text and visually scans for confirming cues, this coordinated set of activities is guided by a trial-and-check process. One observes behaviours like overt self-correction which imply that one source of information is being checked against another in the act of reading (Clay, 1969, 1979a). A similar type of searching, checking and self-correcting was observed in writing, when children were asked to reassemble a cut-up version of stories they had written (Clay, 1980).

How the child handles confirmation and conflict among hypotheses deserves attention. Teachers may assume that children need to experience regularity, with many instances which confirm new learning. Yet Ferreiro's children held fast to their present hypothesis whether the input was regular or irregular, correct or incorrect. They did not shift until *they* noticed a new conflict, that is until *they* needed to change their hypothesis.

Children's very simple hypotheses permit them to find confirmation, even when it does not exist. However, when conflict becomes salient the cognitive energy is found to reach a new hypothesis. For example, in oral language, children gradually master the regular inflections and tend to control the irregular later, and yet they are hearing both in the speech of adults all the time. We should therefore be suspicious of attempts to convince children that language is regular by only allowing them to use regular forms. Donaldson (1978) suggested that there is no reason why children of five cannot understand a system with options or even with exceptions. One only needs to know about two options to understand this principle.

In sum, children, like adults, are active theory-builders, operating on problems and constructing their own solutions. Young children who are encouraged to explore the possibilities of print create meanings and written representations for themselves. As Carol Chomsky (1971) maintains, a child enters the classroom equipped to learn language and able to do so by methods of his own. By five or six years he has constructed a complex system of language rules which enable him to understand and produce sentences in speech and he is beginning to do the same for writing. He builds these rules by a process that is as yet little understood; but his language learning is already innovative and rule-governed. Conflicts between existing assumptions and present experience seem to encourage new discoveries. If we think of the child as a constructor of responses who becomes more rapid and fluent in the production of those early responses, we can understand how he or she may then be able to attend to new information that was not noticed before. When this new information causes enough ripples from mismatches, a shift in concepts may be sought by the child in order to achieve a better match.

INTERRELATIONSHIPS AMONG LANGUAGE ACTIVITIES

Following the review of studies of spontaneous development of skill in writing, I shall in this section review a number of reports which have a bearing on instructional sequences, in particular on what experiences should precede others.

Motor Control and Writing

It has been argued that there are physical reasons why writing must follow after the introduction of reading. Hand coordination is thought to slow the whole process of learning and make it tedious for the child. However, having to coordinate the hand and mind in message construction forces a slow careful analysis, bringing detail into momentary focus in a way that may not happen in rapid reading. The child who has something to say in print is unusually persistent and there are many supports that a teacher can bring to this situation. For example, she may guide him manually and verbally in the forming of letters, using the opportunity to emphasize the distinctiveness of somewhat similar letters. If this is important for some children, then it indicates the value of the motor movement for supporting visual discrimination learning.

Luria, an eminent Russian neuropsychologist, described how a study of injuries to the brain provided him with a theory of complex brain functioning in speech and writing (1970). Particular zones of the brain are responsible for the synthesis into a coherent whole of collections of information from memory and from different senses. Every complex form of behaviour depends upon the joint operation of several areas located in different zones of the brain. It is a combination of cues 'out there', of memories, and of expectations of what might happen next, which enables the person to perform complex actions. In Luria's analysis there is a similarity between reading orally and writing, because both require motor action: to speak is as much to organize movement as to write. The difference for the young writer is that the movements of speech are already well organized and the movements of writing are not. However, writing can also help reading behaviour to become intricately organized. Writing is a means of slowing up the complex activity so that all the pieces can be interwoven. The musician, skilled though he be, will slow up the intricate passage to ensure control; the chorister may be asked to sing the notes of a difficult passage very slowly before he combines them in what seems to be a rapid and intricate cadenza. Luria poetically described a skilled sequence of movement as a kinetic melody of interchangeable links.

Older children who are retarded in reading are usually even further behind in writing achievements. They have the necessary motor control but writing for them is extraordinarily difficult and tedious. Recent theory would suggest that what such children lack are operations or strategies or plans for internalizing and using word forms. Fernald (1943) would have encouraged them to say and trace the words in script form, the slow articulation, the movement and the memory for these being stored as a plan of operation for the whole word. Slowed by the need to carry out the movements, the reader establishes a scanning order, attends to detail in correct sequence, and carries out a slowed but not distorted sound analysis. Her procedures anticipated Lashley's (1951) ideas on learning sequential order and Elkonin's (1973) account of learning to hear the sound sequences in words.

The motor difficulties with writing can usually be overcome by a resourceful teacher of young children. They are only a problem for a very few children. It is interesting to note that school systems which begin formal education at about five years tend to be the ones that allow young children to write early.

Hearing and Writing Stories

When children enter school, they have a tendency to select a topic like whales and write all they know about (Clay, 1975; Sowers, 1979). One example from Sower's study was *Woody Owl* (p.8).

Woody is cute.	He took a worm.	Woody dead.
Woody wake.	Woody good.	Woody nice.

Sowers likens this to the compiling of inventories of 'all that I know' — a stocktaking activity. I attributed such writing to an attempt to make a long statement on a limited repertoire. The writing had a generative quality, I thought. Once the children had gained more control over writing they seemed free to attend to a more creative form of composing.

However, most children's experience with the written dialect before they come to school has been through the stories they have heard. From these they acquire some sense of the forms of language used, the ways in which stories are written, the character types, the building to a climax, the humour or the suspense and the resolution of dilemmas. Stories also offer scope for advancing skills in speculation and the consideration of alternative possibilities.

Work in progress by King and Rentel (1979) attempts to look at the facilitating role of exposure to stories and story structures in children's growth as writers. It seems that they are helped by a sense of framework or supporting fence along which their story can be trained, the framework providing reminders of what comes next as well as support for holding what has already been completed and a sense of how far there is to go. A story schema, internally represented, guiding the temporal flow of the tale, might not be very different from the mental schema I have for a journey which guides my travel from work to home, or my walk through the forest. Little is known about how we carry such plans in our brains, except to say that we cannot visualize them. Story schema are probably one example of the plans which control the serial ordering of ideas in writing, and there must be others that can guide the young writer.

Those who understand children and their growth in language and cognitive processes will find it easy to accept an argument that rich preschool experience with children's literature is a fine preparation for understanding about books and about writing. They may even predict that the best prepared will become the best readers of stories and writers of stories. If that is what educators demand, then ways will be found to read to children in schools, and to share more books with children who missed this experience in their early years.

A caution should be raised, however. The demonstration of one appealing, highly motivating, apparently literary path to more interesting writing in the classroom should not be interpreted as the necessary sequence. There are probably equally exciting, educative experiences which are not dependent on the availability of story books. Such experiences may be more appropriate in some cultural settings, and capable of engendering a spontaneous accumulation of more and more skill. In some cultures the storyteller may inspire sustained solo discourse which could lead to writing. There must be positive sequences for children whose preschool language is not written into child-sized stories in beautiful books. For the linguistically different child for whom the language of children's story books could be too big a leap into the standard written dialect, the telling of stories might be more appropriate.

Non-Fiction Writing

Primary school children structure their stories out of their awareness of story form, their feelings, their own experience, and the language they use most effectively. Often they have more problems with the writing of non-fiction, which is judged on its truthfulness, its logic and what the writer meant to say. Children are more likely to have a scatter of ideas and be casting around for order or structure in this kind of writing.

However, there are practices which can help them. Some programmes expect young children to recount their experiences, to retell how they made a construction (in craft or block-building, for example), or what was seen and done on a class visit. In many classrooms children write their personal news daily. In schools where children are encouraged to consult books of all kinds for information which will answer their questions — on cameras, trees or fire-engines — as the need for knowledge arises, this reading for information leads to retelling of what has been found out and often to writing. How much of this writing is done depends upon the teacher, the programmes and the resources available.

In contrast to such programmes, most schools use a reading book series for instruction, which emphasizes fictional stories for the first two years, only broadening to non-fiction texts in later years. However, it may be important that children have early and successive opportunities for non-fiction writing as well as for story writing, as most of the writing they will do in their lives will be non-fiction, and flexibility in writing modes might with advantage be fostered from the beginning. It may therefore be important to ask the question, 'Does story writing develop planning in non-fiction writing in adequate ways?' and if it does not, to ensure that young children get opportunities to hear non-fictional work read aloud, to read such books themselves and to practice the writing of non-fiction.

Writing requires a process of planning in order to organize the flow of information, to select chucks small enough to be expressed in sentences, and then to choose particular words and phrases (Chafe, 1977). Time sequences (the order of events that occurred) and construction sequences (the steps taken in making something) provide order for some non-fiction writing. Personal experience (what is salient for the individual) may also provide structure for writing. A question posed and answered is yet another kind of plan.

The child who is able to give an oral report on some subject, as in retelling an experience, may be acquiring a framework for non-fictional prose. Sustained discourse is less prompted than dialogue and receives less feedback during the composing process. The cues to the next episode are not what someone else said but what the speaker himself has said so far. Sustained discourse and its effect on writing is a major variable being studied by King and Rentel (1979) in relation to children's writing.

Acknowledging the Audience

The youngest writers put on to paper what is of interest to them. Gradually there is a shift towards recognition that one writes for an audience. At every stage of learning to write one has more to learn about communicating to one's audience.

Graves and his team used small groups of children who worked on writing assignments together to show that group interaction facilitated solo discourse and sustained the ideas in the prewriting and composing phases of a writing episode. Groups who worked together helped each other to select writing modes and influenced the understanding of the assigned writing and interpretation task (Giacobbe, 1980). Talking about their own writing or about literature can assist members of the group to exchange, modify and share points of view from their own experiences, creating a respect for alternative interpretations of experience, and building a clearer awareness of the importance of audience to the writer.

The audience factor is also discussed in the wider framework of literacy programmes by Elsasser and John-Steiner (1977). Drawing on the work of

Freire (1970, 1973) and Vygotsky (1978), they specified cognitive states and social conditions that must exist if fluent writing is to be achieved. Their study assumed an intricate interaction between teachers, learners and social change. The students learned the skills of writing for someone who did not share their frame of reference. They focused in specific exercises on *decontextualizing* and *elaborating* their thoughts. Oral discussion was used to broaden and flesh out ideas: students were asked to tell a stranger about a personal experience, or to write a letter to an editor, or to persuade an imagined audience to change its view. Exercises encouraged writing for a removed and impersonal audience and students discussed:

— what was or was not shared knowledge.
— the information needs of the intended audience.
— the particulars of the writer's experience.
— the linguistic prejudices of the projected audience.

Elsasser and John-Steiner concluded that

> The critical role of dialogue, highlighted by both Freire and Vygotsky, can be put into effect by the conscious and productive reliance upon groups in which learners confront and work through — orally or in writing — issues of significance in their lives. (p.368)

To some extent the imaginative story is a medium in which the writer is protected from the rigour of decontextualizing for an unknown audience. On the other hand, classroom experiences of shared books (which combine story reading, discussions of plots, characters, and illustrations, and exploration of what the author is trying to make us feel and understand) raise issues of audience and the purposes of writing. Young children who are introduced to two books on a similar theme or two books by the same author can begin quite early to verbalize in discussion the ways in which the authors are reaching them.

Dialect Differences

There are special groups of children who write for people who do not share their frame of reference. They are children who enter the schools of a majority culture with personal experience that is rooted in another culture. This can involve a different language or a dialect which is very different from the written dialects of the majority culture. How can they learn to write for someone who cannot share their frame of reference? There are many arguments for and against permitting the use of their own dialect in reading and writing, and other arguments for finding helpful activities for increasing their range of dialects to include the standard one they will find in books.

We encourage children to write as they talk, to express their ideas through the language they control. On the other hand, most teachers, according to McLeod (1979), want their pupils to be able to write in standard English when they need to and to choose whether to write in dialect or not. He suggests that adolescents are likely to achieve competence in standard English more readily if they are familiar with their own dialects in written form than they are if teachers concentrate on the standard dialect alone. This hypothesis rests on the very sensible assumption that in order to be correct, and to be fully confident that they are correct, writers have to be able to recognize alternative forms, to understand that dialect forms are not errors in the normal sense, but also to know when and why they must avoid them. These ideas were developed when McLeod observed adolescent writers in an East London comprehensive school. They apply on a smaller scale to the classroom where the teacher records for school entrants the stories they dictate in their dialect, knowing that before long teaching will offer them alternative ways of saying the same thing.

Learning to write is thus much more complicated when cultural and dialect differences are involved. However, the distinctions between dialects are possibly sharpened by writing in both, and questions of audiences provide motivation for gaining control of a standard written dialect.

Tutoring for Reading Recovery

In almost all schools there are some children who fail to make adequate progress in acquiring literacy. In a special tutoring programme for New Zealand children who had been at school for a year and had not yet responded to the school's reading and writing programme, daily individual tutoring sessions were undertaken in a carefully monitored research study (Clay, 1979a,b). It was a reading recovery programme for children who were not pushing the development of their hypotheses about print in any successful way. By daily individual tutoring, the teachers were able to bring the children back into the mainstream of the work of their classes. There were probably many reasons why the programme worked, and one contributing factor was the writing component. Writing was an essential segment of the daily reading lesson, not a casual extra, or a means of learning words, or a late extension of skill.

Three areas of the children's programme related to early writing. The children composed a short sentence or story to be written, and with the teacher's assistance wrote the words they knew, analysed the regular words which provided them with practice in hearing sounds in words, and copied others supplied by the teacher. They reread their sentences. Then they constructed the sentence again, perhaps twice, from a cut-up version supplied by the teacher. It was in this cut-up story that we noticed the development of careful monitoring and checking. The task seemed to exaggerate the behaviour. The children selected one or two words from the jumbled words, and began the assembly of the sentence. They reread the sentence so far, selected another word, repeated the sentence half-aloud, checking that word, placed it, looked for another word, placed it and reread the sentence. And so the task continued until all the words were used. Selecting the correct word from the pile forced discrimination of similar words in a purposeful activity. Knowing the story, having composed it letter by letter already and read it over, the child had a model in his head which helped him to carry out the checking and to complete the construction exercise. The teacher could prompt checking with a comment like 'something is not quite right' and the children would locate and solve the problem. Writing and reassembling the cut-up story developed self-monitoring behaviours in children who had been slow to learn. Children need little encouragement to check, develop and revise a product that means something to them and teachers can highlight both their successes and salient features they are ignoring, so that new puzzles receive their attention. Most children do not require such specific tutoring, however. The same behaviours emerge spontaneously in their early attempts to write their own scraps of news.

The Interrelatedness of Language Activities

Oral language, reading and writing occur together and support each other in many learning activities: writing stories develops from hearing stories, and from reading them; non-fiction writing and sustained oral discourse seem likely to be related; talking about events which are not related to the present context may assist in the development of a sense of audience; and having someone try to read one's writing certainly does this. Becoming more aware of the sounds of the language within words helps the writer to record unfamiliar words, and the reciprocity of writing and reading has been the basis of one reading recovery programme.

Halliday (1975) has provided an argument for the interrelatedness of language processes which seems to sum up the ideas discussed in this section. He described three aspects of language learning: (1) language learning or constructing the system we call the child's mother tongue, (2) learning through language as the child constructs his/her picture of the world and using language as a social process to acquire and share meaning, and (3) learning about the nature of language itself. He saw all three processes as largely subconscious but brought to the level of consciousness in education so that they can be consolidated and expanded. Learning to read and write are major tasks in such expansion. According to Halliday the three language processes should be allowed to take place side by side because they reinforce each other, and they should take place as social processes shared between the child and significant others. These three processes of constructing symbol systems, using these to explore the world and experience, and exploring the symbols themselves may be, at another level of abstraction, what we understand by education itself, he says. It should be emphasized that Halliday's three language processes cut right across typical curriculum divisions to be discussed in the next section.

LEARNING LANGUAGE IN INTEGRATED ACTIVITIES

In some infant classrooms teachers place an emphasis on integrating language activities. In such classrooms, where creative writing is encouraged, it plays an important part in learning to read. It provides for letters to be selected and built into words which make sentences, reinforcing the understanding, however intuitive, of the hierarchical nature of language. Creative writing provides complementary experiences to those of the reading programme, which focuses on the messages of continuous text and depends less on learning words and letter–sound relationships. In these classrooms *semantic intent* is the central strategy fostered in oral language, reading, writing or listening. All these are seen as active processes. Language learning always occurs in a subsidiary relationship to meaning.

Children in such programmes are active constructors of their own competencies with the teachers as observers and facilitators. These teachers are not always aware of what strategies or stores of knowledge individual children have available but they leave room for children to surprise them.

Integration Leads to Mutual Enrichment

However, there are still further benefits to be gained from a full integration of language activities. If oral language, reading and writing are indeed all outputs from a cognitively managed set of communicative competencies, as De Stephano (1978) argues, each will be enriched and developed by experience in any of the others. This assumes that children learn more about talking because they become readers and writers, and more about reading because they control more speaking options and because they write. They know more about writing when they control more spoken registers and read a wide variety of texts.

There is evidence to support this claim that, in a whole language programme, the responsiveness of the children increases as their learning in one area is facilitated by what is happening in another area.

Oral language and reading. Following a longitudinal study of children's oral language development and progress in reading and writing, Francis (1975) called attention to the interrelationships within these language activities. She reported low correlations between spoken language and reading ability in the early years of schooling (which is supported by New Zealand data) when children can produce and comprehend in speech more complex sentences than they can read. The effects of language differences show up only later as the children come to read more complex prose. Francis suggests that when the stronger correlations emerge it is just as likely that reading is affecting the knowledge of the spoken language as that speech may be affecting reading ability. Chomsky (1972) and Francis agree that learning to read changes the children's understanding of the structure of language. Children who read widely will be responding to a greater range of structures and functions than they encounter in spoken language alone.

Writing and reading. Early writing activities support reading acquisition because they provide many interesting activities to establish and stabilize strategies for analysing words. If a child knows how to scan letters and words, how to study a word in order to write it and how to organize the writing of that word, he or she has the skills to deal with the detail of print. It is probable that early writing serves to organize the visual analysis of print needed in reading and to strengthen important memoric strategies. Motor performance in writing adds another way of knowing about written language, and remembering the movement needed to produce a letter provides another means of error detection. When the child can carry out a slow articulation of words he speaks and finds letter sequences for recording the sound patterns, he has another set of responses for checking his writing or reading. As the child becomes a better reader, aware of more of the redundancies in the written code, he can afford to forget movement as a way of checking on the correctness of a response. However, in those early unsure days, his memories for the words which he has tried to write may provide feedback to both early writing and reading. Later, when the basic processes are established for visual scanning, remembering and linking sound patterns to print patterns on a small writing vocabulary, the reciprocity value of reading and writing probably changes in nature. At that later stage things noticed in reading help with writing, either directly as remembered forms, or indirectly through new language options.

Oral language and writing. A case can also be made for a third effect—of oral language profiting from writing activities. Apparently slow and tedious writing or reading behaviours that occur in the early and difficult stages of this coming-together process might be seen as impeding spoken language growth, so much further advanced, and even causing frustration in the learner. However the slowed-up processes needed in early reading and writing give the learner time to pay more attention to the language he has been speaking without observing—the window-pane is made opaque or mirror-like by such activities (Luria in Elkonin, 1973; Cazden, 1974). So children can turn back on their own language, reviewing in the two-dimensional frameworks of reading and writing what was too elusive for them to observe as speakers. For example, although they may place juncture appropriately in a run of spoken utterances, they still need to discover the relationship between utterances and sentences in order to be able correctly to place full-stops. Learning to write changes the nature of what one attends to and what one can do with texts as one reads. Writing also provides another means for checking on one's formulations and for extending one's range of registers for producing language. Thus the interplay between writing and other language activities adds to one's linguistic awareness — Halliday's third aspect of language learning, learning about language itself.

Towards fluency. Finally, a kind of learning occurs in natural language tasks which is hard to describe and is rarely studied. In early reading and writing, as I have observed it, the child seems to use a simple, perhaps primitive and error-prone system of responses and, because of his attention to conflicts, changes the system so that it becomes gradually more complex, more capable, less error-prone, until finally it emerges as an efficient complex process. This process begins in oral language learning and the potential for improving hypotheses increases as new language activities are learned in reading and writing. Inherent in such a way of learning is a confusing phenomenon. Old learning, well-practised, will be used with minimal attention to cues; new learning will be laboriously studied and worked over until it has found a place in the relationships of the system, and it will be used many times before it can occur on the basis of minimal cues. Every time a child reads a sentence or writes a story every letter sequence and language form in that sentence is, by its use, moving from somewhere on this continuum from novel learning towards use by minimal cues. The hard-to-spell new word may get attention but every other word in the sentence profits by being used, moving further towards fluency, automaticity and flexibility of use.

FROM THEORY INTO PRACTICE

Conflicting Views of Learning

The literature on instruction suggests that there are two contrasting views of learning among teachers. The first view leads to practices in which the introduction of new information is strictly controlled and the aim is to have the child practise each performance perfectly. The learner develops feedback systems which control this continuing perfection. Every item is introduced by the teacher in a controlled sequence designed to prevent the child from making mistakes; the teacher determines how often the child will practise each item and allows the child to discover only those features necessary for the programme. It is as if teachers considered children to be incompetent and themselves to be competent, with a sound knowledge of how to teach and what to teach. When the teacher instructs in a sequence detailed by a theory or a curriculum or a publisher's programme, it is assumed that the present curriculum steps with linear goals will be appropriate for individual children. This view of learning has been most clearly illustrated in reading instruction but programmes for spelling and handwriting apply the approach to the area of writing.

The second view of learning is appropriate for activities where redundancy is high, and this includes all language activities. Children are encouraged to develop behaviours which allow them to attempt novel responses for themselves; they are helped to use a complicated system of feedforward, checking, and feedback processes which allows them to estimate what might work and to detect when an error might have occurred. Learning can occur when the teacher stimulates some activity, establishes a requirement to perform but does not predetermine what the children produce. The children work and monitor their own productions, learning at one and the same time how to push the boundaries of what is known. The children's responses determine the next teaching step in such an approach and the learning can be many-faceted, developing in several directions but always moving towards greater accuracy, more articulate and more extensive productions with emergent new competencies. This happens with very little help in oral language learning, and it can also happen in reading and writing.

In practice, however, reading instruction has traditionally been characterized by a specified, sequenced and deliberately tutored approach in many responsible, accountable education systems. The commonest pattern is for the essential knowledge to be deliberately taught, item by item, with a heavy reliance on the learning principle of association through repetition and practice. The approach has often been stripped of its richness in order to keep many children busy while the teacher works with a small group. Some systems continue the sequenced tuition in reading throughout the primary or elementary school and beyond. Other systems move to a broader English curriculum after about three years, as if acknowledging that further progress accumulates by talking, reading and writing in many varied activities rather than along some known paths that can be sequenced. In some schools, by contrast, an integrated language programme is used from the beginning.

Educators who compare a decoding approach to reading with a whole language approach have shown a slight edge in favour of the children learning to decode acquiring higher scores on outcome measures. This leads proponents to say that we know how to teach children to decode and so research must now turn its attention to the comprehension question: How do we improve the understanding of the older decoder? To educators who aim to have their children reading for meaning and writing for pleasure from the beginning, even if it takes a little longer to read with equivalent decoding skills, there is a strange logic in that argument.

When the teacher introduces learning activities and checks all work for its match to a linear, planned, learning sequence, children are likely to be convinced that the control of their learning lies outside their efforts. Their task is to respond, not to initiate, a stance that may be incompatible with becoming better writers. Work with non-readers suggests that, while a competent child who is 'getting a theory about writing' may survive the intrusion of the teacher's competing theory about reading and spelling with only temporary confusion, the less competent child may submerge his theory construction in the face of authority and put his faith in the teacher. We have tolerated some barren conceptualizations of what language is and how it works in education!

Well-prepared or Not

It is said that only 'good' children will learn in a programme where the items of learning are not specified and sequenced and that the teacher must provide structure for the ill-prepared child. Children like order, we are told. It is maintained that the well-prepared child can be stimulated to teach himself, can do creative, interesting things, can take responsibility for determining his own learning, and that the ill-prepared child is not able to learn or experience these things. He may or must be taught systematically, repetitively, and in logical sequences in a thoroughly responsible and professional manner.

However, it is possible that instructing in this compartmentalized way makes learning more difficult for some children. When we dissect the curriculum and narrow our instructional focus one might expect children of higher intelligence to find it easier to discover interrelationships than children with lesser ability. Instructional emphases could, in fact, construct barriers preventing children from profiting from the overlap in language activities. Instead of focussing on isolated processes, teaching this before that and trusting that somehow children will integrate them as and when necessary, it may be more appropriate to help children to work with the interrelationships across all forms of language activities from the beginning.

Covering the Risks in a Whole Language Programme

The supporters of decoding approaches might argue that a whole language approach produces more failing readers and writers because children who are not becoming constructive linguists slip by unnoticed. A rather consistent approach of schools following from that position has been to move to item teaching, to sequenced, teacher-determined bit-by-bit association for failing children usually in reading alone, because writing takes too much lesson-time. However, the risks of a whole language programme are covered when:

— teachers understand what they are doing and make their own
   choices of tasks and emphases in their interactions with

individual pupils, for whole language approaches do not come ready-made.
— teachers have time and knowledge for observing the children as they read and write, capturing day-to-day shifts in strategies in the complex systems that are operating.
— teachers use procedures which increase the salience of something to be discriminated while leaving the whole language activity fully functioning.

For this approach teachers must be well trained. They must understand language processes well enough to help different children proceed in different ways.

The child's written products provide the teacher with objective evidence of what the child has learned. If teachers watch children at work they have opportunities to see how children organize their behaviour as they write.

— From the correct copying of a word carried out in appropriate sequence we may assume some functional organization in the brain which permits that sequence of actions.
— If we see a child write a new word without a copy we can assume the capacity to synthesize information from several sources.

Observing children as writers will create an awareness in teachers of the directions in which children's writing evolves, and will give those teachers many opportunities to reinforce the child for carrying out profitable operations. Those who do not work alongside children can respond only to the products and may influence the processes that children use to construct those products.

Writing in an Integrated Language Curriculum

There are signs that a new confidence in children as writers is emerging. Wells (1981) believes that we should not miss the opportunity to introduce children to writing concurrently with reading as the most effective means of introducing children to the possibilities that this new medium of communication—written language—makes available. In some classrooms in USA invented spelling is now valued highly. These new advocacies cannot be supported by linear sequenced curricula and do not lend themselves to workbooks or the type of teachers' manual that specifies what should be done today on a day-by-day basis.

If the arguments are accepted for integrating early writing with other language activities in a flexible curriculum geared to the needs of individual children, what are the requirements of the writing component of the curriculum? My suggestions are these:

First, the oral language learning that has so far provided children with a means of understanding the world should be tapped, and reading and writing should be seen as expansions of that language learning. Second, there must be room for the child to make discoveries. These opportunities arise at moments of conflict, when what is 'known' conflicts with what is 'observed'. In this sense it is appropriate that the child should be bothered by his/her own discovery of mistakes and that he/she should seek a solution. Third, the teacher should be an observer-facilitator, who watches closely to find out what the learner is able to do, and then plans activities for individual children that enable them to use their natural skills as language constructors to the full.

Many other requirements could be described, but essential to the success of the programme would be:

— a stimulating, exciting set of activities.
— many opportunities to produce writing.
— teachers knowledgeable about observing.
— teachers who work alongside children providing feedback on their successes.
— teachers who increase the salience of some features to induce mild cognitive conflicts but only at a rate that the child can accommodate.
— teachers who understand the learning potential of errors.
— teachers who observe and reinforce changes in process rather than products.

Above all, what is required is that the programme should start where individual children are, skipping the period of confusion during which they try to figure out what it is that we, the teachers, want them to do and how, if at all, it relates to what they know they can do. School programmes exist which attempt to minimize the discontinuity of preschool with school learning; their focus is on the continuing evolution of the individual child's understanding of language. This approach is manageable because the more competent children need teacher attention at first, but quickly become able to monitor their own writing and learn a great deal from their own efforts, freeing the teacher to give more focussed attention to less competent children who need more reinforcement to support their learning explorations.

Evaluating Whole Language Programmes

Many aspects of the whole language position for which I have argued are untested and it would be unwise to go beyond the information available and attempt to argue that a knowledge of the code is more efficiently arrived at by this approach than by a decoding approach. What evaluation situations would fairly test the accountability of the two types of programme? Children in whole language programmes, where language fluency and negotiations across language skills are developed, may learn more language options more quickly than children in sequenced programmes, age for age and class for class. If the questions are not how many words, or letters, or sounds, or vocabulary items, or even how many comprehension questions or how difficult texts the children can read but, more globally, what amount of change from base rates occurs in sustained oral discourse, in story writing, in transactional writing, in text reading and retelling, in self-monitoring strategies in both reading and writing, in attitudes to discussion, to writing and to reading, and in real-life out-of-school examples of using these activities, then one teaching approach might prove stronger than another. Perhaps another type of evaluation would be to compare current levels of performance in groups taught well by linear sequenced and by whole language approaches and measure the time taken to learn an activity performed well by the other group or to learn a novel activity. Would one group take on a new option more effectively than the other? A third evaluative test of the whole language hypothesis is available in working with children who have already failed in reading and writing. We have provided one demonstration of impressive accelerative learning after one year of school using a body of theory close to that discussed in this paper (Clay, 1980).

In Summary

Whole language approaches, paired with the kind of tutoring which encourages children to push the boundaries of their own learning and to extend the range of language options that they control, may be more efficient for the individual's learning and for school resources than other apparently efficient sequenced programmes. They have potential to be more enjoyable, developing the aesthetic and creative aspects of the human being as well as consolidating correct performances. A common feature of such learning must be tentativeness, a position from which it is easy to change. Increasing flexibility that allows one to select from a variety of language options must be a feature of any aspect of language learning. This then provides us with some important questions to ask ourselves about our writing programmes.

— Have we observed what our children actually do?
— Are we sensitive to what their writing can tell us about them?
— Do our procedures prevent them from making their own discoveries?
— Have we made unnecessary assumptions about teaching sequences?

— What kinds of teacher–child interactions will foster tentativeness, change and flexibility in language use?

If we do release ourselves from subject boundaries and think about the reciprocal opportunities for learning to read that occur in writing, for writing in discussion, for sustained solo discourse from writing for audiences, for learning standard dialects from trying to write for an audience, for spelling from reading and writing, for writing words one has never heard or seen before from other experience with English orthography—in the face of these observations we must conclude that the conditions of writing development are wanting to write, having frequent opportunities to write, being encouraged to draw on one's current resources in any cognitive or linguistic area, and having tutoring situations in which the teacher knows how to let children venture into new territory and recognizes when they have done so.

REFERENCES

Binns, R. A technique for developing written language. In M. M. Clark and T. Glynn (Eds), *Reading and writing for the child with difficulties*. Occasional publication (No. 8), *Educational Review*, University of Birmingham, 1980.

Burrows, A. T. Composition: Prospect and retrospect. In H. A. Robinson (Ed.), *Reading and writing instruction in the United States: Historical trends*. Newark, DE: International Reading Association, 1977.

Calkins, L. M. Children learn the writer's craft. *Language Arts*, 1980, **57**, 207–213.

Cazden, C. B. Play with language and metalinguistic awareness: One dimension of language experience. *Organization Mondiale pour l'Education Prescholaire*, 1974, **6**, 12–24.

Chafe, W. L. Creativity in verbalization and its implications for the nature of stored knowledge. In R. O. Freedle (Ed.), *Discourse production and comprehension* (Vol. 1). Norwood, NJ: Ablex, 1977.

Chomsky, C. Write first: Read later. *Childhood Education*, 1971, **47**, 396–399.

Chomsky, C. Stages in language development and reading exposure. *Harvard Educational Review*, 1972, **42**, 1–33.

Chomsky, C. Invented spelling in the open classroom. *Word*, 1975, **27**, 499–518.

Chomsky, C. Approaching reading through invented spelling. In L. B. Resnick and P. A. Weaver (Eds), *Theory and practice of early reading* (Vol. 2). Hillsdale, NJ: Lawrence Erlbaum, 1979.

Clay, M. M. Reading errors and self-correction behaviour. *British Journal of Education*, 1969, **30**, 47–56.

Clay, M. M. *What did I write?* Auckland: Heinemann, 1975.

Clay, M. M. *Reading: The patterning of complex behaviour*. Auckland: Heinemann, 1979. (a)

Clay, M. M. *The early detection of reading difficulties: A diagnostic survey with recovery procedures*. Auckland: Heinemann, 1979. (b)

Clay, M. M. Early writing and reading: Reciprocal gains. In M. M. Clark and T. Glynn (Eds), *Reading and writing for the child with difficulties*. Occasional publication (No. 8), *Educational Review*, University of Birmingham, 1980.

De Stephano, J. S. *Language, the learner and the school*. New York: Wiley, 1978.

Donaldson, M. *Children's minds*. Glasgow: Fontana/Collins, 1978.

Duckworth, E. Either we're too early and they can't learn it or we're too late and they know it already: The dilemma of 'applying Piaget'. *Harvard Educational Review*, 1979, **49**, 297–312.

Ehri, L. C. The development of orthographic images. In U. Frith (Ed.), *Cognitive processes in spelling*. London: Academic Press, 1980.

Elkonin, D. USSR. In J. Downing (Ed.), *Comparative reading*. New York: Macmillan, 1973.

Elsasser, N., and John-Steiner, V. An interactionist approach to advancing literacy. *Harvard Educational Review*, 1977, **47**, 355–368.

Fernald, G. *Remedial techniques in the basic subjects*. New York: McGraw-Hill, 1943.

Ferreiro, E. *The relationship between oral and written language: The children's viewpoints*. New York: The Ford Foundation, 1978. (a)

Ferreiro, E. What is written in a written sentence: A developmental answer. *Journal of Education*, 1978, **160**(4), 25–39. (b)

Florio, S. *The problem of dead letters: Social perspectives on the teaching of writing*. Working paper, Institute for Research on Teaching, Michigan State University, 1978.

Francis, H. *Language in childhood: Form and function in language learning*. London: Paul Elek, 1975.

Freire, P. *Pedagogy of the oppressed*. New York: The Seabury Press, 1970.

Freire, P. *Education for critical consciousness*. New York: The Seabury Press, 1973.

Giacobbe, M. E. *Who says that children can't write the first week of school*. Unpublished paper, Writing Process Laboratory, University of New Hampshire, 1980.

Gibson, E. J., and Levin, H. *The psychology of reading*. Cambridge, MA: Massachusetts Institute of Technology Press, 1975.

Goodnow, J. *Children's drawing*. Glasgow: Fontana/Open Books, 1977.

Graves, D. H. *Children's writing: Research directions and hypotheses based upon an examination of the writing processes of seven-year-old children*. Unpublished doctoral dissertation, State University of New York at Buffalo, 1973.

Graves, D. H. *Balance the basics*. New York: The Ford Foundation, 1978.

Halliday, M. A. K. Learning how to mean. In E. Lenneberg and E. Lenneberg (Eds), *Foundations of language development* (Vol. 1). New York: Academic Press, 1975.

Harste, J. C. *Communication potential*. Paper presented at the annual convention of the National Council of Teachers of English, 1980.

Henderson, E. H., and Beers, J. W. *Developmental and cognitive aspects of learning to spell*. Newark, DE: International Reading Association, 1980.

King, M., and Rentel, V. Toward a theory of writing development. *Research in the Teaching of English*, 1979, **13**, 243–253.

Lashley, K. S. The problem of serial order in behaviour. In L. A. Jeffress (Ed.), *Cerebral mechanisms in behaviour*. New York: Wiley, 1951.

Luria, A. R. The functional organization of the brain. *Scientific American*, March 1970, pp.66–78.

Marshall, S. *Creative writing*. London: Macmillan Education, 1974.

McLeod, A. *Writing, dialect and linguistic awareness*. Unpublished paper, English Department, Institute of Education, University of London, 1979.

Read, C. *Children's categorization of speech sounds in English*. Urbana: IL: National Council of Teachers of English, 1975.

Sowers, S. *Young writers' preferences for non-narrative modes of composition*. Unpublished paper, Writing Process Laboratory, University of New Hampshire, 1979.

Smith, F. *Understanding reading*. New York: Holt, Rinehart and Winston, 1971.

Vygotsky, L. S. *Mind in Society*. M. Cole, S. Scribner, V. John-Steiner, and E. Souberman (Eds). Cambridge, MA: Harvard University Press, 1978.

Wells, G. *Learning through interaction: The study of language development*. Cambridge: Cambridge University Press, 1981.

Author Index

Page numbers in italics indicate the page on which the full reference appears.

285

Subject Index